AngularJS

Philipp Tarasiewicz & Robin Böhm

AngularJS
Original Title: AngularJS: Eine praktische Einführung in das JavaScript-Framework
Copyright ©2014 by dpunkt.verlag GmbH, Heidelberg, Germany.
Original ISBN: 978-3-86490-154-6

English Translation Copyright ©2014 by Brainy Software Inc.
First Edition: December 2014

ISBN: 978-1-77197-001-3

Printed in the United States of America
Book and Cover Designer: Brainy Software Team

Technical Reviewer: Budi Kurniawan
Translators: Adam Ruebsaat-Trott and Mark Salzwedel
Indexer: Chris Mayle

Trademarks
Oracle and Java are registered trademarks of Oracle and/or its affiliates.
UNIX is a registered trademark of The Open Group.
Apache is a trademark of The Apache Software Foundation.
Firefox is a registered trademark of the Mozilla Foundation.
Google is a trademark of Google, Inc.

Throughout this book the printing of trademarked names without the trademark symbol is for editorial purpose only. We have no intention of infringement of the trademark.

Warning and Disclaimer
Every effort has been made to make this book as accurate as possible. The author and the publisher shall have neither liability nor responsibility to any person or entity with respect to any loss or damages arising from the information in this book.

About the Authors

Philipp Tarasiewicz (philipp.tarasiewicz@angularjs.de) is a freelance technology consultant, author, speaker and coach. For several years he has been specializing in the area of Enterprise JavaScript, especially AngularJS, and providing corporate clients with education and training of employees as well as helping them with new project ramp-ups. Together with Sascha Brink and Robin Böhm, he runs AngularJS.DE, a German AngularJS portal.

Robin Böhm (robin.boehm@angularjs.de) is a passionate software developer, consultant and author in the area of web technologies, specializing in enterprise JavaScript. For several years he has been dealing extensively with the creation of client-side web applications and helping companies with both education and training of employees as well as project implementation. He also co-founded the portal AngularJS.DE.

Table of Contents

Introduction..1
  Who This Book Is For..2
  Prerequisites...2
  Who This Book Is Not For...2
  About This Book...3
  Downloading Examples and Getting An Update...4
  Contacting the Authors..4
Chapter 1: AngularJS Quick Start...**5**
  Hello AngularJS!...6
  Directives: An HTML Element and an Attribute 9
  Filters 16
  Summary 20
Chapter 2: Basic Principles and Concepts...**21**
  Key Concepts 21
  Application Building Blocks..30
  Isolated Scopes...60
  The Relationship to Polymer...71
  Summary..73
Chapter 3: The BookMonkey Project..**75**
  Project and Process Presentation..75
  Requirements...76
  Setting up the Project Environment...77
  Project Start: The Book Details View...81
  The List View...97
  Navigating within the Application...122
  The First Service..132
  Summary..149
Chapter 4: Extending the Application..**151**
  The Administration Area...151
  Creating Categories with Tags..185
  Connecting to A REST Web Service..209

Chapter 5: Project Management and Automation............................**231**
 Node.js: The Runtime Environment for Tools.....................231
 Yeoman: A Defined Workflow...267
Chapter 6: Debugging...**279**
 Chrome Developer Tools...279
 Batarang: Inspecting A Running AngularJS Application......285
Chapter 7: Frequently Asked Questions..............................**295**
 AngularJS Modules...295
 Promises: How Do You Deal with Asynchronicity?............302
 AngularJS and RequireJS: Is This the Right Mix?.............313
 Mobile Devices: Does AngularJS Support Mobile Devices?.............328
Index...**335**

Introduction

AngularJS is a JavaScript framework that helps you create modern client-side web applications. Through its elegant conventions, AngularJS provides solutions to common problems and save you a large amount of code that you would otherwise have to write. With AngularJS you can focus on the actual task, instead.

This book introduces you to AngularJS through a sample project that builds gradually. You will learn about the basic concepts, which allow you to create structured, modular and thus easy-to-maintain applications. In particular, we explain concepts such as modules, scopes, services and directives, and show how you can use them effectively. A separate chapter is devoted to connecting to a REST-based web service. In addition, we discuss tools such as Bower, Grunt, Karma and Yo. These tools can save you time by rendering certain tasks unnecessary. With Yeoman we outline a workflow that defines how these tools can be employed to create a productive environment for developers.

During the preparation of this book, we have a large number of projects implemented using AngularJS. Many of the insights from these practical experiences are included in this book.

After reading this book you should be able to

- understand how you can use each of the modules in AngularJS and how they interact,
- develop modular, structured and easy-to-maintain client-side web applications,
- create quality AngularJS applications through the use of the test-driven development method.

Who This Book Is For

This book is primarily aimed at web developers with experience with JavaScript and have acquired a basic understanding of the language, and who now wish to take their knowledge to the next level through the use of the test-driven development method and techniques for JavaScript code structuring and modularization. Moreover, it will help if you have experience with jQuery. Such skills are not required, but will help you appreciate how a framework like AngularJS plays a role in JavaScript application development.

Prerequisites

You do not need any prior knowledge of AngularJS to understand the content of this book. However, you need a basic understanding of JavaScript. In addition, you should also know both HTML and CSS basics. It would also be advantageous if you had learned the basic concepts of test-driven development.

Who This Book Is Not For

As experience in web environment and specially in JavaScript is required, any developer who has no experience in this area is advised to first work out the basics required before reading. Furthermore, you should not consider it a reference in which you will find all the answers to the AngularJS framework questions. It does not discuss all the features and directives of AngularJS. Instead, it explains and demonstrates the main features and concepts of the framework using small practical examples.

About This Book

The book begins with a quick start in Chapter 1, "AngularJS Quick Start" to explain the framework by presenting some of the core concepts of AngularJS in short examples. This chapter demonstrates the potentials and added value of AngularJS. You should get a sense of why AngularJS is worth using. However, we will not explain the examples in detail. You should read this chapter if you want to quickly produce impressive results and experiment a bit.

Then, it goes further with the basics and concepts of the framework in Chapter 2, "Basic Principles and Concepts." This chapter first explains a few key concepts of AngularJS, including the Model-View-ViewModel pattern (MVVM), two-way data binding, dependency injection and testability. It also presents the individual application modules that AngularJS ships with and with which you can write applications.

Having explained the basics, the book continues with the development of an example project called BookMonkey in Chapter 3, "The BookMonkey Project." This is the main part of the book and it shows how you can create a small web application to browse a book collection using AngularJS . This example demonstrates how the basic concepts and features of AngularJS are used in a real-world application. Therefore, we have made sure that we follow the test-driven development approach when developing this application. In Chapter 4, "Extending the Application" we extend the project to include an admin section and custom directives and explain how to consume a REST web service.

In Chapter 5, "Project Management and Automation" and Chapter 6, "Debugging" we discuss project-related issues such as project management, task automation, debugging and automated tests. In Chapter 7, "Frequently Asked Questions" we answer some of the questions that people asked us many times within a project.

For a complete beginner to AngularJS, it makes sense to first read Chapter 1, "AngularJS Quick Start" and Chapter 2, "Basic Principles and Concepts" to learn the vocabulary of the framework. Building on this knowledge, the practical example in Chapter 3, "The BookMonkey Project" and Chapter 4, "Extending the Project" can be easily updated. Chapters 5, 6 and 7 can be read independently of the previous chapters to prepare for an upcoming project or to familiarize yourself with the tools used in the project.

Downloading Examples and Getting An Update

The examples in this book are available from the publisher's website at

```
http://books.brainysoftware.com
```

These examples were developed with AngularJS version 1.2.10. This version reflects the most current version at the time of writing. However, we will be updating the examples accordingly if there are incompatibilities with future versions of AngularJS.

Contacting the Authors

Since 2013 the authors have been running the portal AngularJS.DE2 (http://angularjs.de). This portal regularly publishes articles on the current issues about AngularJS, and AngularJS developers can network and offer their service. If you need consultants or training for your development team, you can contact the authors directly.

Chapter 1
AngularJS Quick Start

This chapter demonstrates the powerful features of AngularJS in short examples. We also want to show you what typical code snippets in an AngularJS application would look like. The examples were deliberately made simple so that they would be easy to understand and execute without extensive knowledge of the framework. We are not going to explain all the details. Rather, we will keep the explanation short. After working through the book, you will understand the examples in detail.

Two-Way Data Binding: Boilerplate Code Is A Thing of the Past Two-way data binding is certainly one of the more important features that make AngularJS appealing. Two-way data binding ensures that changes in the data model are automatically reflected in the corresponding elements in the view. It also automatically updates the data model when the user makes changes to the related view. This automatic adjustment in both directions is what we call two-way data binding. Thanks to this feature, you can save a lot of boilerplate code that you would otherwise have to write to implement the equivalent synchronization logic. The example in Listing 1.1 shows the feature in action.

Listing 1.1: Two-way data binding with an input field

```
<!DOCTYPE html>
<html ng-app>
<head>
<meta charset="utf-8">
</head>
<body>
<div>
    <label>Name:</label>
    <input type="text" ng-model="yourName">
    <hr>
    <h1>Hello {{yourName}}!</h1>
```

```
</div>

<script src="lib/angular/angular.js">
</script>

</body>
</html>
```

The simple HTML file in Listing 1.1 contains an input field and an output in the form of an **h1** heading. If you run this example in a browser (see Figure 1.1), you will learn that the headline is updated automatically every time you type something in the input field. This is two-way data binding.

Figure 1.1: Output from the code in Listing 1.1

Hello AngularJS!

For two-way data binding to work in the example, you need the **ng-model** attribute in the input field. In the world of AngularJS, this unknown HTML attribute is called a directive. The **ng-model** directive establishes two-way data binding between the input field and the variable **yourName**. Thanks to the directive, the value of the variable changes automatically when the value of the input field changes. Where the variable is defined is not important.

The expression in the curly braces within the **h1** tags is AngularJS's mechanism to generate output. To be precise, you use expressions to output variable values. Expressions are also subject to two-way data binding. If the value of the variable **yourName** changes, the expression is re-evaluated, which eventually leads to the view automatically being updated. In this way the AngularJS framework transfers the content of the input field to the **h1** tag automatically.

We should mention the **ng-app** directive at this point, which in the example annotates the **html** tag. You use this directive to tell AngularJS which part of the DOM (Document Object Model) should be considered an AngularJS application. When you add the directive in the **html** tag, you are telling AngularJS to operate on the entire DOM because the **html** tag is the root node. Alternatively, you can add **ng-app** to a DOM node within the **html** tag and make the DOM subtree an AngularJS application. In the latter case, all expressions outside the subtree will be left untouched and ignored.

You can also annotate multiple sibling nodes in the DOM with **ng-app** to define multiple independent AngularJS applications in an HTML document. For the majority of applications, this makes little sense because the individual applications have no ways of interacting with each other. Nevertheless, we should mention this because the official AngularJS website (at http://angularjs.org) exploits this property to present a myriad of self-contained examples.

A Second Example

Even with only two-way data binding, many applications can be implemented elegantly without writing a single line of JavaScript code. We will prove it by presenting a color picker as a more complex example. A color picker is a user interface (UI) component that lets the user select a color easily by providing immediate visual feedback that reflects the current RGBA values of a color.

Listing 1.2: Two-way data binding with HTML5 sliders

```
<!DOCTYPE html>
<html ng-app>
<head>
    <meta charset="utf-8">
</head>
<body ng-init="r=255; g=0; b=123; a=0.7">

R:<input type="range" name="color_r"
        min="0" max="255" step="1" ng-model="r"><br>
G:<input type="range" name="color_g"
```

```
        min="0" max="255" step="1" ng-model="g"><br>
B:<input type="range" name="color_b"
        min="0" max="255" step="1" ng-model="b"><br>
A:<input type="range" name="color_a"
        min="0" max="1" step="0.01" ng-model="a">

<div style="width: 300px; height: 100px;
        background-color:
        rgba({{ r }}, {{ g }}, {{ b }}, {{ a }});">

</div>

<script src="lib/angular/angular.js"></script>
</body>
</html>
```

Listing 1.2 shows a simple color picker. In its basic design, this example is similar to the previous example. We define four HTML5 sliders by assigning "range" to the **type** attribute of four input tags. We also provide a value range for each of the input tags using the **min** and **max** attributes. We need three sliders to control the red, green and blue values of the color picker and the fourth to control the alpha channel (transparency). The **step** attribute specifies the increment.

Also in this example we use the **ng-model** directive to bind the sliders and the corresponding scope variables **r**, **g**, **b** and **a**. Again, it is two-way data binding. Expressions can also be used, and this time we are using expressions not to generate direct output, but to set the individual components of the CSS **background-color** property of the **div** element, in which the color preview is to be rendered.

The result is quite impressive. Basically, we are using four sliders to control the four individual components of the **rgba** property based on the scope variables **r**, **g**, **b** and create two-way data binding. As shown in Figure 1.2, we managed to create a simple color picker with live color preview almost effortlessly. Every time we move one of the four sliders, the color of the **div** element changes.

Note that there is a slight difference between the current example and the previous example. In the current example, we use the **ng-init** directive in the body tag to assign initial values to variables **r**, **g**, **b** and **a**.

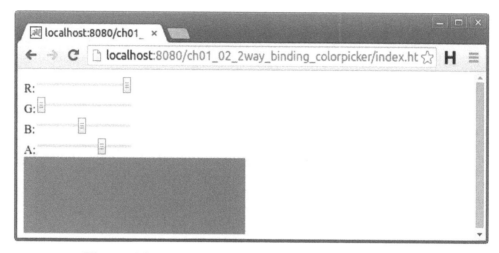

Figure 1.2: The color picker example in Listing 1.2

ng-init

Writing initial values in a template should be avoided in larger projects, as it would mean shifting some of the logic into the template. We are only using it in our example to avoid having to initialize values using JavaScript code.

Directives: An HTML Element and an Attribute

Directives are another powerful feature and one of the unique features of AngularJS. As you have seen in the previous two examples, directives are ubiquitous in AngularJS. The framework itself is based very heavily on this concept.

With directives you can extend your own HTML elements and attributes. You can use this technique for many interesting things. For instance, you can define your own tag collection and use the tags to describe many parts of the application declaratively. Or, you can write a reusable library that extends HTML to a variety of specialized UI components essential to your application. Imagine tags like **<chart>**, **<spreadsheet>** or **<input auto-complete="data">**. You would then encapsulate the needed logic within the directives.

An Example

In the following example, we create a **<color-picker>** tag that encapsulates the logic from the Color Picker example, thus making it reusable. We have decided that our directive must meet two requirements. First, there must be a way to configure the initial color of the Color Picker. Second, we want to be notified when the color changes so that we can respond to it in some form. The template in Listing 1.3 shows how we create our **<color-picker>** directive that meets the requirements.

Listing 1.3: Using the color picker directive

```
<!DOCTYPE html>
<html ng-app="colorPickerApp">
<head>
    <meta charset="utf-8">
</head>

<body ng-controller="MainCtrl">

<h1>AngularJS Quickstart ColorPicker</h1>
<color-picker init-r="255"
        init-g="0" init-b="0" init-a="1.0"
        on-change="onColorChange(r,g,b,a)">
</color-picker>

<script src="lib/angular/angular.js"></script>
<script src="scripts/colorPickerApp.js"></script>

</body>
</html>
```

Our **color-picker** directive looks exactly like standard HTML tags, employing the usual tag syntax and setting some user-defined attributes. In particular, the attributes are **init-r**, **init-g**, **init-b**, **init-a** and **on-change**. Following one of the requirements, we use the **init** attributes to initialize the RGB and alpha values of the Color Picker.

We use the **on-change** attribute to specify a callback function that will be called upon a color change. The callback function allows us to respond to color change from outside the tag. In Listing 1.3 we tell the directive that **onColorChange()** is the callback function to invoke. The **onColorChange** function is defined in the **MainCtrl** controller and AngularJS knows this because we have annotated the **body** tag with the **ng-controller** directive. We will explain about **ng-controller** later and for now you should not worry about it.

> **Note**
> A callback function is a function that a component passes to another component so that the former will get notified when an event of interest occurs in the latter, giving the first component a chance to respond to the event.

In the template in Listing 1.3, we also annotate the **html** tag with the **ng-app** directive. The **ng-app** directive specifies a module to be loaded. If, as in the previous examples, no module is specified, AngularJS will use the default module. For small examples this is perfectly acceptable. In larger applications with several modules, however, not specifying a module does not work because the framework will not know which module to load after the browser has finished loading the DOM. We want to follow best practices and therefore in the code in Listing 1.3 we tell AngularJS that the framework should load the **colorPickerApp** module after the browser has finished loading the DOM. As such, we need to define this module and the aforementioned **MainCtrl** controller in our JavaScript code. Take a look at the code in Listing 1.4.

Listing 1.4: The definition of the colorPickerApp module including the MainCtrl controller

```
var colorPickerApp = angular.module('colorPickerApp', []);

colorPickerApp.controller('MainCtrl', function ($scope) {
    $scope.onColorChange = function(r,g,b,a) {
        console.log('onColorChange', r, g, b, a);
    };
});
```

What is interesting about the definition in Listing 1.4 is the fact that the AngularJS **MainCtrl** controller has a scope. The concept of the scope have already been introduced in the first example. A scope defines all variables and functions that must be valid in a particular context. It is responsible for making sure that two-way data binding can be used in this context.

In the framework, there are components for which a new scope will be created when the components are called. A controller is one of these components. In the code in Listing 1.4 AngularJS passes the controller its scope. In this scope, you can access the internals of the controller through the given **$scope** parameter. In the code we also define within the scope of the **MainCtrl** controller the callback function **onColorChange()**. The function takes four parameters (**r**, **g**, **b** and **a**) and is called by our **color-picker** directive every time the color changes. The **onColorChange** function does not do much; it simply writes something to the browser console.

Let's now define the actual **color-picker** directive. We start with a template behind the **<color-picker>** tag in Listing 1.5.

Listing 1.5: Defining the template for the color-picker directive

```
R:<input type="range"
        min="0" max="255" step="1"
        ng-model="r"><br>
G:<input type="range"
        min="0" max="255" step="1"
        ng-model="g"><br>
B:<input type="range"
        min="0" max="255" step="1"
        ng-model="b"><br>
A:<input type="range"
        min="0" max="1" step="0.01"
        ng-model="a">

<div style="width: 300px; height: 100px;
        background-color:
        rgba({{ r }}, {{ g }}, {{ b }}, {{ a }});">
</div>
```

As you can see in Listing 1.5, the template is identical to the template from the Color Picker example in Listing 1.2).

Directive Definition

Let's now look at the most interesting part of the example, the actual definition of the directive, which is printed in Listing 1.6.

Listing 1.6: The definition of the color-picker directive

```
colorPickerApp.directive('colorPicker', function () {
    return {
        scope: {
            r: '@initR',
            g: '@initG',
            b: '@initB',
            a: '@initA',
            onChange: '&'
        },

        restrict: 'E',
        templateUrl: 'colorPickerTemplate.html',
        link: function(scope) {
            var COLORS = ['r', 'g', 'b', 'a'];

            COLORS.forEach(function(value) {
                scope.$watch(value, function(newValue, oldValue) {
                    if (newValue !== oldValue) {
                        if (angular.isFunction(scope.onChange)) {
                    scope.onChange(generateColorChangeObject());
                        }
                    }
                });
            });

            var generateColorChangeObject = function() {
                var obj = {};

                COLORS.forEach(function(value) {
                    obj[value] = scope[value];
                });

                return obj;
            };
        }
    };
});
```

For now we will not discuss the code in Listing 1.6 in detail, and will only touch on some key aspects to highlight how the directive is implemented.

Take a look at the call to the **directive()** function in the first line of Listing 1.6. We use **directive()** to register a new directive. The first parameter to **directive()** is the name of the directive you want to register. This name is directly responsible for how the corresponding HTML tag or attribute is called and represents the directive in our templates. Here we can already see a special feature in this example. The HTML tag for our Color Picker is **<color-picker>** and the directive name is **colorPicker**. The mapping of the directive name to the HTML element or attribute follows an AngularJS internal rule that is explained below.

As a second parameter, the **directive()** function expects a function that returns either a function or an instance of the so-called directive definition object (DDO) with certain properties. At this stage, the difference between these two return types is not important. In most cases, you define directives in such a way that you return a DDO, which describes the behavior of the directive based on certain object properties. In this example, we define our **color-picker** directive using such an object. There are a number of properties that you can set in the configuration object to achieve certain behavior, including **scope**, **restrict**, **templateUrl** and **link**.

Rules for Directive Name and Tag/Attribute Mapping

If the name of the directive consists of two or more words, use the camel case notation, e.g. ColorPicker. For the corresponding HTML tag or HTML attribute, the snake case notation is used and the colon (:), hyphen (-) or underscore (_) can all be used as separators. In other words, color:picker, color_picker, or color-picker can all be used to refer to the **colorPicker** directive. However, you usually use the hyphen as a delimiter.

In addition, there are two other ways AngularJS may invoke a directive, namely by using the prefix **data-** or the prefix **x-** . The reason behind this is so that older browsers only allow these self-defined tags or attributes if they have these prefixes. Thus, we could refer to our color picker with **<data-color-picker>** or **<x-color-picker>**. Knowing this naming convention is important when creating a directive to avoid nasty surprises.

The templateUrl property

The **templateUrl** property specifies a URL to the directive's template. In Listing 1.6 we refer to our previously defined template, the **colorPickerTemplate.html** file.

The restrict property

The **restrict** property indicates what HTML elements will be affected by the directive. The valid value for **restrict** is a string containing the letters E, A, C, or M. The meanings of the letters are:

- E – HTML element or tag
- A – HTML attribute
- C – CSS class
- M – HTML comment

A combination of these four characters is also acceptable. For instance, the string "EA" causes the directive to affect HTML tags and HTML attributes and ignore CSS classes and HTML comments.

The scope property

You use the **scope** property to specify whether instances of the directive get their own scope. In the context of directives there is also a special form of scope: the isolated scope. An isolated scope separates the scope inside a directive from the scope outside, and then map the outer scope to a directive's inner scope. We will not go into detail here, and will only explain some relevant aspects of the example.

The link property

You define the core feature of your directive with the **link** property. This is the so-called link function. To put it simply, AngularJS executes the link function of each directive instance exactly once and thus allows you to define initialization code for each instance. Typically, you would register an event handler or, if necessary, perform DOM manipulation in the link function. Therefore, in the link function we can implement the logic that will be called at each function callback when the value of a slider changes in our Color Picker, resulting in a new color. In fact, we are not listening to the changes in the controller, but in the corresponding scope variables **r**, **g**, **b** using what are called observers (watchers).

In summary, we have now created a new HTML tag, **\<color-picker\>**, that we can reuse in our AngularJS applications.

Filters

Although the templating in AngularJS plays an important role, the framework does not have a template engine. The reason for this is the fact that ordinary HTML, along with expressions and directives, is powerful enough to do the tasks of a typical template engine.

Moreover, the framework offers formatting and collection filters. We will explain these filters by discussing the date filter, which is a formatting filter. With this filter, you can format a date.

Listing 1.7: Using the date filter

```
<!DOCTYPE html>
<html ng-app="dateApp">
<head>
    <meta charset="utf-8">
</head>

<body ng-controller="DateCtrl">
Today's date:
{{ now | date:'dd. MMMM yyyy' }}<br> And the time is:
{{ now | date:'HH:mm:ss' }}

<script src="lib/angular/angular.js"></script>
<script src="scripts/dateApp.js"></script>

</body>
</html>
```

Listing 1.7 shows an example of the date filter. You can see that all instances of the date filter—like all other formatting filters—are embedded in expressions. The syntax is similar to the pipe syntax in various Unix shells. You basically use the pipe character ("|") to tell AngularJS that an expression needs to be processed by a filter before being evaluated and its result displayed. The filter comes right after the pipe. Just as it is common in all common Unix shells, multiple filters can be connected in series and processing is done from left to right.

What the date filter does at this point is pretty obvious. Before the value of the scope variable **now** is returned, the date filter tries to format it based on the given format string. The string may contain date or time components to use. In order for the filter to work, the scope variable **now** must fulfill a requirement. You must assign to it one of the following values:

- a **Date** object
- a string or number object specifying the number of milliseconds that have lapsed since 01/01/1970.
- a string containing a valid date in ISO 8601 format, eg a date that follows the following pattern: yyyy-MM-DDTHH: mm: ss.SSSZ

Now to complete the source code, the **dateApp** module and **DateCtrl** controller is presented in Listing 1.8.

Listing 1.8: The definition of the DateApp module and the DateCtrl controller

```
var DateApp = angular.module ("DateApp", []);
dateApp.controller ("DateCtrl", function ($scope, $timeout) {
  $scope.now = 'Loading...';

  var updateTime = function() {
    $timeout(function() {
      $scope.now = new Date();
      updateTime();
    }, 1000);
  };

  updateTime();
});
```

As you can see in Listing 1.8, the scope variable **now** has an initial value of "Loading ...". This value, however, does not meet the requirement of the date-filter and is thus initially ignored by the filter. Then we define the function **updateTime()** in our controller. This function assigns a new **Date** object to the scope variable **now** every second. We use AngularJS's **$timeout** service instead of calling the JavaScript functions **setTimeout()** or **setInterval()** directly. The reason is that **$timeout** triggers the mechanism internally, ensuring that the framework, in the context of two-way data binding, checks to what extent the values of our scope variables have changed and updating the view accordingly. The result is that we get an updated time output in our view every second.

In addition to the filters that AngularJS brings with it, you can implement your own filters. Therefore, you can encapsulate output formatting that you need in our application in a filter and reuse it. To demonstrate this, let's write a formatting filter that truncates text longer than a certain number of letters and appends three periods (...) to the end of a truncated piece of text. We call this filter **truncate** and present it in Listing 1.9.

Listing 1.9: The definition of the truncate filter

```
dateApp.filter ('truncate', function () {
    return function (input, charCount) {
        var output = input;
        if (output.length > charCount) {
            output = output.substr(0, charCount) + '...';
        }

        return output;
    };
});
```

Listing 1.9 shows the definition of our **truncate** filter. In AngularJS you define a filter by calling the **filter()** function. This function takes two parameters. The first parameter is a string that contains the name of the filter. As the second parameter, the function expects a function that returns a function. The whole thing may sound a bit complicated at this point, but as you have already seen in the previous examples, the use of anonymous functions and functions of a higher order for the definition of an application component is a common pattern in AngularJS.

Crucial to the definition of a filter is the so-called **filter** function. In Listing 1.9, this is the function that resides in the filter logic and which we ultimately return. The framework calls this function every time the expression, in which the filter is used, is re-evaluated. We obtain the previously evaluated value of the expression as the first parameter. And using the second parameter, we can optionally access the parameters of the filter. As we have already seen in the date filter, many filters take a parameter or two. For instance, the **date** filter takes a string that contains a date format.

Our **truncate** filter too takes a parameter. The parameter should specify the maximum number of characters at which our filter will start truncating. The actual implementation of the filter itself is rather trivial. We check whether the string exceeds the specified maximum number of characters and, if so, cuts the string and adds three periods.

To wind up, the code in Listing 1.10 shows how to use the **truncate** filter that we just defined.

Listing 1.10: Using our truncate filter

```
<!DOCTYPE html>
<html ng-app="dateApp">
<head>
    <meta charset="utf-8">
</head>#

<body ng-controller="DateCtrl">
Today's date:
{{ now | date:'dd. MMMM yyyy' }}<br>

And the time is:
{{ now | date:'HH:mm:ss' }}<br>
{{ 'This is an example for a long text' | truncate:18 }}

<script src="lib/angular/angular.js"></script>
<script src="scripts/dateApp.js"></script>

</body>
</html>
```

As can be seen in Listing 1.10, we use the **truncate** filter just like we did the **date** filter. In this case, however, we are not using a scope variable.

Instead, we define an input string directly within the expression. This is good enough for our purpose.

The result is the string is truncated to 18 characters and three periods are appended to it.

Summary

- Two-way data binding is a mechanism in AngularJS to update a view automatically when a value bound to it changes.
- The whole thing also works in the opposite direction. If user interaction causes a change in the view itself, the framework ensures the change is propagated in the scope.
- We can use directives to create new HTML elements and attributes. For instance, we can create reusable components that can be used across applications.
- In AngularJS two types of filters exist: the formatting filter and the collection filter.
- AngularJS comes with default formatting filters, such as **date**, **uppercase** and **lowercase**.
- The collection filter is used in conjunction with the **ngRepeat** directive and will be explained in more detail in an upcoming chapter.
- Now that you got your first taste of AngularJS, it should now be clear to you how AngularJS can help you create modern web applications.

Chapter 2
Basic Principles and Concepts

Before we cover AngularJS in detail, we will start with an overview of the fundamental concepts of the AngularJS framework. This is particularly important because someone wishing to understand how AngularJS works needs to first understand a number of basic principles. After completing this chapter you will be able to understand the most important terms in the world of AngularJS and understand how the framework uses certain proven patterns and best practices to facilitate the development of client-side web applications.

Key Concepts

The AngularJS framework is based on some proven design patterns. In this section we present these patterns and explain their purpose in the context of AngularJS.

Model-View-Controller or Model-View-ViewModel?

The Model-View-Controller pattern

One of the most fundamental architectural patterns in software engineering is certainly the Model-View-Controller (MVC) pattern. Any developer who has written applications that include a graphical user interface must have used or at least heard about this pattern, which was first used in Smalltalk. In 1979 Trygve Reenskaug, a Norwegian computer scientist, formulated this pattern after recognizing that it is useful for GUI applications to separate responsibilities in terms of data storage, business logic and presentation and outsource them in separate layers.

Since the emergence of the first dynamic websites that dynamically assembled a response for each HTTP request, the MVC pattern has experienced a major boom. It was quickly recognized that it is useful to apply the MVC division of responsibilities to the realm of server-side web applications. Whether it is Ruby on Rails, Zend Framework or Spring MVC, every relevant web framework requires MVC as the basic architectural pattern. In this case, the pattern of its basic philosophy is quite simple.

As already mentioned, there is a strict division between data management (model), presentation (view) and business logic (controller). The original idea is that the user interacts with a view component (e.g. GUI) and user input is processed by a controller component. This controller component has the responsibility to check the entered data before processing it to make sure that the data conform with certain business rules, and to ensure that the model component manipulates the underlying data model accordingly. Furthermore, there is a communication mechanism between the model component and the view component that allows the view component to be notified of any changes in the model. As a result, the view component is ultimately responsible for ensuring that the user gets to see the current state of the data.

In the context of the classical round-trip based web application, the practical implementation of the MVC pattern usually means an application contains a collection of controllers, each processing requests on a certain URL. Once a client (usually a browser) sends an HTTP request to the server, the request is processed by the controller, which is responsible for the processing of the called URL. This controller now has the aforementioned responsibilities: data validation, data processing according to some business logic and reporting of possible manipulations to the model layer, which usually manifests itself in the form of a database and the appropriate access objects. Moreover, the controller has the task of merging the data and the HTML template, which uses the framework used to assemble an HTTP response. This HTTP response, in the form of dynamically generated HTML, is then sent to the client.

The generated HTML code that the browser ultimately receives for display is, in principle, part of the view component. The fact that the web in its original form is based on the round-trip principle and thus any form of

HTTP communication requires that the client send a request and the server respond, means no smooth communication channel between the data storage layer and the HTML code displayed in the browser (view component) can be established. Thus, the view component of a classic web application is solely in the context of updating an HTTP response that must be preceded by an HTTP request. As such, interactivity suffers.

In summary, it is safe to say that in classic round-trip based web applications, the model, controller and a large part of the view logic reside on the server. This type of software is known as a thin client.

Although the round-trip-based processing is perfectly fine in classic web applications with little interactivity, to create modern applications you need a large part of the logic to be on the browser. The server in this kind of architecture is used only as a data source and memory by providing application data via a REST-based interface to the application running in the browser. Consequently, it is obvious, even in these so-called fat clients how the MVC pattern can be applied has to be considered.

The Model-View-ViewModel Pattern

The fact is the MVC pattern plays a predominant role in the browser. All popular JavaScript frameworks, including AngularJS, use this pattern as the basic approach to structure the application. However, often used in the area of client-side web application is an extended version of the MVC pattern: the Model-View-ViewModel pattern, or MVVM for short.

Originally, the MVVM pattern came from the Adobe Flex and Microsoft Silverlight environments. It has now established itself in the JavaScript world. Because the model layer, i.e. the application data, first of all is on the server and is externally served via a REST API, it makes sense to introduce a proxy layer on the client, which returns only the actual data that is currently used. This proxy layer is called a ViewModel.

Often the data needs to be transformed in a certain way before being fed to the display. Such data transformation is also the responsibility of the ViewModel. Finally, it also defines the functionality that we need within a display. So you could, for instance, define a function in a ViewModel that contains the logic for handling a button click. Figure 2.1 illustrates the relationship.

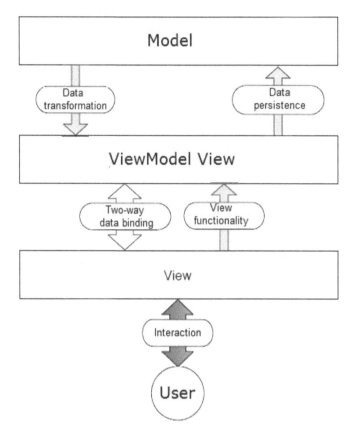

Figure 2.1: The Model-View-ViewModel pattern

In connection with MVVM, the concept of two-way data binding is also used frequently. You will learn this in detail later in the next section. In summary, the ViewModel layer has two primary tasks:

1. Providing and transforming a section of the application data that is located on the server
2. Providing the required functionality in the context of a display.

The actual implementation of the ViewModel concept is done using scopes in AngularJS. Scopes are covered in the next section.

> **MVVM in applications without the backend**
> Even if you are dealing with an application that does not need to communicate with a backend, it makes sense to use the ViewModel concept. On the one hand, the concept of two-way data binding is built on top of the ViewModel layer. On the other hand, in most cases your application will still have a data source whose data needs to be transformed in a certain way before it is displayed.

Two-Way Data Binding and Scopes

Two-way data binding is a mechanism for automatically updating the data model when the user changes something in the GUI. The reverse route, in which automatic updates of views occurs in response to changes in the underlying data model, is also covered by the concept. The meaning of the name of this concept is data binding in two directions.

Because this concept is an integral part of AngularJS, we can save a lot of code we would otherwise have to write to implement the appropriate update logic itself. If you compare AngularJS with jQuery, you will learn that in jQuery you would have to register on DOM elements an event listener that will invoke a callback function when the event is triggered. The jQuery callback function would then modify the corresponding variable of the data model. Also, with jQuery the binding in the opposite direction must be taken care of manually. In other words, when your variable changes, you would have to implement some logic to update the value of the corresponding DOM element. It would involve a lot of so-called "boilerplate code," dirty application logic that you can spare yourself in AngularJS thanks to two-way data binding.

In AngularJS the implementation of two-way data binding is essentially based on scopes. A scope consists of the set of all variables and functions that are defined in a particular context. The context is a specific part of the DOM (Document Object Model). It is important to understand that AngularJS can establish two-way data binding only for variables or functions that are defined in a scope. It is equally important to recognize that the framework creates a root scope for an application.

Another feature of scopes is the fact that they can inherit from each other through prototypes and thus form a hierarchy. Semantically, this corresponds to prototypal inheritance in JavaScript, which is a common way of offloading common data and logic in a higher-level construct to avoid redundancy.

If Scope B is inherited from Scope A, in plain English that means in the context of Scope B not only can you access the variables and functions defined in B, but also the variables and functions defined in A. However, note that the same named variables or functions can be overriden. Thus, if the same variable or function exists in both A and B, then the variable or function from Scope B hides the identically named variable or function in Scope A. In the context of Scope B then you can only guarantee a detour to access an identically named variable or function in A.

Isolated Scopes

In AngularJS you can define isolated scopes. Isolated scopes allow you to control exactly how to grant access to variables or functions from the parent scope. This particular form of scopes is primarily used in directives. With isolated scopes you can make sure that self-contained and reusable components do not accidentally collide when accessing shared variables. Any resulting errors are very difficult to identify in general, which is why you should always strive for this seclusion in this context. The concept of directives is presented later in this chapter.

In addition to the scopes in two-way data binding, you need a mechanism to decide when to synchronize the user interface and the data model. You usually have the choice between dirty checking and an observer-based solution. AngularJS uses dirty checking.

As the name implies, dirty checking essentially consists of an algorithm that examines all relevant scopes for the current view to find polluted variables and, upon finding a discrepancy between the view and the ViewModel, executes some synchronization logic. Be warned that this algorithm is run frequently and, as such, must be highly optimized with regard to execution time, so as not to negatively affect the application responsiveness. Luckily, you do not have to worry about when this algorithm is executed as the framework takes cares of this. Nevertheless, you should keep in mind how this routine works so that you do not run into performance problems within your application. The most important rule that you should note is that you simply define data and functions in a scope when you actually need this in the view. All unnecessary data and functions in the view that are still defined in a scope increase the time taken to perform dirty checking without adding any value.

Inversion of Control and Dependency Injection

AngularJS also makes use of inversion of control (IoC) and automatic dependency injection (DI). Various platforms such as Java and .NET have for years offered a wide range of possibilities in order to use these patterns seamlessly in applications. Thanks to AngularJS, these concepts can now be found for the first time in client-side web applications.

The concepts address a fundamental problem in software development: How do you manage application components so that they are decoupled from the existing dependencies and so that you can achieve a high degree of flexibility and interchangeability? These are finally two important characteristics of high-quality software because they are responsible for ensuring that applications are testable and easy to adapt. Testable in the sense that you can easily write unit tests for your components.

JavaScript developers who have not used IoC and DI probably ask these questions: What is actually inverted? What are the advantages here? What is the difference between IoC and DI? And why are these patterns so essential for producing high quality software? For answering these questions we will talk briefly about IoC and DI.

To resolve an application component's dependencies, in JavaScript you have four options:

- Manual instantiation with the **new** operator
- Integration via a global variable
- Flexibility and interchangeability
- Testability

If you think about it, the first three options are more detrimental than helpful when it comes to dealing with dependencies. The first option means that at design time you have to write code that instantiates a fixed component that is difficult, if possible at all, to change at runtime. The integration over a global variable comes with similar disadvantages and makes the application's global namespace messy. The third solution through a service locator is—although better than the first two—not optimal, because you have to somehow access the service locator and request an instance of the actual dependency. By making use of the indirection provided by the service locator, dependency is decoupled from the component. However, you now have to obtain an instance of the service locator, which basically means you are simply moving the original problem. Therefore, the optimal solution would be to return the responsibility of object creation to the environment. This provides the basis of a convention that automatically determines what dependencies are needed by an application component and hand them to the component at runtime. As such, you do not need to rewire your application component when different dependencies are needed. You just leave this task to the environment.

Your component is no longer responsible for generating its dependencies, but this responsibility has been transferred to the environment. Thus, we speak of inversion of the control flow. In fact, it is this attribute that makes the IoC principle very important in software engineering and on so many levels.

To find an independent and unmistakeably comprehensible name for the IoC pattern in the context of dependency resolution of application components, the name dependency injection (DI) was chosen. DI is thus a special form of IoC.

Talking about the benefits of this pattern, you have to realize what opportunities arise in terms of flexibility and interchangeability, if you decide to use DI in your application. If you have no hard-coded dependencies anymore within an application component and have passed the responsibility of resolving dependencies to the environment, in a test you can tell the environment that it should give you a mock object instead of an actual object. Of course you can implement the mock object yourself. In a test it is a very simple matter to specify how certain dependencies should behave, allowing you to test a component in isolation.

In a test scenario, you obviously have a huge advantage as you can replace the actual implementations of certain dependencies transparently by using DI without re-compiling your application. Your software thus remains flexible and individual components remain interchangeable.

The test scenario presents a tremendous advantage, because you can replace the actual implementations of certain dependencies with little effort by using DI. Your software thus remains flexible and individual components remain interchangeable.

As you will see later in this book, DI is a central theme in AngularJS and provides you with an elegant handling of dependencies in most application components. Similarly, DI occurs naturally in tests. You can just replace dependencies for production with mock objects in a test.

Testability

Unlike most other JavaScript frameworks, AngularJS was designed from the start with a strong emphasis on testability. The basic design and the consistent utilization of dependency injection allow you to test all application building blocks in isolation as well as in the integration scenario extensively. The test-driven development approach allows you to implement client-side web applications. For all AngularJS application modules—especially for controllers, services, directives and filters—there is a concept for unit tests. In addition, you can use ngScenario to as a comprehensive domain specific language (DSL) to define end-to-end tests (E2E tests).

These are tests in which an individual application is regarded as a black box. Using DSL functions you can trigger user interaction and check the results if they meet expectations. The example in Listing 2.1 shows an example E2E test for fictitious user login.

Listing 2.1: E2E-Test for user login

```
describe('User Login', function() {
  it('should successfully login the user', function() {
    input('user').enter('John');
    input('password').enter('123asd');
    element(':button').click();
    expect(element('h1').text()).toEqual('Hello, Tom!');
  });
});
```

In addition, AngularJS brings its own mock service implementations that you can use to produce a given condition for a test. There is, for example, the **$httpBackend** mock object for the **$http-Service**, which prevents a genuine request to a REST-based backend and only checks whether the corresponding function of the **$http-Service** has been called. At the same token, you can easily emulate a REST-based backend and consider what would happen if a real REST service returns a particular record.

Summary of Key Concepts

- AngularJS is based on the Model-View-ViewModel pattern (MVVM).
- The ViewModel layer is implemented in the framework using scopes.
- A very important feature in AngularJS is two-way data binding. It ensures that views are updated automatically when certain data is changed in the scopes. Also, the updating in the opposite direction is carried out automatically.
- Two-way data binding is based on scopes. All data for this type of data binding must be defined in a scope.
- Another key concept that is ubiquitous in AngularJS is dependency injection, i.e., the automatic resolution of dependencies.
- AngularJS is designed from the ground up with testability in mind. Each design decision within the framework strongly motivates a developer to write clean and testable source code.

Application Building Blocks

AngularJS defines a set of application modules with clearly specified functions. Typically, an application consists largely of a composition of these building blocks. In this section we present these modules briefly to introduce you to the concept of AngularJS and explain how these components relate to each other.

Module

In AngularJS a module represents the largest structure that encapsulates a set of related application components. In particular, it serves as a container for controllers, services, directives and filters. Conforming with the definition of module in software engineering, an AngularJS module should have at least the following properties:

- high internal cohesion
- clearly defined API
- high degree of reusability

Also at the module level AngularJS uses dependency injection. Therefore, other modules can be easily integrated as dependencies of a module. AngularJS automatically provides dependency resolution, as long as this module has been previously included with a **<script>** tag in the **index.html**.

An AngularJS application contains at least one module, which is automatically initiated and executed by the framework when the DOM is fully loaded. Using the **ngApp** directive you can tell AngularJS which of your modules is the start module. Many examples in the Internet are based on a single module, which contains all of the application components (controllers, services, directives, filters), which are necessary for the sample. This minimal type of composition is sufficient for most small sample applications. In a large project with multiple teams, however, you should think how you can divide parts into modules such that a high degree of reusability can be achieved. Contrary to what the official AngularJS Developer Guide (at http://docs.angularjs.org/guide/module) says that modules should be defined in terms of the contained technical components, our own experience dictates that a technical definition usually proves to be more useful in large projects. So, in a fictional application with a module called user management, in which the complete aspect of user management is implemented, there are almost always more modules than just the **app-controllers** module, the controller that contains all parts of the application.

In addition to your own application modules, there are a wide range of open source modules that are implemented and managed by third parties for

AngularJS. These include modules such as angular-translate, Angular UI and AngularStrap.

The Controller

The controller contains the design requirements for scopes and thus defines the data and logic needed for a particular view. A controller instance gets its own scope in which variables or functions are defined. These variables and functions can then be accessed from within the view. As already mentioned, scopes can inherit from each other prototypally and thus form a hierarchy. A large part of this hierarchy is built on top of AngularJS when you nest controllers in your application.

In AngularJS controllers have a close connection to services. A service is obtained once again using dependency injection. This also means that you can replace a service with a mock implementation in a test.

When implementing a controller, you should adhere to certain guidelines. Controller implementations should be focused and their source code meaningful. This means that you should encapsulate any complex logic in a service that you then inject into your controller via dependency injection. Furthermore, controllers should not hold any data, but only provide references to data in their scopes. The actual data storage should in turn be encapsulated in a service that acts as a data access object. Any operation that engages in manipulating the DOM in a controller is a taboo. Whenever you find yourself needing to perform DOM manipulations, you should first consider whether you can instead change the default directives as **ngRepeat**, **ngShow** or **ngClass**. If you get into the situation of having to actually perform DOM manipulations, do this in a separate directive.

The Model

Unlike in many other JavaScript frameworks, in AngularJS data-holding objects, the so-called models, are ordinary JavaScript data types. This means that your models do not have to inherit from certain framework classes and no other conventions have to be followed. The definition of an ordinary object or array of primitive data types is sufficient to meet the requirements of AngularJS models. As mentioned before, AngularJS uses the concept of two-way data binding to synchronize models with their corresponding representation in a view. At this point we should mention again that this two-way data binding can only be applied to a model if the model is defined in a scope. In the example in Listing 2.2, you see how some valid model definitions, which include two-way data binding, can be established.

Listing 2.2: Model definition in a controller scope

```
angular.module('myApp')
.controller('MyCtrl', function ($scope) {
  // a simple JavaScript object
  $scope.user = {
    name: 'John Doe',
    age: 27,
    email: 'john@doe.com'
  };

  // a simple JavaScript array
  $scope.family = [
    'James Doe', 'Clarissa Doe', 'Ted Doe'
  ];

  // a primitive value
  $scope.loggedIn = true;
});
```

Routes

A typical problem in single page applications (SPA) is the addressing of individual parts of the application via a URL in conjunction with the browser forward and backward functions. In this context, we also speak of deep linking. This aspect, which has a trivial solution for classic round-trip-based web applications, requires increased expense in client-side web applications. Fortunately, modern browsers offer a History API that allows you read and write access to the browsing history. This way, you can programmatically change the URL according to your application state, such as in the address bar of the browser, without a complete reload of the application.

Despite the simplicity of the History API, AngularJS goes a step further to abstract the logic in the form of routes. As such, you can conveniently map URLs on templates with their associated controllers.

Listing 2.3: Route definition for an AngularJS application

```
angular.module('myApp').config(function ($routeProvider) {
    $routeProvider
        .when('/', {
            templateUrl: 'templates/mainTemplate.html',
            controller: 'MainCtrl'
        })
        .when('/user/:userId', {
            templateUrl: 'templates/userDetailsTemplate.html',
            controller: 'UserDetailsCtrl'
        })
        .when('/user', {
            templateUrl: 'templates/userOverviewTemplate.html',
            controller: 'UserOverviewCtrl'
        })
        .otherwise({
            redirectTo: '/'
        });
});
```

Listing 2.3 shows a route definition. You can use **$routeProvider** to define a mapping between a specific template URL and a controller by calling the **when()** function. The call to the **otherwise()** function defines a fallback mechanism that applies to all requests that do not match the predefined routes. As pointed out in the example, a route may also contain a variable in its definition. Thus, the route **/user** can either be called without a path parameter or with the path parameter **userId**. If it is called with a parameter, you can access the parameter passed in the corresponding **UserDetailsCtrl** controller. Chapter 3, "The BookMonkey Project" explains how this works.

> **Routes**
> Because now the route functionality has been outsourced to an independent module, to use routes in an AngularJS application, you must include the **ngRoute** module and specify it as a dependency of your application module. The exact procedure is explained in more detail in Chapter 3, "The BookMonkey Project."

> ## The AngularJS UI-Router Module
> Using the **ngRoute** module for managing routes is not sufficient in
> certain applications. If you want to nest a view within another view, for
> instance, you quickly find **ngRoute** reaching its limit. Fortunately,
> since **ngRoute** is an independent module and thus no longer part of the
> core of the framework, you can use an alternative module for routing.
> A very popular routing module is UI Router, which can be downloaded
> from https://github.com/angular-ui/ui-router. This module allows you
> to define nested states and views. A new version of the router is
> planned that will combine the advantages of both the old and new
> versions.

Therefore, routes make a AngularJS application a full single page
application and enable application users to use deep linking. Users can
easily share an application link that enables the application to render in a
certain state.

Views, Templates and Expressions

In the context of AngularJS you often hear the terms views, templates and
expressions. Now it is important to clarify the difference between these
terms, especially because the demarcation of views and templates is slightly
blurred and often leads to ambiguities.

Views and Templates

A template is an HTML fragment that contains a part of the HTML page,
which the browser interprets and renders for display. Therefore, you you
define the look of your user interface with templates. In AngularJS a
template may contain expressions and directives.

A view is a part of the user interface. It is created at runtime when
AngularJS compiles the necessary templates for the applicable part and
replaces all expressions as well as directives with concrete values or DOM
nodes. Formally speaking, a view is the result of an instantiated template.

Or more accurately: A view is the combined result of instantiated templates, because most of your application views are based on multiple templates.

In everyday conversation, views and templates are used more or less interchangeably. However, it is sometimes necessary to understand the difference.

Listing 2.4 shows a simple template.

Listing 2.4: A simple AngularJS template

```
<div>
  <p>Hello, John Doe!</p>
</div>
```

As you can see, the template in Listing 2.4 is simply an HTML code. However, as you can see later, it can contain expressions and directives.

Expressions

Expressions are used in a template primarily to access data defined in a scope. So if you look at the **MyCtrl** controller again (see Listing 2.5), you can edit the new template to generate the user's name from the scope (see Listing 2.6).

Listing 2.5: Our MyCtrl controller

```
angular.module('myApp')
.controller('MyCtrl', function ($scope) {
  $scope.user = {
    name: 'John Doe',
    age: 27,
    email: 'john@doe.com'
  };

  $scope.family = [
    'James Doe', 'Clarissa Doe', 'Ted Doe'
  ];

  $scope.loggedIn = true;
});
```

Listing 2.6: A template with a simple expression

```
<div>
  <p>Hello, {{user.name}}!</p>
```

```
</div>
```

As you can see in the template in Listing 2.6, an expression is written in the curly braces. Within these parentheses you can use a subset of JavaScript to generate output. However, the expression cannot be easily evaluated using the JavaScript **eval()**. Therefore, there are special notes with regard to expressions:

1. The evaluation is carried out not like **eval()** against the global **window** object, but against the scope that is valid in the context of the template.
2. Expressions that evaluate to **undefined** or **null** do not generate output because potential exceptions such as **ReferenceError** or **TypeError** are caught and ignored.
3. Control flow statements such as conditional statements or loops cannot be used.

You can also perform simple calculations in expressions (See Listing 2.7).

Listing 2.7: A simple computation in an expression

```
<div>
  <p>
    Hello, {{user.name}}!<br>
    Five years ago you were
    {{user.age - 5}} years old.
  </p>
</div>
```

We have mentioned that expressions exist primarily for evaluating scope data in templates. In conjunction with two-way data binding, this means AngularJS ensures that an expression is automatically evaluated again when the corresponding scope value has changed. Thus, the framework automatically updates the views if the underlying data has changed.

What makes expressions so powerful is the fact that you can use a formatting filter to reformat data. A more detailed explanation can be found in the subsequent subsection.

Filters

In AngularJS there are two types of filters. In the previous chapter we mentioned the formatting filter. On the other section of the same chapter, we discussed the collection filter, which can be used in conjunction with the **ngRepeat** directive to filter or transform a collection. The collection in this context is either an array or an object hash.

Formatting Filters

You use the formatting filter within expressions to format or transform the result of an expression. You can use the pipe syntax in an expression, as shown in Listing 2.8.

Listing 2.8: A filter applied to an expression

```
<div>
  <p>
    Hello, {{user.name | uppercase}}!<br>
    Five years ago you were
    {{user.age - 5}} years old.
  </p>
</div>
```

In the example in Listing 2.8, the **uppercase** filter is applied to the evaluated expression **user.name**. Part of the filter set which ships with AngularJS, this filter transforms a string to uppercase. The resulting output of this template in the view would be the string in Listing 2.9.

Listing 2.9: The result of the uppercase filter

```
Hello, JOHN DOE!
Five years ago you were
22 years old.
```

In addition to the **uppercase** filter, AngularJS includes other useful formatting filters, which we will discuss later. In addition, you can define your own formatting filter. Listing 2.10 shows an example.

Listing 2.10: The alternatingCase filter

```
angular.module('myApp').filter('alternatingCase', function () {
```

```
    return function (input) {
        var output = '',
            tmp;

        for (var i = 0; i < input.length; i++) {
            tmp = input.charAt(i);
            if (i % 2 === 0) {
                output += tmp.toUpperCase();
            }
            else {
                output += tmp.toLowerCase();
            }
        }

        return output;
    };
});
```

The **alternatingCase** filter may seem contrived, but its sole purpose of existence is to educate. All the filter does is alternate the case of the input string. The programming interface for the formatting filter is very simple. It receives the result of an evaluated expression as a function parameter and can then do anything to the input. Finally, it returns an output that is then displayed.

Listing 2.11: Using the alternatingCase filter

```
<div>
  <p>
    Hello, {{user.name | alternatingCase}}!<br>
    Five years ago you were
    {{user.age - 5}} years old.
  </p>
</div>
```

Listing 2.12: The result from the alternatingCase filter

```
Hello, JoHn dOe!
Five years ago you were
22 years old.
```

Collection Filters

In addition to formatting filters, which are used in expressions, there are also collection filters. In terms of the API, collection filters have the same structure as formatting filters, but they are used in a different context in conjunction with the **ng-repeat** directive.

At this point you do not yet know what directives are and what you can do with them. However, we should mention that the **ng-repeat** directive is used in a template to output the elements of an array or an object hash. You can think of **ng-repeat** as the declarative counterpart of the loop.

Listing 2.13: Using ng-repeat

```
<div>
Family members of {{user.name}}:
<ul>
<li ng-repeat="member in family">{{member}}</li>
</ul>
</div>
```

In the example in Listing 2.13, the scope variable **family** references a string array that contains the names of family members. The **ng-repeat** directive makes sure that each element is rendered as an **<li>** tag in the view. As a result, you have a view that displays the family members of John Doe. The HTML code generated at run time by the **ng-repeat** directive is printed in Listing 2.14.

Listing 2.14: The HTML code result in the view

```
<div>
  Family members of John Doe:
  <ul>
    <li>James Doe</li>
    <li>Clarissa Doe</li>
    <li>Ted Doe</li>
  </ul>
</div>
```

The question that immediately springs to mind is: Can we filter this output so that only a subset of the collection is returned? This is exactly where the collection filters come into play. They ensure that the collection filtered based on certain elements or their elements are transformed in a certain way. In conjunction with **ng-repeat** we use the pipe notation again. The following example demonstrates the **filter** filter of AngularJS. Admittedly, this filter has not been very thoughtfully named, but it serves its purpose.

Listing 2.15: Using filters within ng-repeat

```
<div>
    Family members of {{user.name}}:
    <ul>
        <li ng-repeat="member in family | filter:'clarissa'">
            {{member}}
        </li>
    </ul>
</div>
```

We use the **filter** filter here because we want to print only the names of family members that contain the word **clarissa**. The filter is not case-sensitive.

There are other collection filters in the standard repertoire of AngularJS, including **limitTo** and **orderBy**. As both affect the output of a collection, what they do should be clear from their names. Nonetheless, we present an example application that use them later in this book and explain them in more detail.

If none of these filters meets your needs, you can define a new collection filter. In the following example, we define a separate collection filter called **endsWithDoe**. With this filter, we want to ensure that only items ending with the string **Doe** are returned.

Listing 2.16: Our endsWithDoe filter within ng-repeat

```
angular.module('myApp').filter('endsWithDoe', function () {
  return function (inputArray) {
    var outputArray = [];

    angular.forEach(inputArray, function(item) {
      if (item.length >= 3
      && item.substring(item.length - 3) === 'Doe') {
        outputArray.push(item);
      }
    });

    return outputArray;
  };
});
```

As you can see in the example in Listing 2.16, the API for collection filters is very similar to the API for formatting filters. The only difference is that in our filter function in this example, we get an array as input (rather than a string as in formatting filters), and AngularJS accordingly expects the filter function to return an array. Within a filter function you can manipulate the output array to achieve the desired behavior, or build a completely new array. In the **endsWithDoe** filter we choose the latter alternative. For the sake of completeness, the following example shows how to use our own collection filter. To explain the effects, we should also complement the original array to names that do not end with the string **Doe**.

Listing 2.17: Adding members to our array

```
angular.module('myApp').controller('MyCtrl', function ($scope) {
  $scope.user = {
    name: 'John Doe',
    age: 27,
    email: 'john@doe.com'
  };

  $scope.family = [
    'James Doe', 'Clarissa Doe', 'Ted Doe',
    'Burk Smith', 'Samantha Jones', 'Bill Brooks'
  ];

  $scope.loggedIn = true;
});
```

Listing 2.18: Using our endsWithDow filter with ng-repeat

```
<div>
    Family members of {{user.name}}:
    <ul>
        <li ng-repeat="member in family |
          endsWithDoe">{{member}}</li>
    </ul>
</div>
```

If you run this example, you will find out that only three names, all ending with **doe**, are returned, even though the output array now contains six names.

Finally, we should do refactoring to make our filter more generic. It should not only be able to filter the string "Doe," but any arbitrary string.

Since the Filter API supports filter parameters, we can easily incorporate this change. In addition, we should also rename our filter **endsWith**.

Listing 2.19: The endsWith filter with parameters

```
angular.module('myApp').filter('endsWith', function () {
    return function (inputArray, endsWith) {
        var outputArray = [],
            subString,
            hasMinLen,
            isSubStringMatching;

        angular.forEach(inputArray, function(item) {
            hasMinLen = item.length >= endsWith.length;
            subString = item.substring(item.length
                - endsWith.length);
            isSubStringMatching = subString === endsWith;

            if (hasMinLen && isSubStringMatching) {
                outputArray.push(item);
            }
        });
        return outputArray;
    };
});
```

Essentially, AngularJS calls our filter function with a second parameter if we use filter parameters. We can now use it to adjust our logic according to the second parameter. The temporary variables **subString**, **hasMinLen** and **isSubStringMatching** are not necessary and were only introduced in order to avoid long lines in the function body.

For the sake of completeness, the new version of our templates is shown in Listing 2.20.

Listing 2.20: Using our endsWith filter

```
<div>
    Family members of {{user.name}}:
    <ul>
        <li ng-repeat="member in family |
          endsWith:'Doe'">{{member}}</li>
    </ul>
</div>
```

The difference here is the fact that we call the **endsWith** filter by passing a string parameter ("Doe"). The result in the view is the same as the example of the **endsWithDoe** filter. However, thanks to our refactoring, the **endsWith** filter has become reusable and can be potentially used in other parts of the application.

Services

Through its flexible AP, services can be used for a variety of tasks. As already mentioned, controllers should be made as thin as possible, which means that you usually outsource complex routines and algorithms to services. In fact, a service can be used not only by controllers, but pretty much by any application component. Some services can be used in other services. The integration of a service is done basically by using dependency injection.

Services have some special features that you need to consider when implementing an application. An essential property of services is the fact that each service is instantiated only once in an application. Thus, each service follows the Singleton pattern. The so-called *injector* in AngularJS ensures that each time you submit a service via dependency injection, the same instance is always reused. Thus, services are particularly suitable for logic and data reuse in more than one controller.

Another characteristic of services is the interchangeability and the definition of a clear and stable API associated with services. It is important that you design the public interface of your services so that you can easily replace an implementation. This is an important characteristic particularly with regard to the testability and the flexibility of your application, so you can, for example, define a service that will ensure that your application data is persisted. You could offer the typical CRUD operations in its public API. During the development of the overall system you could initially begin offering an implementation based on the HTML5 Local Storage API. When the backend is ready, you could replace the service implementation so that the service addresses a REST endpoint and stores the data on a server.

Besides the aspect of interchangeability and flexibility, the example just mentioned showcases another application of services. It makes sense to use services in an AngularJS application as data access objects because they can be fed to every controller that need the corresponding data.

Listing 2.21 shows the definition of a service.

Listing 2.21: The definition of a log service

```
ngular.module('myApp').factory('log', function() {
  // Service Implementation
  var log = function(level, message) {
    console.log('[' + level + '] ' + message);
  };

  // Public API
  return {
    error: function(message) {
      log('ERROR', message);
    },
    info: function(message) {
      log('INFO', message);
    },
    debug: function(message) {
      log('DEBUG', message);
    }
  };
});
```

Listing 2.21 shows a simple service which defined a pretty rudimentary logging API and offers an implementation based on **console.log()**. The service implementation does not come close to a level that makes it useable in production, and is deliberately kept simple for educational purpose.

The interesting thing about this snippet is that we did not define the service using a function called **service()**. Instead, we used the **factory()** function. In fact, in AngularJS a service can be defined in one of several ways. Among them a service can be registered using the **service()** function. You usually use this method only for a specific application, namely if you want to register a property of an existing class as a service instance.

Specifically, there are five methods for defining a service. Table 2.1 contains an overview that briefly highlights these five methods.

The most common form is the so-called *factory* method, which we used in Listing 2.21. In addition to **factory()**, you can define a service using the **value()**, **constant()**, **provider()** and **service()** functions.

Service definition	API	Description
Provider	provider(...)	Basic API for defining a service that can be configured during the configuration phase. Must provide a **$get()** function that returns the appropriate service instance. Can be called using a constructor function or an object.
Factory	factory(...)	Built on top of the Provider API. Abstracted from the aspect of configurability to allow a more convenient service definition if configurability is irrelevant.
Constructor function	service(...)	Built on top of the Factory API. Instantiates the service instance using the **new** operator in conjunction with the given constructor. Thus, an instance of an existing class can be registered as a service.
Value as service	value(...)	Built on top of the Factory API. Allows the registration of a value as a service. The value can be a primitive type, an object or a function.
Constant as service	constant(...)	Registers a constant value as a service. The value cannot be changed at runtime.

Table 2.1: The five methods for service definition

Now, of course, you might ask this legitimate question: What is the difference between all these service definition methods?

As shown in Figure 2.2, the various service definition methods are mostly built on top of each other. The **providerCache** and **instanceCache** serve as a basic container for the provider or service instances of your AngularJS application. Using the **provider()** function you can access the **providerCache** and register a provider this way. Therefore, a service provider is a component that must define a **$get()** function, which is eventually called by the framework and must return a service instance. The singleton instances of your services are managed in the **instanceCache**. Before the actual service object is instantiated, however, you can configure the service object in the configuration phase of your application using a provider. You do not have this option with the other methods. Thus, the service definition for a provider is the most powerful but at the same time the most complex way to obtain a service instance.

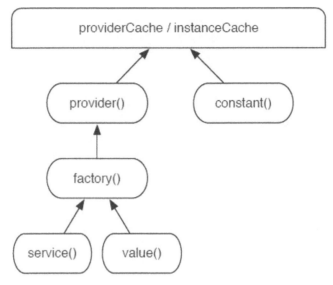

Figure 2.2: The service ecosystem

A service factory, which we have used in the definition of our **log** service, internally uses the **provider()** function and simplifies the definition by abstracting from the aspect of configurability. This way, you can create a service definition by simply defining a factory function that returns a service object. The downside is that you can no longer configure your service.

Figure 2.2 also shows that the **service()** and **value()** functions are in turn built on top of a factory. Therefore, the **service()** function expects a constructor function next to the service name. Internally, the **service()** function creates a service factory, which eventually instantiates the service object using the passed constructor function. The fact that the instantiation is done internally using the **new** operator allows you to work within the constructor to define your service object. This means that you can register an instance of an existing class as a service instance quite simply.

The **value()** function is the simplest but also the most primitive way of obtaining a service definition. As the name implies, the **value()** function registers a value as a service. In this case, the value can contain a primitive data type such as a number or boolean. However, any objects or functions can thus be easily deployed as a service and be available throughout the application via dependency injection. From a purely technical point of view, the **value()** function creates a factory, which in turn encapsulates and returns the passed value in a service instance. Thus, internally the **value()** function uses the **factory()** function.

In addition to service definition methods that build on top of each other, there is also the **constant()** function. This function registers a constant value as a service. This means the registered value cannot change at run time. Therefore, the **constant()** function has direct access to both **providerCache** and **instanceCache** containers.

Now we will breathe a little life to the dry theory and clarify the description with some sample service definitions.

Based on our **log** service in Listing 2.21, which we have defined using a factory, we will now implement the same service using a provider in order to still be able to do some small configuration.

Listing 2.22: The log service definition with a provider

```
angular.module('myApp').provider('log', function() {
  /* Private state/methods */
    var prefix = '',
        suffix = '';

    // Service Implementation
    var log = function(level, message) {
        console.log(prefix + '[' + level + '] ' + message + suffix);
    };

    /* Public state/methods */
    // Configuration methods / Public methods
    this.setPrefix = function(newPrefix) {
        prefix = newPrefix;
    };

    this.setSuffix = function(newSuffix) {
        suffix = newSuffix;
    };

    this.$get = function() {
        // Public API
```

```
        return {
            error: function(message) {
                log('ERROR', message);
            },
            info: function(message) {
                log('INFO', message);
            },
            debug: function(message) {
                log('DEBUG', message);
            }
        };
    };
});
```

Listing 2.22 shows the definition of our **log** service with a provider. What is interesting in this code is the fact that we call the **provider()** function with the service name and a constructor function for the provider. As can be seen in Table 2.1, instead of a constructor function, we could alternatively pass an object that needs to be similarly constructed. In particular, this object would also have a function called **$get()**. This function will be called by AngularJS when the framework needs to create the appropriate service instance, as soon as it is requested for the first time as a dependency. In this case, this function is called exactly once for each service, because, as already mentioned, services are singleton objects.

Anyway, at this point we have chosen the alternative with the constructor function. In general, this option is also commonly used, because it allows you to define variables that you cannot access from outside. Specifically, in this example the **prefix** and **suffix** variables, which contain a prefix or suffix for our log messages. Also, the **log** variable that references the function, which is the basis of our API implementation, is "private" and not reachable from the outside.

On the other hand, the **setPrefix()** and **setSuffix()** provider functions, which are defined by using **this**, are public and during the configuration phase (in a **config()** block) are called to make the necessary settings for the service, namely define a prefix or suffix for all our log messages. The **$get()** function is also open to the public and thus potentially accessible from the outside. As already mentioned, this function has a special meaning within AngularJS and should therefore not be called from your own application code.

> **Functions in JavaScript**
> In JavaScript, functions are a very powerful construct on which you
> can map many proven software engineering concepts and paradigms.
> In particular, in your provider definition, for example, you employ the
> concept of constructor, which you use to define an anonymous class.

After preparing our provider to enable us to set a prefix or suffix, we should
now turn to the actual configuration.

Listing 2.23: The configuration of our log provider in a config() block

```
angular.module('myApp').config(function (logProvider) {
    logProvider.setPrefix('[myApp] ');
    logProvider.setSuffix('.');
});
```

Listing 2.23 shows a possible configuration of our **log** service. To configure
the service, we take the previously defined provider **logProvider** passed by
the framework (via dependency injection). We use the **setPrefix()** and
setSuffix() public instance methods to set the strings that will contain the
prefix and suffix of every log message.

> **The Configuration Block**
> Previously in this chapter we used a **config()** block to configure
> application routes using the **$routeProvider** component. You use a
> configuration block to perform configuration before the actual
> application start of our services by using the appropriate service
> provider. For this purpose, you can make the appropriate provider
> available through dependency injection by supplementing the service
> name with the string "Provider".
> It is important to note that in a configuration block you actually pass
> the service provider and not the actual service. The latter would not
> work because the framework, with some exceptions, only allows
> providers to be injected in a configuration block.
> You may still want to invoke a function of the actual service instance
> at the start of the application, for example to start a recurring task, so
> you still provide AngularJS with a special construct, a **run()** block.

After our **log** service is configured, we present an example, which shows
how we can use the service in a controller.

Listing 2.24: Using our log service

```
angular.module('myApp').controller('MyCtrl', function($scope, log) {
  log.debug('MyCtrl has been invoked');
});
```

Listing 2.24 shows how easily we can use our **log** service in a controller, by
simply specifying its name as a parameter to the controller function. We can
then access the functions that belong to the public API. In the case of the
log service, the functions are **debug()**, **info()** and **error()**, of which only
debug() is used to produce output in the browser console.

Directives

Directives are probably the most interesting feature in AngularJS because
the framework manifests its unique selling point through this feature. You
can use directives to expand the HTML vocabulary. This means that you
can invent new HTML tags and attributes. Using directives you can hide
complex logic behind a tag or an attribute. Without doubt this concept is
therefore one of the crucial aspects of AngularJS.

A major advantage is that for the first time you can create reusable web
components using directives. For instance, you can write a directive to
encapsulate certain UI widgets used frequently in your application and thus
eliminate much of redundant code that would otherwise have to be written.
By using a directive this way you can, for instance, create organization-
wide component libraries with a consistent "look and feel." You can also
ensure that repetitive components do not have to be developed again.

Using directives, applications can also be described declaratively. You
can design tags or attributes with names that are already known to a
developer. Thus they have a semantic value. New developers can get a first
idea of an application without having to look deep below the surface.
Existing developers in your team will be pleased with the resulting clarity
and related maintenance.

Directives are a powerful feature that is responsible for making sure that application code is structured and reusable. Unfortunately, the whole thing comes at a price, in the form of a very complex API.

Naming Convention

To illustrate the concept of directives in a realistic example, we now represent our **colorPicker** directive from the previous chapter and discuss its details.

Listing 2.25: The definition of the colorPicker directive

```
angular.module('myApp').directive('colorPicker', function () {

});
```

As you have learned in the prevoius chapter, you can define a directive using the **directive()** function. This function takes two parameters, the name of the directive and a factory function. Do not confuse the factory function here with the factory in the context of services.

By convention a directive name starts with a lowercase letter and follow the camel case notation if the name consists of several words. The illustration on the HTML tag or attribute defined by a directive is done through the mapping of camel case notation against the snake case notation. For example, **spreadsheet**, **chart** or **colorPicker** are valid directive names. The corresponding HTML tags would be **<spreadsheet>**, **<chart>** and **<color-picker>**. In the case of colorPicker, you can also use **<color:picker>** and **<color_picker>**. Since AngularJS uses the colon (:), hyphen (-) and underscore (_) as delimiters.

As already mentioned in the previous chapter, there are two other valid ways to call a directive, by using the **data-** or **x-** prefix. The reason for this is older browsers will only allow user-defined tags and attributes if they are prefixed by one of these prefixes. Therefore, you can also use **<data-spreadsheet>** or **<x-spreadsheet>** in your templates.

Directive Naming

It is important that you recognize and understand this naming convention to avoid any nasty surprises when creating your own directives. In particular, it is not recommended to give a directive a name that does not comply with the implicit convention.

Definition with A Link Function

AngularJS expects the factory function, which you pass as the second parameter, to return either a function or a directive definition object. If you return a function, then this function is called the link function of the directive. In the case of a directive definition object, you can control in very fine granularity how the directive should behave through a lot of properties. Thus, returning a function (link function) represents a simple case and returning a directive definition object represents a complex case.

Listing 2.26: The definition of the colorPicker directive through the return of a link function

```
angular.module('myApp').directive('colorPicker', function () {
  return function(scope, element, attrs) {
    console.log("It's me, colorPicker!");
  }
});
```

In Listing 2.26, we first consider the simple case where we return a function (a link function) in the factory function of our colorPicker directive. For each instance of our directive, the link function is called exactly once. Thus, within the link function you can register event handlers to perform DOM manipulations and perform other routines that are specific to that instance. In short, the link function allows you to perform an initialization for each instance of the directive. When calling a link function, AngularJS passes at least three parameters:

1. **scope**. A reference to the valid scope for this directive.
2. **element**. A reference to the DOM element affected by this directive.
3. **attrs**. A reference to an object, by which you can access the HTML attributes of the DOM element.

The implementation of our link function in Listing 2.26 simply writes a message to the browser console. In order to view this minimal directive in action, we need to write a small template that uses the directive.

Listing 2.27: Using the colorPicker directive in a template

```
<div color-picker></div>
<div color-picker></div>
<div color-picker></div>
```

Listing 2.27 shows a sample template that uses our minimal **colorPicker** directive. As you can see in the template, we have created a new HTML attribute with our minimum directive definition. The attribute does not have to reside in a **div** tag and can be used in any other tag. So if you implement a directive by simply returning a link function within the factory function, then by default you create a new HTML attribute. To make the example feasible, we will also create a minimal application that contains three files.

1. **index.html**. The entry point and base template of our application.
2. **app.js**. The module definition of our application.
3. **color-picker.js**. The definition of our **colorPicker** directive.

Listing 2.28: The index.html of our minimum colorPicker application

```
<!DOCTYPE html>
<html ng-app="colorPickerApp">
<head>
    <meta charset="utf-8">
</head>

<body>

<div color-picker></div>
<div color-picker></div>
<div color-picker></div>

<script src="lib/angular/angular.js"></script>
<script src="scripts/app.js"></script>
<script src="scripts/directives/colorPickerDirective.js"></script>

</body>
</html>
```

Listing 2.28 shows the **index.html** of our minimal AngularJS application. It serves as the entry point for the browser and defines the basic template of our application. To prevent this example from getting unnecessarily complex, we have inserted the example template in Listing 2.27 in our base template.

Listing 2.29: The app.js of our minimalist colorPicker application

```
var colorPickerApp = angular.module('colorPickerApp', []);
```

Listing 2.29 shows the module definition of our **colorPickerApp** module, which AngularJS loads automatically when the browser has finished loading the DOM. The instruction for AngularJS to do so can be found in the **ngApp** directive in the **index.html**.

Listing 2.30: The color-picker.js file of our minimal colorPicker application

```
colorPickerApp.directive('colorPicker', function() {
  return function(scope, element, attrs) {
    console.log("It's me, colorPicker!");
  }
});
```

Last but not least, we still need our minimal definition of our **colorPicker** directive (the **color-picker.js** file), which is shown in Listing 2.30.

The Project Structure of the Example

For the example, we have renamed the **myApp** temporary module **colorPickerApp**. In addition, we have created a **scripts** subdirectory for the JavaScript files. This directory contains the **app.js** file (that contains our module definition) and a subdirectory named **directives** that contains the **color-picker.js** file. This file includes our minimum directive definition. This structure corresponds to the structure that is automatically generated by the Yo tool when we create our application components with Yo. It has proved that for a single-module application, i.e. an application that has only one single module, it is helpful and applicable as best practice.

Definition with A Directive Definition Object

As mentioned in the previous section, you can define a directive by returning a link function in the factory function. Let's now take a closer look at the directive definition object (DDO). This type of definition is much more complex, but allows for a very fine-grained description of the behavior of a directive. You have learned such a definition in the previous chapter when we developed a **colorPicker** directive using such a DDO. Therefore, our discussion of this type of definition is also based on the colorPicker example.

Let's get started. We will convert the directive that returns a link function from the previous section to a DDO.

Listing 2.31: The definition of the colorPicker directive using a directive definition object

```
colorPickerApp.directive('colorPicker', function() {
  return {
    link: function(scope, element, attrs) {
      console.log("It's me, colorPicker as DDO!");
    }
  };
});
```

Listing 2.31 shows the definition of our **colorPicker** directive using a DDO. In this form, this definition is equivalent to the definition in Listing 2.30. You can also define a link function in the DDO by assigning the function to the **link** property.

Next, we want to change our directive so that instead of defining an HTML attribute, it will define an HTML tag. We do this by using the **restrict** property of the scope in the DDO.

Listing 2.32: Defining the scope using restrict

```
colorPickerApp.directive('colorPicker', function() {
  return {
    restrict: 'E',
    link: function(scope, element, attrs) {
      console.log("It's me, colorPicker as DDO!");
    }
```

```
    };
});
```

Listing 2.32 shows that we set the scope to **E**, which restricts the directive to HTML elements or HTML tags. Now we can only use the directive as an HTML tag. As such, we need to modify our template to that in Listing 2.33.

Listing 2.33: Using the colorPicker directive as an HTML tag

```
<color-picker></color-picker>
<color-picker></color-picker>
<color-picker></color-picker>
```

The value of the **restrict** property has to be a string that contains one or more letters from the set {'E', 'A', 'C', 'M'}. The letters have the following meaning:

- **E**. HTML element or HTML tag
- **A**. HTML attribute
- **C**. CSS class
- **M**. HTML comment

Therefore, directives can also be used in conjunction with a CSS class or an HTML comment.

It is essential to note that for most directives there is certain logic or a certain markup hiding behind the corresponding HTML tag or attribute. You usually implement the logic in the link function. As for the markup for a directive, you normally use the **template** or **templateUrl** property. For both properties, AngularJS expects a string value. You can use the **template** property to set the template markup directly as a string within the DDO. On the other hand, the **templateUrl** property expects a URL to the template.

> ## Directive Templates
> As a guide, short templates are defined directly in the DDO while longer templates are stored in a separate file and referenced by **templateUrl**.

In our colorPicker example, we work with a more complex template, so we store it in a separate file and set a reference to it in the **templateUrl** property.

Listing 2.34: Referencing the template of the colorPicker directive

```
colorPickerApp.directive('colorPicker', function() {
  return {
    templateUrl: 'templates/colorPickerTemplate.html',
    restrict: 'E',
    link: function(scope, element, attrs) {
      console.log("It's me, colorPicker as DDO!");
    }
  };
});
```

Listing 2.34 indicates that the template for our **colorPicker** directive can be found in the **colorPickerTemplate.html** file, which is located in the **templates** subdirectory. This is the same template we had in the previous chapter. For your reading convenience, however, we print it again in Listing 2.35.

Listing 2.35: The template definition of the colorPicker directive

```
R:<input type="range"
       min="0" max="255" step="1"
       ng-model="r"><br>
G:<input type="range"
       min="0" max="255" step="1"
       ng-model="g"><br>
B:<input type="range"
       min="0" max="255" step="1"
       ng-model="b"><br>
A:<input type="range"
       min="0" max="1" step="0.01"
       ng-model="a">

<div style="width: 300px; height: 100px;
       background-color:
       rgba({{ r }}, {{ g }}, {{ b }}, {{ a }});">
</div>
```

Our colorPicker is now complete and the example will work. You can see in your browser that AngularJS creates three instances of the color picker. If you take a close look, however, you will find two major flaws.

So far, our color picker has no initial value. As a result, initially there is no color preview because the corresponding **r**, **g**, **b** and **a** scope variables are initially undefined and therefore the CSS **background-color** property cannot be rendered. Only after we have moved every slider at least once, will the variables be assigned appropriate values and a color preview appear.

On top of that, our color picker is not a self-contained component and has an unpleasant effect on the surrounding context. This is to say that the three instances are not independent. If we move, say, the **r** controller for one instance, the **r** controllers of the other two instances will move at the same time. The reason for this is that at this stage the instances do not have a scope yet. Thus, each color picker instance is currently still bound to the **r**, **g**, **b** and **a** variables from the root scope and modifies these values when a slider moves. This situation is visualized in Figure 2.3 again. The resulting two-way data binding leads to the interaction of colorPicker instances.

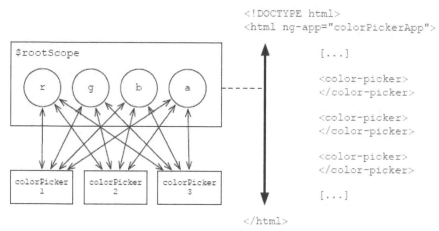

Figure 2.3: colorPicker instances access the root scope

Independent Scopes for Directives

Before we look at the problem with the initial values, we first need to make sure our **colorPicker** instances have their own scopes.

Listing 2.36: Defining an independent scope for the colorPicker directive

```
colorPickerApp.directive('colorPicker', function() {
  return {
    scope: true,
```

```
      templateUrl: 'templates/colorPickerTemplate.html',
      restrict: 'E',
      link: function(scope, element, attrs) {
        console.log("It's me, colorPicker as DDO!");
      }
   };
});
```

Listing 2.36 shows that the directive instances receive their own scope by setting the **scope** property of our DDO to **true**. So, if you run the example, you will see that the color picker instances no longer interfere with each other. Each instance has its own scope, in which the **r**, **g**, **b** and **a** variables are defined. This means that two-way data binding works on the variables in each instance's own scope, leaving the root scope untouched.

This solution makes us one step closer to a self-contained and reusable component. However, there is still a bitter aftertaste.

An instance of our **colorPicker** directive has its own scope, but that scope currently still inherits a prototype of its parent scope, which in this case is still the root scope. This means we can access the variable scope and function of the parent scope in our **colorPicker** directive and can potentially manipulate them. If we intend to create a self-contained and reusable component, then the current **colorPicker** directive is obviously not ideal. Sooner or later we may rely on certain features or variables from the parent scope and thus become dependent on the parent. As a result, our component can only function if it lives in this context. It is not a self-contained and reusable component.

In addition, inadvertent manipulation of a variable from the parent scope may lead to nasty and hard to identify errors, which will ultimately cause time-consuming debugging sessions.

To avoid this problem and provide a clean break from the parent scope, AngularJS introduces the concept of isolated scopes.

Isolated Scopes

You can create an isolated scope within a directive. Although an isolated scope is still part of the valid scope hierarchy of an application, such a scope does not inherit a prototype of its parent scope. This means that you have no way of accessing data or logic of the parent scope from within a directive's isolated scope. Accordingly, you cannot inadvertently modify the parent scope. This means the isolated scope is a key concept when creating reusable and self-contained components.

Listing 2.37: Defining an isolated scope for the colorPicker directive

```
colorPickerApp.directive('colorPicker', function() {
  return {
    scope: {},
    templateUrl: 'templates/colorPickerTemplate.html',
    restrict: 'E',
    link: function(scope, element, attrs) {
      console.log("It's me, colorPicker as DDO!");
    }
  };
});
```

As shown in Listing 2.37, we tell AngularJS to create an isolated scope for our directive by assigning an empty object ({}) to the **scope** property of the DDO. Therefore, at this point we have a reusable color picker without dependencies on any context. We may still inadvertently manipulate a variable from the parent scope when implementing the directive logic in the link function. This constellation of the scope hierarchy can be seen in Figure 2.4.

So far, so good. However, as already mentioned, with the isolated scope you can access data and functions of the parent scope. And if you think carefully about it, you will find that the majority of reusable components need to connect to their context. These connections can be useful for several purposes. One of them is for a component to receive data from its surrounding context.

Our colorPicker requires such access to its context. On the one hand, we want to pass initial values. On the other hand, we want to notify the environment when the colorPicker has changed a color value internally. So what now?

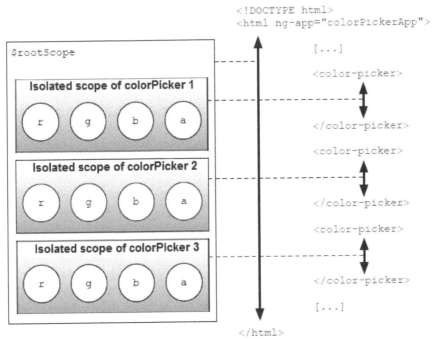

Figure 2.4: colorPicker instances with isolated scopes

Despite the adjective isolated in isolated scope, AngularJS allows you controlled connections to the parent scope. There are three ways you can make such a connection. Probably the most often used connection is the one that establishes a two-way data binding to a variable in the parent scope. The framework also provides you the opportunity to create a unidirectional connection to the parent scope as well as to call a function defined in the parent scope within the directive. In the latter case, you can even call the directive function and pass internal data.

In our colorPicker directive we use the unidirectional link to set initial values and the function to notify the environment of the change of a color value. Listing 2.38 shows the whole thing.

Listing 2.38: The definition of an isolated scope with controlled connections to the parent scope

```
colorPickerApp.directive('colorPicker', function() {
  return {
    scope: {
      r: '@initR',
```

```
      g: '@initG',
      b: '@initB',
      a: '@initA',
      onChange: '&'
    },
    templateUrl: 'templates/colorPickerTemplate.html',
    restrict: 'E',
    link: function(scope, element, attrs) {
      console.log("It's me, colorPicker as DDO!");
    }
  };
});
```

Listing 2.38 shows how you can establish a number of connections to the parent scope, despite using an isolated scope. As such, you can access the data and functions of the parent scope. The main factor is that you no longer assign an empty object to the **scope** property of the DDO. Instead, you specify a configuration object. The key in this configuration object is how you specify which scope variables from the directive's isolated scope should connect to the parent scope. As already mentioned, there are basically three forms. These are specified by the prefixes =, @ and &.

- =. Indicates that the scope variable in the isolated scope of the directive that is specified as the key is to establish a two-way data binding to a variable in the parent scope.
- @. Indicates that the scope variable in the directive's isolated scope that is specified as the key is to establish a one-way data binding to the parent scope.
- &. Indicates that the scope variable specified as the key should reference a function in the parent scope and be able to invoke the function and pass internal data from the directive.

This will become clear when you look at how you use the colorPicker directive definition in Listing 2.38.

Listing 2.39: Using the colorPicker directive by specifying initial values

```
<color-picker init-r="255"
    init-g="0"
    init-b="0"
    init-a="1.0">
</color-picker>
```

> ## Connecting to the Parent Scope
> The string that follows a prefix specifies which HTML attribute of the directive HTML tag contains information about which variable or function from the parent scope of the connection should be involved. If the corresponding HTML attribute name used as the key is the same as the name of the variable in the isolated scopes, then you can omit the string following the prefix. In Listing 2.38, this is shown by the **onChange** scope variable.

Listing 2.39 shows a section of the template that uses our **colorPicker** directive. We also want to pass data to the directive despite it having an isolated scope. In this case, the data we are passing are the initial values for the individual color components. The HTML attributes used here, **init-r**, **init-g**, **init-b** and **init-a**, which correspond to our directive definition in Listing 2.38, must be specified in snake case notation. Because the scope variables for the color components are **r**, **g**, **b** and **a** (and not **initR**, **initG**, etc.), we need the HTML attributes in addition to the connection type (here: @) in camel case notation, hence **initR**, **initG**, **initB** and **initA**. The unidirectional binding works well here because we only want to set initial values, and thus do not need data binding in two directions. Figure 2.5 illustrates the relationship again.

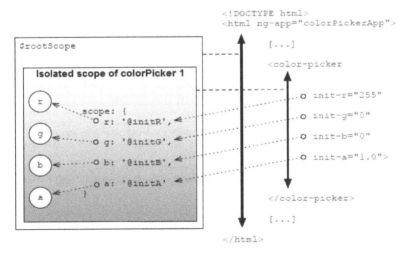

Figure 2.5: Unidirectional binding for scope variables r, g, b and a

Unidirectional Binding

Using unidirectional binding you can pass data from a parent scope to a directive that has an isolated scope. This type of binding is especially useful when the directive only consumes the data and the higher-level controller is not interested in any changes. We call it one-way binding because data exchange occurs only in one direction, from the parent controller to the directive. By contrast, you use two-way data binding if you not only want to pass data to the directive, but are also interested in changes to this data.

Using unidirectional binding in this example merely means you can use HTML attributes to pass fixed values to the **colorPicker** directive. Often, however, you want to be notified if the value of the variable has changed in the parent scope. In this case you do not assign a fixed value to the HTML attribute. Instead, you assign an expression that is constantly re-evaluated when the scope variable changes in the parent scope. So something like this:

```
<color-picker init-r="{{r}}"></color-picker>
```

Within the directive you can then observe the scope variable **r** and execute certain logic in response to changes. Practically, you use the **$observe()** function on the **attrs** object, that AngularJS passes as the third parameter of the link function.

We now have an insulated scope assigned to our colorPicker directive to turn it into a self-contained and reusable component. In addition, we have defined five controlled connections to the parent scope. Specifically, these are the four unidirectional connections (**initR**, **initG**, etc.), with which we can pass initial values to a color picker instance, and a working link (&) that we will subsequently use to call a callback function when a color changes.

Before we discuss the implementation of the link function, we will first introduce the **MainCtrl** controller, in which we define the callback function. The key point is we can have this callback function in spite of having an isolated scope by using **onChange**.

Listing 2.40: The definition of the MainCtrl controller with the handleColorChange() callback function

```
colorPickerApp.controller('MainCtrl', function ($scope) {
    $scope.handleColorChange = function(r,g,b,a) {
        console.log('handleColorChange', r, g, b, a);
    };
});
```

Listing 2.40 shows the implementation of the **MainCtrl** controller just mentioned. The **handleColorChange()** function, which we define in the controller scope, represents the callback function that we want to make accessible to the **colorPicker** directive. In this example, we respond to a color change in the color picker with a simple console output. In addition, we provide the value of each color component for review.

To maintain a good style, we define this controller in a separate file named **mainCtrl.js**. We also create a directory called **controllers** under the **scripts** directory for our controller. The **mainCtrl.js** file is then saved in the **controllers** directory. We have to modify our **index.html** file so that it will load the newly created **mainCtrl.js** file. In addition, we still have to use the **ngController** directive to determine for which DOM section of the controller a new scope should be defined. We have to make sure that the DOM element that initiates the section is a parent element of our colorPicker instance. Therefore, we add the **ng-controller** attribute to the **<body>** element. The result of these changes can be seen in Listing 2.41.

Listing 2.41: The index.html with the ngController directive

```
<!DOCTYPE html>
<html ng-app="colorPickerApp">
<head>
    <meta charset="utf-8">
</head>

<body ng-controller="MainCtrl">

<color-picker init-r="255" init-g="0" init-b="0" init-a="1.0">
</color-picker>

<script src="lib/angular/angular.js"></script>
<script src="scripts/app.js"></script>
<script src="scripts/directives/colorPickerDirective.js"></script>
```

```
<script src="scripts/controllers/mainCtrl.js"></script>

</body>
</html>
```

Next, we change how we call the **colorPicker** directive so that we can pass a callback function. The relevant part of the **index.html** is shown in Listing 2.42.

Listing 2.42: Supplementing the colorPicker call by specifying the callback function

```
<color-picker init-r="255" init-g="0" init-b="0" init-a="1.0"
        on-change="handleColorChange(r, g, b, a)">
</color-picker>
```

We use the **on-change** attribute to pass a reference to the **handleColorChange()** function to our **colorPicker** instance. Again, the snake case notation is used because we have written the **onChange** scope variable that will contain the reference in the directive definition. Recall that the mapping of names from the DDO to the corresponding HTML attributes is done by replacing the camel case notation with the snake case notation.

To check the connection function created, we should conduct a brief test and call the **handleColorChange** function via the **onChange** attribute in the link function of the **colorPicker** directive. Listing 2.43 prints the corresponding source code.

Listing 2.43: Call to the handleColorChange function via the onChange reference

```
colorPickerApp.directive('colorPicker', function() {
  return {
    scope: {
      r: '@initR',
      g: '@initG',
      b: '@initB',
      a: '@initA',
      onChange: '&'
    },
    templateUrl: 'templates/colorPickerTemplate.html',
    restrict: 'E',
    link: function(scope, element, attrs) {
      console.log("It's me, colorPicker as DDO!");
      scope.onChange();
```

```
    }
  };
});
```

The scope hierarchy and the scenario just described are summarized in Figure 2.6. The rectangles with rounded corners symbolize scope variables that reference a function.

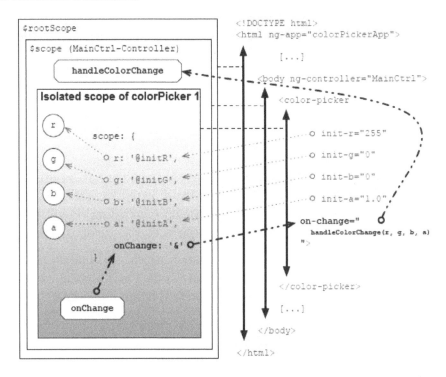

Figure 2.6: The connection function for the onChange scope variable

If you run the example, you will get the expected output in the console like the one shown in Figure 2.7.

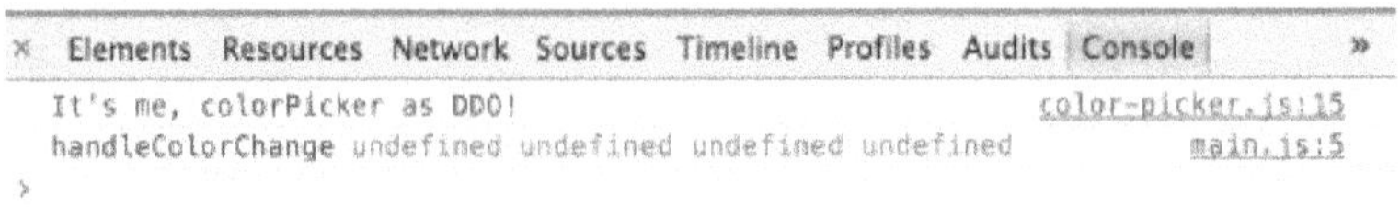

Figure 2.7: The console output in Chrome

This means that despite the isolated scope in our **colorPicker** directive we can create a working link to the parent scope and to the scope of the **MainCtrl** controller, and thus can reach the **handleColorChange** function through the **onChange** scope variable. The output contains the color components but so far the value is **undefined**. However, it is also clear that is because we did not pass parameters in our call within the directive.

Well, now we can devote ourselves to the final requirement and implement the link function so that the **handleColorChange** callback function is only called on color changes. The final implementation of the link function is shown in Listing 2.44.

Listing 2.44: The final implementation of the link function of our colorPicker directive

```
colorPickerApp.directive('colorPicker', function() {
return {

  [...]

  link: function(scope, element, attrs) {
    var COLORS = ['r', 'g', 'b', 'a'];

    COLORS.forEach(function(value) {
      scope.$watch(value, function(newValue, oldValue) {
        if (newValue !== oldValue) {
          if (angular.isFunction(scope.onChange)) {
            scope.onChange(generateColorChangeObject());
          }
        }
      });
    });

    var generateColorChangeObject = function() {
      var obj = {};

      COLORS.forEach(function(value) {
        obj[value] = scope[value];
      });

      return obj;
    };
  }
};
});
```

Basically, the implementation is quite simple. First, we define an array that contains the names of our scope variables for the individual color values. We do this solely to keep the following source code clearer and shorter. Then, we iterate over this array (using **forEach**) and use **scope.$watch** to register a watcher for each color component. The **$watch** function expects two parameters. The first parameter is the name of the scope variable to be monitored for changes. To the second parameter we pass a function that will be invoked in the event of a change. The framework passes two parameters, **newValue** and **oldValue**, which contains the new and old values of the scope variable, respectively. We then check if the two values are equal and, if they are not, call the **handleColorChange** callback function, which can be reached through the **onChange** scope variable. Before that, we make sure that **onChange** actually references a function.

Now we introduce another AngularJS convention. The **handleColorChange** callback function is defined to take four parameters, namely the individual color components **r**, **g**, **b** and **a**. With the function, we can transfer these parameters to a parameter object. Figure 2.8 shows how such a parameter object would look like.

```
// parameter object          [...]

{                             <color-picker
    r: VALUE_FOR_r,               [...]
    g: VALUE_FOR_g,               on-change="handleColorChange(r, g, b, a)">
    b: VALUE_FOR_b,
    a: VALUE_FOR_a,           </color-picker>
}                             [...]
```

Figure 2.8: The parameter object when calling handleColorChange

Basically the key parameters of the object must match the parameter names in the template, so that the parameters are ultimately transferred correctly. In Figure 2.8 the necessary matching items are shown in bold. In our implementation, we use a small helper function called **generateColorChangeObject** to generate this parameter object.

At this point we are done. Using a directive we have created a self-contained and reusable component called colorPicker. It can be used in a template by specifying **<color-picker>**. Because AngularJS registered this directive under some other names, it can also be used using **<color:picker>** and **<data-color-picker>**. In addition, we may pass initial values to our color picker using HTML attributes. Finally, we have implemented a mechanism that informs the parent component by calling a callback function to notify a color has changed.

If you run the example and move any of the sliders, you will get a bunch of console output that should be similar to the one in Figure 2.9.

×	Elements	Resources	Network	Sources	Timeline	Profiles	Audits	Console	»
	handleColorChange 247 0 0 1.0							main.js:5	
	handleColorChange 243 0 0 1.0							main.js:5	
	handleColorChange 236 0 0 1.0							main.js:5	
	handleColorChange 234 0 0 1.0							main.js:5	
	handleColorChange 229 0 0 1.0							main.js:5	
	handleColorChange 223 0 0 1.0							main.js:5	

Figure 2.9: The final console output in Chrome

Besides the DDO properties mentioned here, there are other properties that you can use to control the operation of the directive. You can surely imagine that the potentials of directives are still far from being exhausted with the example presented here. However, in order to explain every single nuance of directives, you would need another book that explains this concept. Table 2.2 shows the overview.

The Relationship to Polymer

Although the concept of directives and the associated creation of independent HTML elements make AngularJS unique, admittedly the concept still has weakness. Despite the level of isolation you can achieve with isolated scopes, instances of a directive are still part of the DOM. It means not only can you refer to the corresponding HTML element in the DOM, you can also formulate a CSS selector to select the DOM element defined by the HTML template of the directive. In other words, in directives you can only have isolation at the data level. At the DOM level, however, you can easily write a script that modifies the inner working of a directive, which can ultimately lead to nasty errors.

DDO property	Valid values	Description
link	A function with a maximum of four parameters	Definition of the link function that for each directive instance is called exactly once. AngularJS passes the following 3 or 4 parameters to the function, depending on the **require** property: - **scope**. The scope - **element**. HTML element - **attrs**. Access to the HTML attributes - **ctrl**. The controller (if require is set)
compile	A function with a maximum of three parameters	Definition of the compile function that for each directive (not instance!) Is called exactly once. AngularJS passes the function three parameters: - **tElement**. Template element - **tAttrs**. Access to template attributes - **transclude**. Link function for the transclusion
restrict	string	Restriction of the scope whose value can be Attributes (A), Elements (E), CSS classes (C), comments (M) or a combination of them
template	string	Definition of the HTML template
templateUrl	string	Definition of the URL to the HTML template, if the template is located in a separate file
scope	boolean or object	Scope definition
replace	boolean	Indicates whether or not the directive tag will be replaced by the directive template
require	string	Definition of a controller dependency of another directive
controller	function	More complex directives can have their own controller
transclude	boolean	Definition of a transclusion, if we are allowing an innerHTML field when calling the directive in the directive tag. Used in connection with the **ngTransclude** directive
terminal	boolean	Indicates whether the directive is to be processed in the template directive
priority	number	Determines the processing order when several directives act on the same DOM element. Directives with higher priority are processed before those with lower priority. If two directives have the same priority, the order of processing is not defined.

Table 2.2: The overview of DDO properties of directives

However, there is a reason for this weakness. In the initial phase of AngularJS, shadow DOM, custom elements, templates, etc, which would allow for isolation and encapsulation at the DOM level, were not even in the first draft of any W3C specifications. Thus, you had to live with this limitation and implement the concept of directives without this kind of isolation.

At the time of writing this book, we were one step closer. There were already W3C specifications even though they were not yet implemented in any browser. At least, there were first drafts, so that dedicated developers can use polyfills or shims. These are small software artifacts that compensate for functionality not available natively with the appropriate emulation of the same API. New browser functionality can thus be made available to a certain extent even in older browsers.

At this point, the Polymer project (http://polymer-project.org) comes into play. Polymer provides a polyfill for the aforementioned W3C specifications and supports the use of the functionality discussed, some even in older versions of Internet Explorer. Polymer goes a step further by defining genuine self-contained and reusable components on the basis of the specifications mentioned. Of course, it is also possible to use Polymer to develop your own components that have these properties.

Because of this, it is obvious that you should try to use the Polymer approach in the implementation of the directive. In fact, the developers of AngularJS have announced that the directive functions will be based on Polymer in a future version of AngularJS.

Summary

- A module represents the coarsest structure in AngularJS. It serves as a container for a controller, filter, service and directive. In addition, it can have as many **config()** and **run()** blocks.
- You use a controller to define an independent scope for a DOM. You should try to keep a service slim and outsource complex logic to a controller.

- Unlike most other JavaScript frameworks, the model layer consists of ordinary JavaScript constructs such as objects or primitive data types. Nevertheless, the framework can offer the feature of two-way data binding using these ordinary JavaScript structures by employing dirty checking for changes.
- Routes make an AngularJS application a single page application and provide us with deep linking.
- Views are instances of templates and are generated at run-time, when the framework has processed the required templates. The template is the HTML code of our application.
- There are two types of filters in AngularJS, the collection filter and the formatting filter.
- The collection filter is used in conjunction of the **ngRepeat** directive to filter or transform the underlying collection.
- The formatting filter is used in conjunction with expressions to format or transform an evaluated value before being output.
- A service is a singleton that contains the bulk of an application's logic. It can be used for a variety of tasks, including to act as data access objects.
- Directives are at the heart of AngularJS and are therefore the unique feature of the framework. They allow us to define new HTML elements and attributes. These elements or attributes can create their own template and have their own logic.

Chapter 3
The BookMonkey Project

After discussing the basic concepts of AngularJS, we now want to use what we know so far to build a real-world application with AngularJS. We will also base it on specific use cases to introduce other mechanisms that make AngularJS great.

Project and Process Presentation

The project that we are implementing is called BookMonkey. It is a small web application to browse a book collection, view detailed information about a book and tag a book to put it in a category. There will also be an administration area that allows an administrator to manage the database.

The implementation will be carried out in iterative steps. The order of these steps is chosen such that they will provide the highest educational value. For example, even if it would be preferable in a real project, the test-driven development approach will not be the first step. We could shed light on many aspects of a popular approach and might lose focus on the core functionality of the framework. Therefore, we will introduce the test-first approach only in some future steps.

In order to make the goals of the individual steps tangible, there is a user story to be met at each iteration.

The project backend system is not the subject of this chapter. However, we have created a rudimentary backend implementation based on Node.js that you can use.

Requirements

To run the examples in this project, you need a modern browser. We tested the examples in Chrome and recommend the latest version of this browser. However, every other browser that implements the ECMAScript language standard version 5 or later should be able to run the project easily. Google Chrome can be downloaded for free from this site.

```
http://www.google.com/chrome/
```

In addition, the example should be loaded from a local web server. For this purpose, you can use the **http-server** module of Node.js. This module can be downloaded from this site.

```
http://npmjs.org/package/http-server
```

Using **http-server** you can start an HTTP server from any directory. Before you can install the **http-server** module, however, you need a current version of Node.js and npm installed on your machine. You can download Node.js for free from its official website:

```
http://nodejs.org/download
```

> **npm**
> npm is now an essential part of Node.js and is thus automatically installed from the Node.js installation routine.

After Node.js and npm have been successfully installed, you can install the **http-server** module by using npm. Use this command on the console to install it:

```
npm install -g http-server
```

After a successful installation, you can start **http-server** using this command on the console:

```
http-server
```

By default a lightweight HTTP server will be started on port 8080. The HTTP server will deliver all files located in the directory where the server is running.

You also need Karma to run the tests. Karma is also installed as a Node.js module. Its official website is this.

```
http://karma-runner.github.io
```

Use the following console command to install Karma.

```
npm install -g karma
```

Finally, you need to install the Karma support for the ngScenario framework. This is the test framework for E2E testing that AngularJS brings with it. Use this command on the console to install it:

```
npm install-g karma-ng-scenario
```

Setting up the Project Environment

Before you begin the actual application development, you first need to set up the project environment. To do this, create a new directory named **bookmonkey**. In this directory, you define a basic structure by creating two subdirectories called **app** and **test**. This way, you separate tests, which you will write later, from the actual application. In the **app** directory, create an HTML file named **index.html**. This file is delivered as the default page by most web servers when the user does not reference a specific file in the address bar. Thus, it serves as the entry point into the application. The content of this file is shown in Listing 3.1.

Listing 3.1: The initial index.html of our application

```
<!DOCTYPE html>
<html>
<head>
    <meta charset="utf-8">
    <title>BookMonkey</title>
</head>
<body>
    <h1>Hello BookMonkey</h1>
</body>
</html>
```

Now change directory to the **app** directory and start the aforementioned HTTP server using this familiar command:

```
http-server
```

The command should return a successful message and tell you the port number on which the server is started.

```
Starting up http-server, serving ./ on port: 8080
Hit CTRL-C to stop the server
```

This statement simply states that you can stop the server by pressing CTRL+C. Of course, you need to leave it run for now.

You can now browse to this URL to retrieve your currently static HTML page:

```
http://localhost:8080
```

Figure 3.1: The output of the initial index.html page

If you see something similar to Figure 3.1 in your browser, you have successfully completed this step and can proceed with the AngularJS integration.

In the next step we want to integrate AngularJS in our project. In this project we use AngularJS version 1.2.10. The library we can be downloaded from its official website here.

```
Http://code.angularjs.org/1.2.10/angular.js
```

In the project the file is stored under the path **app/lib/angular/angular.js**. To do this you need to create a **lib** directory under the **app** directory. The **lib** directory in turn has a subdirectory called **angular**. While you are at it, you should also download the **ngRoute** module from http://code.angularjs.org/1.2.10/angular-route.js and put the file as

app/lib/angular-route/angular-route.js. You will need this module to use the routing functionality of AngularJS.

> ### AngularJS 1.3 and Internet Explorer 8
> In the upcoming version of 1.3, the AngularJS support for Internet Explorer 8 (IE8) will be terminated. This decision was made to allow the framework to download new extensions quickly without incurring substantial additional work associated with IE8.

Next, you need to include the framework using a **<script>** tag in your **index.html** page. You should add this tag to the end of our **<body>** tag. The **<script>** tag for including the **ngRoute** module (**angular-route.js**) should follow immediately. To quickly check if AngularJS is mounted correctly, we extend our **index.html** page to a simple two-way data binding. For this purpose, we have to tell AngularJS in which DOM section we want to create a AngularJS application. We know that we have to use the **ngApp** directive, and by annotating the **<html>** tag with the **ng-app** attribute, we define it for the entire DOM. Thus, we tell AngularJS that it should consider and evaluate the entire range as an AngularJS application. Finally, we build a simple example of a bidirectional data binding in order to make sure that our AngularJS was mounted correctly.

Listing 3.2: Our application now needs AngularJS

```
<!DOCTYPE html>
<html ng-app>
<head>
    <meta charset="utf-8">
    <title>BookMonkey</title>
</head>

<body ng-init="name='BookMonkey'">
    <h1>Hello {{ name }}</h1>
    <input type="text" ng-model="name" />

    <!-- Scripts -->
    <script src="lib/angular/angular.js"></script>
    <script src="lib/angular-route/angular-route.js"></script>
</body>
</html>
```

Here we create a new text field and use the **ngModel** directive to bind it to the scope variable **name**. We also replace our heading with the expression **Hello {{name}}** and give the **ngInit** directive the initial value for scope variable **name**. Our **index.html** page should now look like that in Listing 3.2.

Figure 3.2: The output of our index.html after including AngularJS

If you reload our browser window, the page should look like that in Figure 3.2. It already supports interaction. If you change the text in our box, the text in the header will also be updated immediately. The two-way data binding works. This means you have successfully integrated AngularJS in our project.

Using the Downloaded Project
Alternatively, you can use the accompanying project that you downloaded from the publisher's website. In this case, change directory to **ch03_01_project_init/app** and start http-server from there.

Why use automatic update at this point? And, what exactly is happening here? Because we annotate the **<html>** with the **ngApp** directive, AngularJS will evaluate all directives and expressions within this DOM section. In practice this means the whole DOM is evaluated. By using the **ngInit** directive in the **<body>** tag, we put the scope variable **name** in the scope and assign to it the string "BookMonkey". Since we have previously used no constructs, we initialize the variable in the so-called **$rootScope**. Each AngularJS application has such a **$rootScope** and it always represents the root of the resulting scope hierarchy, hence the name **$rootScope**.

The expression **Hello {{name}}** in the **<h1>** tag triggers AngularJS to use the scope in this area. Practically, the framework checks if the scope variable **name** is defined in **$rootScope**, and, if so, displays its value. In addition, the expression is evaluated every time the value of the scope variable **name** has changed.

By using the **ngModel** directive in the **<input>** tag, we establish two-way data binding on the scope variable **name**. Thus, any change to the scope variable name will be reflected in the **<input>** field. The same is also true in the opposite direction. If the input field changes, the scope variable **name** will also be automatically updated.

Project Start: The Book Details View

Now that we have laid the foundation for the project and successfully integrated AngularJS, we now need to take care of the BookMonkey project. To this end, we introduce more concepts and mechanisms of the framework to solve relevant problems. So let's look at our first task, which we define in the form of a user story:

> As user Michael, I want detailed information on a book that will tell me more about the book.

The central aspect of this story is the display of detailed information about a particular book. For this purpose, we should first make a wireframe of the view (see Figure 3.3).

Based on this wireframe we try to derive a data model that leads us directly to a JSON structure. We opt for the data model in Listing 3.3.

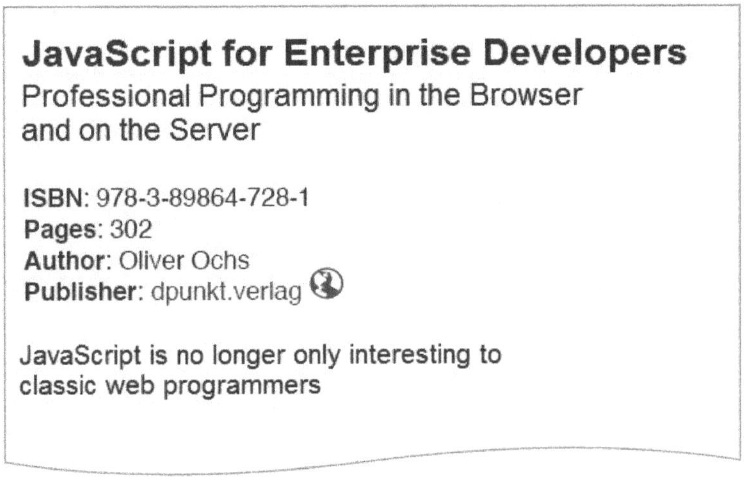

JavaScript for Enterprise Developers
Professional Programming in the Browser
and on the Server

ISBN: 978-3-89864-728-1
Pages: 302
Author: Oliver Ochs
Publisher: dpunkt.verlag

JavaScript is no longer only interesting to
classic web programmers

Figure 3.3: The wireframe of the Details view

Listing 3.3: The data model for the detailed view of a book in JSON format

```
{
  "title"    : "JavaScript for Enterprise Developers",
  "subtitle" : "Professional Programming in the Browser"
       + "and on the Server",
  "isbn"     : "978-3-89864-728-1",
  "abstract" : "JavaScript is no longer only interesting to"
       + " classic web programmers.",
  "numPages" : 302,
  "author" : "Oliver Ochs",
  "publisher": {
    "name" : "dpunkt.verlag",
    "url" : "http://dpunkt.de/"
  }
}
```

Using the Downloaded Project
To test the code in this section, you can use the accompanying project that you downloaded from the publisher's website. To do this, change directory to **ch03_02_details_view/app** and start http-server from there.

The Template for the Details View with Expressions

We continue with the creation of a template for this view. For this purpose, we create a new directory called **templates** for our templates in the **app** directory. In this new directory we create an HTML file named **book_details.html**. This file will contain the definition of the template.

Listing 3.4: The template for the book Details view

```
<h2>{{ book.title }}</h2>
<h3>{{ book.subtitle }}</h3>
<p>
  <ul>
    <li>ISBN: {{ book.isbn }}</li>
    <li>Number of Pages: {{ book.numPages }}</li>
    <li>Author: {{ book.author }}</li>
    <li>
      Publisher:
      <a ng-href="{{ book.publisher.url }}"
        target="_blank">
        {{ book.publisher.name }}
      </a>
    </li>
  </ul>
</p>
<hr>
<p>
  {{ book.abstract }}
</p>
```

Listing 3.4 shows the HTML code of the template for the book Details view. We use expressions **{{book.title}}**, **{{book.subtitle}}**, etc to display relevant accounting information. In order for these expressions to be evaluated successfully, the scope variable **book** must be in the scope that is valid for this view, and **book** must point to an object that contains the corresponding properties (**title**, **subtitle**, etc). We will define the scope for this view using a controller. However, first let's look at yet another feature of the template in Listing 3.4.

> **Internationalization**
> In the example used here, we do not tackle internationalization.
> However, there are some AngularJS modules that can handle it. The
> best known and most widely used module is ng-translate from Pascal
> Precht. It can be easily adapted to existing service structures, has
> extensive documentation and is still actively being developed. You can
> download this module from http://pascalprecht.github.io/angular-
> translate.

Templates with ngBind and ngBindTemplate

Consider the HTML template in Listing 3.5.

Listing 3.5: Displaying book information with ngBind

```
<h2 ng-bind="book.title"></h2>
<h3 ng-bind="book.subtitle"></h3>
<p>
  <ul>
    <li ng-bind-template="ISBN: {{ book.isbn }}"></li>
    <li ng-bind-template="Number of Pages:
       {{ book.numPages }}"></li>
    <li ng-bind-template="Author: {{ book.author }}"></li>
    <li>
      Publisher:
      <a ng-bind="book.publisher.name"
        ng-href="{{ book.publisher.url }}"
        target="_blank">
      </a>
    </li>
  </ul>
</p>
<hr>
<p ng-bind="book.abstract">
</p>
```

In Listing 3.5 we have largely replaced the expressions with special **ngbind** attributes. The **ngBind** directive that defines the **ng-bind** attribute is
also part of the standard repertoire of the framework. Technically, the
directive binds the value of a scope variable that is specified as an attribute

value to an annotated HTML element. Finally, using this directive produces the same output as with the equivalent expressions. Compared to an expression, however, the **ngBind** directive has two decisive advantages:

1. Before AngularJS finishes evaluating an expression, the expression can be seen as it is on the view. This does not happen with **ngBind**.
2. When generating output from expressions, AngularJS always creates a new DOM element to replace the old DOM element that contains the old value, if the value of the corresponding variable scope has changed. If you instead use the **ngBind** directive to generate output, the framework creates no new DOM element and instead updates the text content of the existing DOM element with the new value of the scope variable. Compared to an expression, **ngBind** has a performance advantage and usually consumes lower memory within our application.

In addition, the template in Listing 3.5 also uses a directive that is related to **ngBind**, the **ngBindTemplate** directive. As the name of the directive implies, you can use it to define a template for the text content of an HTML element. The **ngBindTemplate** directive is useful when we want to generate output that combines a static string with the value of a variable scope. In addition, **ngBindTemplate** can also produce output that mixes the values of multiple scope variables, because we can specify multiple expressions with this directive. The **ngBindTemplate** directive also has the same advantages as **ngBind** over simple expressions.

Defining the Application Module

After optimizing the template, we now want to implement the controller that provides the scope for this view and resides in the scope of the **book** variable with a corresponding **Book** object. In addition, we want to create our first route. To do this we need to extend our project structure and the **index.html** file. The new version of our **index.html** file is shown in Listing 3.6.

Listing 3.6: An advanced version of index.html

```
<!DOCTYPE html>
<html ng-app="bmApp">
<head>
```

```
  <meta charset="utf-8">
  <title>BookMonkey</title>
</head>
<body>
  <header>
    <h1>BookMonkey</h1>
  </header>

  <div ng-view>
  </div>

  <!-- Scripts -->
  <script src="lib/angular/angular.js"></script>
  <script src="lib/angular-route/angular-route.js">
  </script>
  <script src="scripts/app.js"></script>
  <script
    src="scripts/controllers/book_details.js">
  </script>
</body>
</html>
```

Listing 3.6 shows a module, specified using the **ngApp** directive, which
AngularJS should load automatically when the DOM has finished loading.
Once the browser has loaded the DOM, the **bmApp** module should be
started. At this point we can already anticipate that our BookMonkey
application will only have one module. Within this module we will
therefore define and implement all application components.

The First Route

Looking at the **<script>** tags in Listing 3.6, we realize we need two more
JavaScript files: **app.js** and **book_details.js**. The **app.js** file will contain the
definition of our **bmApp** module and route definition. In the
book_details.js file we will implement the **BookDetailsCtrl** controller that
provides the data and functionality for the book Details view. To do this we
first create in a directory named **scripts** under the **app** directory. In this new
directory we will store the entire JavaScript source code of the
BookMonkey application. Next, we create a file called **app.js** in the **scripts**
directory. Below the **scripts** directory we also create a directory called
controllers, in which we create the **book_details.js** file. At the same time,

we will also implement another controller in our application and store it in the **controllers** directory. In addition to the **controllers** directory, later in the next steps we will also create more directories in the **scripts** directory for directives, services and filters.

Listing 3.7: The definition of bmApp module and the first route in app.js

```
var bmApp = angular.module('bmApp', ['ngRoute']);

bmApp.config(function ($routeProvider) {
    $routeProvider.when('/books/:isbn', {
        templateUrl: 'templates/book_details.html',
        controller: 'BookDetailsCtrl'
    });
});
```

Listing 3.7 shows the source code for **app.js**. In the first line we define our **bmApp** module with the **module()** function from AngularJS. It is important that the module name is passed as the first parameter. The module name corresponds to the name used for the **ngApp** directive in the **index.html** file. The second parameter is an array, which other AngularJS modules for our **bmApp** module will depend on. Because we want to use routes in our BookMonkey application, we need to insert the **ngRoute** module at this point. This module is available, because we have included the **angular-route.js** file in our **index.html** file (see Listing 3.6).

Furthermore, we use **$routeProviders** to configure our first route in a **config()** block. Recall that we may use dependency injection to inject a service provider to configure the **config()** block in the configuration phase of our application. This means that we can use **$routerProviders** to configure the routes of the **$route** service. As mentioned in the previous chapter, routes are URL mappings on a template. Optionally, as shown in our example, we can also specify a controller. The **$route** service, which at runtime evaluates which route is active, works closely with the **ngView** directive, with which we have annotated the **<div>** container in the **index.html** file (See Listing 3.6). The configured templates will be loaded depending on the current URL in the **innerHTML** attribute of this **<div>** element. In addition, if a controller has been configured for a route, a new scope will be created for the template and the controller's constructor function will be called. This relationship is illustrated in Figure 3.4.

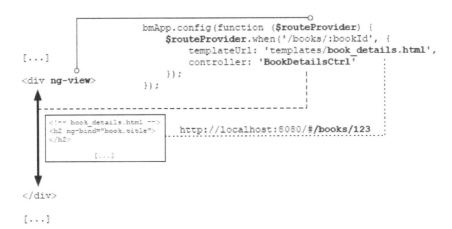

Figure 3.4: The relationship between the ngView directive and $routeProvider

Looking at the **/books/:isbn** route, which is mapped to the detail view of a book, there is still a small feature. You can specify a path parameter with a colon. In this route, **isbn** is a path parameter. This means that this part of the URL can be a variable and will still be mapped to the configured template and controller. In a later stage of development of the book details, we can use the **isbn** path parameter to access the appropriate book. Within the **BookDetailsCtrl** controller, access is made possible by via the so-called **$routeParams** service.

A Separate Scope with the BookDetailsCtrl Controller

In the rudimentary implementation of **BookDetailsCtrl** in Listing 3.8, we are not interested in the ISBN yet. Rather, we want to assign a **Book** object to the scope variable **book** so that we can produce the first working version of the Details view. Recall that a controller for a DOM element defines its own scope. This is also true for the **BookDetailsCtrl** controller. In the DOM section of the template (**book_details.html**) AngularJS creates a new scope every time the route is invoked. In this scope, we can access the inner part of the constructor function of the controller. In the scope we finally set the **book** variable with a **Book** object containing all the properties specified in the template with the **ngBind** or **ngBindTemplate** directive.

Listing 3.8: The implementation of BookDetailsCtrl

```
bmApp.controller('BookDetailsCtrl', function($scope)
{
  $scope.book = {
    title : 'JavaScript for Enterprise Developers',
    subtitle :
      'Professional Programming in the Browser'
        + ' and on the Server',
    isbn : '978-3-89864-728-1',
    abstract : 'JavaScript is no longer only'
        + ' interesting to classic web programmers',
    numPages : 302,
    author : 'Oliver Ochs',
    publisher: {
        name : 'dpunkt.verlag',
        url : 'http://dpunkt.de/'
    }
  };
});
```

Now if you type a URL that matches the defined route in your browser, you should see the first version of the Details view like that in Figure 3.5. A possible URL is:

```
http://localhost:8080/#/books/123
```

Of course, you can also pass a value other than **123** as the path parameter. Because we have not yet handled the **isbn** path parameters when creating the Details view, the same Details view is always rendered.

First, the Test

As mentioned earlier, it is very important to embrace the test-driven development approach. From this perspective we have already made a mistake, because we did not write the test before the actual implementation. We therefore want to write a first simple test at this point to show that using the **ngBind** or **ngBindTemplate** directive in the template will produce the same result as the expression.

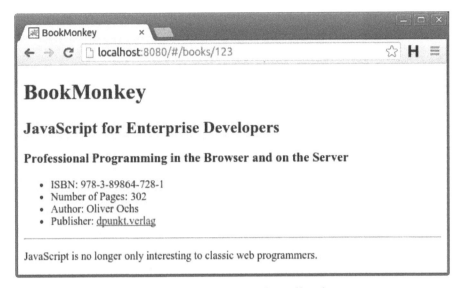

Figure 3.5: The Book Details view

We have a directory named **test** in our BookMonkey main directory for the tests we will write. Now in the **test** directory we will create two subdirectories named **unit** and **e2e**. In the **unit** directory we will store our unit tests, while in the **e2e** directory we will render E2E testing.

In summary, you use unit tests to test small application units isolated from the rest of the application. Examples of such units are controllers, services, directives and filters. In unit testing you run part of their logic and then check if the results of this execution are as expected. To write a genuine isolated test, the dependencies of the application units are usually mocked. This means you replace the real implementation of a dependency with a mock object. A mock object is an object that has the same public API provided for the tested application unit. Instead of an actual implementation, a mock object provides an implementation that returns some hardcoded values. Based on these hard-coded values, you can determine how a dependency should behave in the test case. AngularJS brings with it its own mock implementations, to save you a lot of work when conducting testing.

In E2E testing, however, you should think of your application as a black box. You have no access to the internal state of your JavaScript code and can thus formulate no expectations on the basis of this condition. Rather, you can only formulate expectations which relate to the state of the DOM.

Using a domain specific language (DSL) you can control how a potential user should behave. This way, you can put the application in a particular state and then check the DOM to find out if the application is behaving correctly.

At this point we want to examine our template for the Book Details view by using an E2E test. For this, however, we have to expand our template again to make it able to easily reference the corresponding DOM node whose content we want to check in the test.

Listing 3.9: Extending our template to include CSS classes

```
<h2 ng-bind="book.title" class="bm-book-title"></h2>
<h3 ng-bind="book.subtitle"
    class="bm-book-subtitle"></h3>
<p>
  <ul>
    <li ng-bind-template="ISBN: {{ book.isbn }}"
      class="bm-book-isbn"></li>
    <li ng-bind-template=
"Number of Pages:{{ book.numPages }}"
      class="bm-book-num-pages"></li>
    <li ng-bind-template="Author: {{ book.author }}"
      class="bm-book-author"></li>
    <li>
      Publisher: <a ng-bind="book.publisher.name"
        ng-href="{{ book.publisher.url }}"
        target="_blank"
        class="bm-book-publisher-name">
      </a>
    </li>
  </ul>
</p>
<hr>
<p ng-bind="book.abstract" class="bm-book-abstract">
</p>
```

Listing 3.9 shows the markup of our template after the extension. As you can see, there are HTML elements that contain the relevant book information, supplemented by CSS classes (such as **bm-book-title**). This allows us to formulate short CSS selectors to reference these HTML elements and check its contents in the E2E test.

Before writing the actual E2E test, we need to create a subdirectory named **templates** in the **e2e** directory. We also need to create a **book_details.spec.js** file in **templates** and define the E2E test for book details in the file.

File Names and Structures for Tests

It is common to use the extension **.spec.js** for all test files. In addition, the structure of the test directory should resemble the structure of the application in the **app** directory.

Listing 3.10: E2E test for the template

```
describe("E2E: book details view", function() {

  beforeEach(function() {
      browser().navigateTo('/');
  });

  it('should show the correct book details', function() {
    browser().navigateTo('#/books/978-3-89864-728-1');

    expect(element('.bm-book-title').html()).toBe(
      'JavaScript for Enterprise Developers'
    );
    expect(element('.bm-book-subtitle').html())
      .toBe( 'Professional Programming in the Browser'
          + ' and on the Server'
    );
    expect(element('.bm-book-isbn').html())
      .toBe( 'ISBN: 978-3-89864-728-1'
    );
    expect(element('.bm-book-num-pages').html())
      .toBe( 'Number of Pages: 302'
    );
    expect(element('.bm-book-author').html())
      .toBe( 'Author: Oliver Ochs'
    );
    expect(element('.bm-book-publisher-name')
      .html()).toBe( 'dpunkt.verlag'
    );
    expect(element('.bm-book-publisher-name')
      .attr('href')).toBe( 'http://dpunkt.de/'
    );
```

```
    expect(element('.bm-book-abstract').html())
      .toBe( 'JavaScript is no longer only interesting '
         + ' to classic web programmers.'
    );
  });
});
```

Listing 3.10 shows the E2E test for the book details (See **book_details.spec.js**), which checks whether the data from the scope is returned correctly. If you are familiar with Jasmine testing framework (http://pivotal.github.io/jasmine) , you will probably immediately see the parallels. In fact, AngularJS **ngScenario**, which is used for E2E testing, was designed based on Jasmine.

> ### The Protractor Framework
> The Protractor project, which can be downloaded from http://github.com/angular/protractor, is a framework for defining E2E tests. It is similar to **ngScenario**, but it is based on the WebDriver specification, which allows much more control over the browser. The official documentation of AngularJS mentions that Protractor Karma will replace the AngularJS E2E environment in the future. There are differences in the configuration of the test environment and in some parts of the API. However, the concepts for defining E2E tests described here can be applied similarly and are generally valid.

Basically E2E tests are constructed the same way as unit tests. You start out with a **describe()** function that the test suite defines. The first parameter to the function is a name for the test suite. The second parameter contains an anonymous function within which you define the test cases. A single test case defined with the **it()** function expects as its first parameter a string that expresses the expected behavior in natural language. The second parameter is an anonymous function in which the test case is defined. It is characteristic of such a test case that it first creates a condition, then it executes the tested functionality and concludes with one or more **expect()** function that formulates the expected post-conditions. If several test cases require the same condition or you want to perform certain logic before each test case, then you can use the **beforeEach()** function. This function expects a single parameter, a function that will be executed before each test case. In our E2E Test Suite in Listing 3.10, we use the **beforeEach()** function to navigate to the home page of the application before each test case. The specific call looks like this.

```
browser().navigateTo('/')
```

At the current stage of development, that is our only condition that could potentially be relevant for all test cases in the test suite. Because we only define one test case, we could encode this precondition directly in the test case. However, we may add more test cases that require this condition in the future. Looking ahead, we have therefore put this in the **beforeEach()** function.

In our single test case, we navigate to the same URL, which we have opened manually in the browser. However, this time we add a path parameter to a real ISBN to prepare for this test case for future development. Finally, we will use it to display the details of the corresponding book.

```
browser().navigateTo('#/books/978-3-89864-728-1');
```

Internally, our application should now be loaded according to the route configuration of the **BookDetailsCtrl** controller and the template for the Details view (**templates/book_details.html**). Then, the book information should be available in the DOM. Subsequently, we can start by using the **expect()** function to formulate our post-conditions. Since we have provided the appropriate HTML elements with meaningful CSS classes in our template, we can now use the **element()** function in conjunction with the appropriate CSS selector (e.g. **bm-book-title**) to reference the necessary DOM elements. What follows is calling a matcher. In ngScenario, a matcher has the same semantics as in Jasmine. There are basic matchers like the **toBe()** matcher, which only compares the types of two objects. More complex matchers include the **toContain()** matcher, which is provided by **ngScenario**. This matcher checks if a string is part of another string. You can also use **toContain()** to ensure that a certain element is contained in an array. A complete list of matchers and the descriptions of the complete API of **ngScenario** can be found at http://docs.angularjs.org/guide/dev_guide.e2e-testing.

We have now defined our first test suite. To execute the E2E testing suite, we now need a runtime environment. In the AngularJS world, Karma has established itself as the test execution environment, because the project virtually started when the AngularJS developers themselves were looking for a suitable tool for AngularJS. You have installed Karma at the beginning of this chapter and can use it from now on as the runtime environment for unit and E2E testing.

> **Karma**
>
> The most popular test execution environment was probably Testacular, which was renamed Karma after it became the official test environment for the AngularJS framework.

To run the test suite in Listing 3.10, you need a configuration file for Karma. At this point, don't worry about what configuration options Karma provides. This aspect will be discussed in Chapter 5, "Project Management and Automation." If you have created a project structure exactly as described, you can easily use the configuration file in the accompanying zip file. To this end, copy the **karma-e2e.conf.js** file in the **bookmonkey** directory. And, while you're at it, you can also copy the **karma.conf.js** file in the same directory. The **karma.conf.js** file is the configuration file you need to run the unit tests, while **karma-e2e.conf.js** is the configuration for running the E2E testing.

Now, to perform the E2E test suite for a book's details, change directory to the root directory of the BookMonkey application (**bookmonkey**) and start Karma with the following command:

```
karma start karma-e2e.conf.js
```

> **Executing the E2E Tests**
>
> According to our configuration for the E2E tests (**karma-e2e.conf.js**) Karma assumes that the BookMonkey application can be reach at http://localhost:8080. This means **http-server** must be running on port 8080 before Karma can execute the tests. Karma will load the application from this URL and perform the E2E tests.

If you have not made a mistake, Karma should give you feedback on the successful execution of a test case.

```
Chrome 30.0.1599: Executed 1 of 1 SUCCESS (0.908 secs / 0.699 secs)
```

The aim of this E2E testing is to show that the **ngBind** or **ngBindTemplate**
directive can return the same output as the template that uses simple
expressions.

To verify this claim, you can create another Book Details view template
with expressions. However, do not forget to decorate the HTML elements
with the corresponding CSS classes. Otherwise your CSS selectors from the
E2E test will no longer work. The new template can be seen in Listing 3.11.

Listing 3.11: A template that uses expressions for the tests

```
<h2 class="bm-book-title">{{ book.title }}</h2>
<h3 class="bm-book-subtitle">{{ book.subtitle }}</h3>
<p>
<ul>
    <li class="bm-book-isbn">ISBN: {{ book.isbn }}</li>
    <li class="bm-book-num-pages">
Number of Pages: {{ book.numPages }}</li>
    <li class="bm-book-author">Author: {{ book.author }}</li>
    <li>
        Publisher:
        <a ng-href="{{ book.publisher.url }}"
            target="_blank" class="bm-book-publisher-name">
            {{ book.publisher.name }}</a>
    </li>
</ul>
</p>
<hr>
<p class="bm-book-abstract">{{ book.abstract }}</p>
```

If you run the E2E test again, you will see the same output with simple
expressions.

Summary

- You use expressions to return values for a template.
- You can use expressions to output the current values of variables from
  the scope, which are valid for the template in its current state.
- Expressions are subject to two-way data binding. This means they
  will be re-evaluated when the value of the scope variable changes.

- Whenever possible, you should choose the **ngBind** or **ngBindTemplate** directive over expressions for performance reasons.
- You can use the **ngHref** directive to create a hyperlink that contains an expression. AngularJS then ensures that the link is active only when the template is processed and the corresponding expression evaluated.
- With **$routeProvider** you can configure application routes in a **config()** block.
- The **ngView** directive is used to annotate an HTML element to tell the framework which route template should be loaded.
- You use E2E tests to script simulated user behavior for your application and to formulate certain expectations based on the DOM.
- Angular comes with its own test framework called **ngScenario**.

The List View

After we have created a basic Details view successfully, we now want to take care of the List view. This view will show a list of books that the user can select to view in the Details view. You can use the List view for multiple purposes. For instance, you can show the search results (See Figure 3.6). As another example, the List view can also be used in the Administration area to facilitate the admin management.

BookMonkey

| Search |

Name	Autor	ISBN
Javascript for Enterprise Dev.	Oliver Ochs	978-3-89864-728-1
Node.js & Co.	Golo Roden	978-3-89864-728-1
CoffeeScript	Andreas Schubert	978-3-89864-728-1

Figure 3.6: The proposed List view

The central aspect of this section deals with the **ngRepeat** directive. You use this directive to render a list-like structure like an array in a template. The **ngRepeat** directive provides a series of functions to filter or arrange the output.

We also formulate a user store for the List view.

> As user Michael, I want to be able to view a list of books to give me an overview.

> **Using the Downloaded Project**
> To test the code in this section, you can use the accompanying project that you downloaded from the publisher's website. To do this, change directory to **ch03_03_list_view/app** and start http-server from there.

First, the Test

We mentioned that we wanted to continue with the test-first approach. In this section, we first examine the tests for the List view by creating the **book_list.spec.js** file in the **test/e2e/templates/** directory and defining an E2E test suite in the file.

Listing 3.12: Preparing the E2E test to verify the List view

```
describe("E2E: book list view", function () {

    // Define the array of books in the expected order.
    // Sorted by title.
    var expectedBooks = [
        {
            title: 'CoffeeScript',
            isbn: '978-3-86490-050-1',
            author: 'Andreas Schubert'
        },
        {
            title: 'JavaScript for Enterprise Developers',
            isbn: '978-3-89864-728-1',
            author: 'Oliver Ochs'
        },
        {
```

```
            title: 'Node.js & Co.',
            isbn: '978-3-89864-829-5',
            author: 'Golo Roden'
        }
    ];

    // Derive an array that only contains titles
    // for easier expectation checks.
    var orderedTitles = expectedBooks.map(function(book) {
        return book.title;
    });

    [...]

});
```

Listing 3.12 shows the basic structure of the test suite. Before we write the actual test cases, we define some auxiliary constructs to simplify the implementation of the test cases. The relevant auxiliary construct at this point is the **expectedBooks** book array. In this array, we define what we expect to see as a book entry in the List view, namely an object with **title**, **isbn** and **author** properties. In particular, in this definition it is important that the **Book** objects are in the expected order, so we can easily check in the test case if the List view has the entries sorted correctly. Here we have chosen to define the lexical order based on the book title.

In addition, we use the **map()** function to derive from the **expectedBooks** array a second array named **orderedTitles**, in which we only store the book titles in the same order. The **orderedTitles** array is an auxiliary construct for the subsequent test cases.

Listing 3.13: The beforeEach() block of the E2E test suite to verify the List view

```
describe("E2E: book list view", function () {

    [...]

    beforeEach(function () {
        browser().navigateTo('#/books');
        browser().reload();
    });

    [...]
```

```
});
```

Listing 3.13 shows the continuation of our test suite in Listing 3.12. Just like the E2E test for the book details, here we use a **beforeEach()** block to produce the precondition for our tests. In this case we are telling Karma to navigate to the **/books** route and reload the document before each test case. The reloading is necessary because we will change the view state in some future test cases. Thus, we make sure that the view is in its original state before the execution of each test case. Simply navigating to the **/books** route is not enough here, because the initial state is not usually produced when we navigate between the same URLs.

Listing 3.14: The test case for verifying the correct number of books

```
describe("E2E: book list view", function () {

    [...]

    var selector = 'table.bm-book-list tr';

    it('should show the correct number of books', function () {
        expect(repeater(selector).count()).toEqual(
                expectedBooks.length);
    });

    [...]

});
```

We continue in Listing 3.14. Since we need the CSS selector in several test cases, we store it in a variable called **selector**.

We now use the **it()** function and a repeater to write our first test case to test if the List view has as many items as the **expectedBooks** array has the **Book** objects. The repeater is a construct that **ngScenario** provides to conveniently retrieve information from the tabular DOM-like structures, most of which were generated using the **ngRepeat** directive. Examples of such tabular DOM structures include an HTML table. It is characteristic of such a structure that repeats a specific DOM pattern several times. An HTML table is therefore a perfect example of such a structure, because each row (**<tr>**) usually has the same number of columns (**<td>**) and thus has a consistent structure.

Based on the CSS **selector**, which we passed to the repeater as a parameter, we have implicitly determined that the List view should be based on an HTML table. This way, we can use the repeater to determine how many entries are included in our list view. The relevant function for this on the repeater is **count()**. Thus, we can now formulate our expectation for this test.

It continues with the next test, which checks whether the entries in the List view are sorted correctly on the book title in descending order.

Listing 3:15. A test case for verifying the correct order

```
describe("E2E: book list view", function () {

    [...]

    it('should show the books in the proper order', function() {
        // Are they in the expected order
        // (ascending sorted by title)?
        expect(repeater(selector).column('book.title')).toEqual(
            orderedTitles);
    });

    [...]

});
```

The corresponding test case is shown in Listing 3.15. Again, we use a repeater to read the information from the DOM. However, this time we use the **column()** function of the repeater, in which we can see again that a repeater is practically the supplementary test construct for the **ngRepeat** directive. The **column()** function takes as a parameter a data binding expression, which is exactly the fragment which we would use in conjunction with the **ngBind** directive to produce template output. At this point we determine that this expression should read **book.title**. Afterward, we will have to work with the following expression in the implementation to generate the output:

```
ng-bind="book.title"
```

Using the **column()** function we can easily read the values of the table columns that contain book titles. The function returns an array containing the corresponding column values of all rows. Therefore, we can use the

toEqual() matcher to compare if the returned array corresponds to our **orderedTitles** array. If this expectation is fulfilled, then it means that the list entries match the order that we have manually specified in the **expectedBooks** array because the **orderedTitles** array was derived from the **expectedBooks** array.

The toEqual Matcher

The **toEqual()** matcher performs a comparison based on the AngularJS **angular.equals()** function. This function uses a more complex algorithm to check the equality of two objects. Among other things, it checks whether individual elements in two arrays match. Using this matcher and the repeaters we can easily write a relatively complex expectation.

What we are still missing before we proceed to the actual implementation of the List view, is the last test case that verifies that the author and ISBN are returned correctly after the book title. The test case can be found in Listing 3.16.

Listing 3.16: Test case for verifying the correct list contents

```
describe("E2E: book list view", function () {

    [...]

    it('should show the correct book information', function() {
        // Do the other book details (isbn, author) match?
        for (var i = 0, n = expectedBooks.length; i < n; i++) {
            expect(repeater(selector).row(i))
                .toEqual(
                    [
                        expectedBooks[i].title,
                        expectedBooks[i].author,
                        expectedBooks[i].isbn
                    ]
                );
        }
    });
});
```

The special feature of this test case is that we use a new aspect of the repeater, the **row()** function. The name says it all. This function takes a table row index as parameter and returns an array containing column values in that row. Therefore, we can easily express the expectation using a for loop that the book title, author and ISBN in a line must always be equivalent to the corresponding definition in the **expectedBooks** array. We have thus defined the last expectation on the list view. Therefore, we can now create an implementation as expected. Before we do that, we should run the E2E tests again and make sure that the tests from the test suite we just created fail because there is still no implementation.

```
karma start karma-e2e.conf.js
```

The corresponding negative feedback should look like this.

```
Chrome 30.0.1599: Executed 4 of 4 (3 FAILED)
                              (1.217 secs / 0.971 secs)
```

Our E2E test for the Details view is still "green," while the three tests we just defined failed. In the output we can also find out which tests failed.

The Infrastructure for the List View

Having defined the E2E tests for the List view, we now need to first create the infrastructure before we get started with the actual implementation. This means we have to create the appropriate files and configure an additional route in our **app.js** file. We will start with the route. For this we need to expand the **app.js** file to that in Listing 3.17.

Listing 3.17: A new route for the List view

```
var bmApp = angular.module('bmApp', ['ngRoute']);

bmApp.config(function ($routeProvider) {
    $routeProvider.when('/books/:isbn', {
        templateUrl: 'templates/book_details.html',
        controller: 'BookDetailsCtrl'
    })
    .when('/books', {
        templateUrl: 'templates/book_list.html',
        controller: 'BookListCtrl'
    });
});
```

We use the **when** function to configure another route so that all calls to
/books are directed to the List view, which of course has its own template
(**book_list.html**) and controller (**BookListCtrl**). Therefore, we need to
create these two files and include them in the **index.html** file using
<script> tags. We will create the **book_list.html** file in the **app/templates/**
directory and the **BookListCtrl** controller in a separate file named
book_list.js in the **app/scripts/controllers/** directory.

The BookListCtrl Controller

The **BookListCtrl** controller implementation is similar to the
implementation of the **BookDetailsCtrl** controller (See Listing 3.18).

Listing 3.18: The BookListCtrl controller

```
bmApp.controller('BookListCtrl', function ($scope) {
    $scope.books = [
        {
            title : 'JavaScript for Enterprise Developers',
            isbn : '978-3-89864-728-1',
            author : 'Oliver Ochs',
            [...]
        },
        {
            title : 'Node.js & Co.',
            isbn : '978-3-89864-829-5',
            author : 'Golo Roden',
            [...]
        },
        {
            title : 'CoffeeScript',
            isbn : '978-3-86490-050-1',
            author : 'Andreas Schubert',
            [...]
        }
    ];
});
```

We populate the **books** scope variable with an array of **Book** objects.
Before we upload this information from the server in the next step, for now
we content ourselves with a static definition. We should also note that for

the sake of clarity, we have omitted irrelevant book information in Listing 3.18.

The ngRepeat Directive: Displaying An Array in the Template

To display output from a list-like structure like an array in a template, we have to use the **ngRepeat** directive. Besides displaying the output, this AngularJS directive can also filter, transform and assign a list. You will learn all these aspects in the sections to come.

For this purpose, we first implement the simplest version of our template, to have at least three books returned by the array. This version of the template is shown in Listing 3.19.

Listing 3.19: The template for the List view, employing the ngRepeat directive

```
<table class="bm-book-list">
    <tbody>
        <tr ng-repeat="book in books">
            <td ng-bind="book.title"></td>
            <td ng-bind="book.author"></td>
            <td ng-bind="book.isbn"></td>
        </tr>
    </tbody>
</table>
```

As specified in the E2E test, we are expanding the list view in the form of an HTML table on (**<table>**). We also annotate this table with the **bm-book-list** CSS class. Now comes the interesting part with regard to the **ngRepeat** directive. As shown in Listing 3.19, we use the **ngRepeat** directive as an attribute to the HTML element that will be generated repeatedly as the output of the **books** array. The DOM subtree of the HTML element, including the HTML element itself, considers the directive a template that will be instantiated once for each element of the underlying array. So in this case, we want to ensure that a table row (**<tr>**) is rendered for every **Book** object in the **books** array, because we are using the directive with the **<tr>** tag.

The **ngRepeat** directive expects a structured expression, such as "book in books" in this case. The expression describes which array is to be iterated over and the name of the variable that can be used to access the array element from within the loop in each iteration. Here we specify that the array referenced by the scope variable **books** is to be iterated over and the loop variable **book** is how the loop can access the array element at each iteration. Thus, at each iteration we have access to the individual book details such as the book title (**book.title**), author (**book.author**) and ISBN (**book.isbn**). This relationship is illustrated again in Figure 3.7. You can also see in the diagram which DOM section in the scope of the **BookListCtrl** controller is valid.

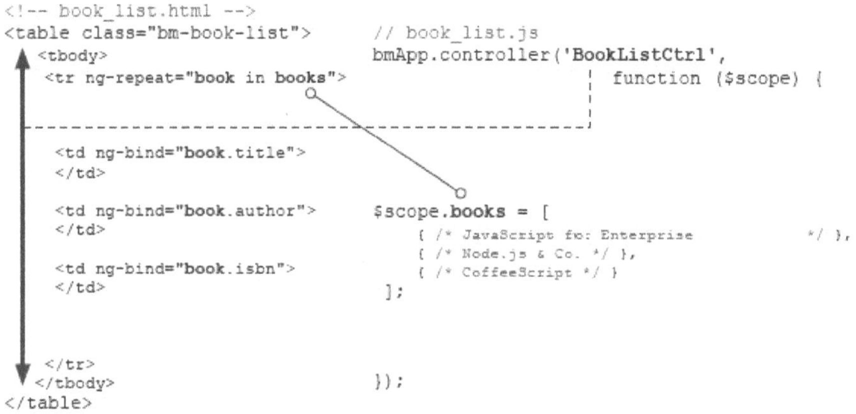

Figure 3.7: ngRepeat iterates over a book array in the controller scope

Consequently, we can use the **ngBind** directive again to produce the actual output. The relationship between the **ngRepeat** directive and the repeater from the E2E test is shown in Figure 3.8.

One of the anomalies of **ngRepeat** is that the construct is also subject to two-way data binding. This means AngularJS automatically create new DOM elements at runtime when the content of the underlying array changes. In our case, this means we just need to add new **Book** objects in the **books** array at runtime to obtain a current list view of books.

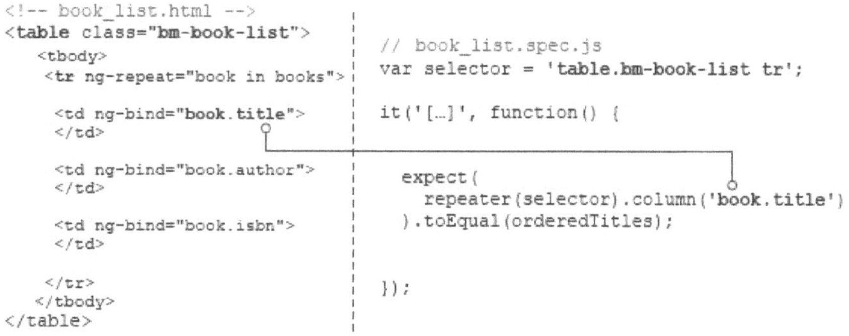

```
<!-- book_list.html -->
<table class="bm-book-list">          // book_list.spec.js
    <tbody>                           var selector = 'table.bm-book-list tr';
      <tr ng-repeat="book in books">
                                      it('[…]', function() {
        <td ng-bind="book.title">
        </td>
                                        expect(
        <td ng-bind="book.author">        repeater(selector).column('book.title')
        </td>                            ).toEqual(orderedTitles);

        <td ng-bind="book.isbn">
        </td>

      </tr>                            });
    </tbody>
</table>
```

Figure 3.8: The relationship between ngRepeat and the repeater

The second anomaly of **ngRepeat** is that it creates a new scope for each element of the array it is iterating over. This fact has no impact on our current List view example. However, it is important to know this background information to avoid any nasty surprises when creating more complex views. This aspect is especially appreciated when you render form fields using the **ngRepeat** directive. You should always make it clear in which scope you bind a field to a variable.

The fact that the **ngRepeat** directive creates a scope for each element of the underlying array leads, in the case of our application, to the list in Figure 3.9. To understand the aspect better, we have added the resulting HTML code from **ngRepeat** in the figure.

You can see in Figure 3.9 that AngularJS defines the scope variable **book** in each of the scopes produced by the **ngRepeat** directive. The scope variable **book** references the corresponding **Book** object.

To see the List view, direct the browser to the following URL.

```
http://localhost:8080/#/books
```

If you did not make a mistake, you should see the List view like that in Figure 3.10.

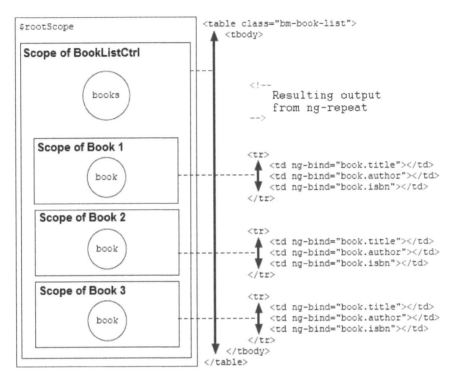

Figure 3.9: The scope hierarchy when displaying the List view

Figure 3.10: The List view

If you get the same output as that in Figure 3.10, then logically one of the three E2E tests will also be "green." Finally, you can verify the correct number of books by using the familiar Karma call:

```
karma start karma-e2e.conf.js
```

Now only two tests are failing, as shown in the following output:

```
Chrome 30.0.1599: Executed 4 of 4 (2 FAILED)
                                    (1.233 secs / 0.983 secs)
```

The test, which tests the number of books, should pass now. You can move on to make the other two tests "green."

The orderBy Filter: Determining the Sort Order

As already mentioned, you can use the **ngRepeat** directive to sort an array based on certain criteria. You can use the **orderBy** filter that ships with AngularJS.

So let's now extend our template for the List view, so our books will be sorted by book title in ascending order. We have formulated the corresponding E2E tests to meet this requirement. The extension can be seen in Listing 3.20.

Listing 3.20: Determining the sort order with the orderBy filter

```
<table class="bm-book-list">
    <tbody>
        <tr ng-repeat="book in books | orderBy: 'title'">
            <td ng-bind="book.title"></td>
            <td ng-bind="book.author"></td>
            <td ng-bind="book.isbn"></td>
        </tr>
    </tbody>
</table>
```

You can use a collection filter by expanding the structured **ng-repeat** expression accordingly. For this purpose, you use the pipe notation, just like you would a formatting filter. The pipe notation follows the name of the collection filter (here: **orderBy**). After the name comes a colon that separates the filter with a list of parameters for the filter. You can use static values as well as reference scope variables. As an alternative to the code in

Listing 3.20, you could also define a variable named **booksOrderedBy** in the scope of the **BookListCtrl** controller and assign the string "title" to it. The resulting **ng-repeat** expression would then look like this:

```
ng-repeat="book in books | orderBy: booksOrderedBy"
```

Here, the **orderBy** filter is also subject to two-way data binding. This means that you just have to change the value of the scope variable **booksOrderedBy** at runtime to sort the books by a different property, such as the ISBN.

In particular, the **orderBy** filter takes two parameters. The first parameter is a comparison predicate, which you can specify in a couple of different ways.

- If you pass a reference to a function defined in the currently valid scope, then this function is understood to be a getter function and its return value interpreted as a comparison value of each element. Sorting will then be based on the comparison value in each case, using comparison operator >, < or ==. The filter will pass the corresponding array element to the function, so you, in the case of an object, can easily have access to certain properties of the object and return them as reference values.
- If you pass a string, this string is interpreted as an AngularJS expression and will finally be evaluated on each element of the array to determine the comparative value. Consequently, this specification of the comparison predicate makes sense only for arrays that contain objects. In addition, you can prefix it with a minus or plus sign to have the array elements sorted in ascending (+) or descending (-) order. Without a prefix, by default the elements will be sorted in ascending order.
- You can specify an array of getter functions or expressions. You use the first predicate for comparison. If two elements of the array are equal, the next predicate is used to evaluate the two elements. If, after being compared with the second predicate, the two elements are still equal, the next predicate is used for comparison, and so on.

The second parameter to the **orderBy** filter is optional. If you pass **true** as the second parameter, the sorting done with the help of the first parameter will be reversed. If you do not supply a value, it is assumed sorting should not be reversed.

In our extended template in Listing 3.20, we use the second option for specifying the comparison predicate. We pass the string "title", which indicates that sorting should be based on the **title** property of our **Book** objects.

Thus, we have specified sorting in the E2E Test with this small extension. As such, the remaining two test cases should also pass now. The manual version in the browser should display the correct order (see Figure 3.11).

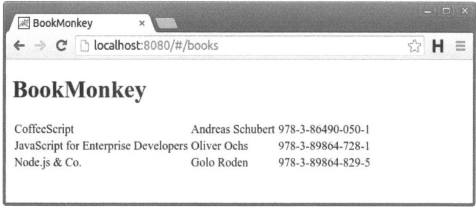

Figure 3.11: Sorting the books in the List view

Next, we want to use the first option to specify a comparison predicate, to achieve the same effect of sorting. We do this by changing the **ng-repeat** expression as follows:

```
ng-repeat="book in books | orderBy: getBookOrder"
```

Now **getBookOrder** must be a variable in the currently valid scope and references a function that returns the comparison value for each **Book** object from the **books** array. The currently valid scope is still the scope of the **BookListCtrl** controller. This means we have to expand the implementation of this controller to that in Listing 3.21.

**Listing 3.21: The BookListCtrl controller with the getBookOrder()
function**

```
bmApp.controller('BookListCtrl', function ($scope) {
  $scope.books = [
    [...]
  ];

  $scope.getBookOrder = function(book) {
    return book.title;
  };
});
```

Every time the **getBookOrder()** function is called, the **orderBy** filter
passes the corresponding **Book** object as a parameter to the function.
Because we want to sort by book title, we return the book title as a
comparison value.

At this point that is all we have to do to define the comparison predicate
using a getter function. To verify this solution to the sorting problem, we
can rerun our E2E test suite.

```
Chrome 30.0.1599: Executed 4 of 4 SUCCESS (1.401 secs / 0.532 secs)
```

That's it. All tests should pass.

Invoking A Filter Programmatically

So far we have only used the **orderBy** filter with the **ngRepeat** directive.
This is a common way to use the filter. However, you might also want to
call a filter programmatically in order to use it within a controller or a
service as an auxiliary function. The good news is you can do this in
AngularJS. Let's look at how to do it.

**Listing 3.22: Calling the orderBy filter programmatically in the
BookListCtrl controller**

```
bmApp.controller('BookListCtrl', function ($scope, $filter) {
  $scope.books = [
    [...]
  ];

  $scope.getBookOrder = function(book) {
    return book.title;
```

```
};

// This is just to demonstrate the programmatic usage of a filter
var orderBy = $filter('orderBy');

var titles = $scope.books.map(function(book) {
  return {title: book.title};
});

console.log('titles before ordering', titles);

// This is the actual invocation of the filter
titles = orderBy(titles, 'title');

console.log('titles after ordering', titles);
});
```

As shown in Listing 3.22, to invoke a filter programmatically you use the **$filter** service, which AngularJS can pass to you via dependency injection. To achieve this, add a parameter named **$filter** to the constructor. This is how you tell AngularJS that you need the **$filter** service in the constructor.

The **$filter** service consists solely of a function that returns a reference to the filter function of this filter, which you can obtain by passing the filter name to the function. What we do in Listing 3.22 is call **$filter('orderBy')** to get the reference to the filter function of the **orderBy** filter. We store this reference in a local variable **orderBy**. We can now call the logic in the **orderBy** filter with **orderBy()**.

To see a programmatic call in action, we define a new array named **titles** and populates it with data from our **books** arrays using the **Array.map()** function. The new array contains only book titles. At first the elements in this array are in the same order as the **Book** objects in **books**. After we apply the filter function of the **orderBy** filter on this array, however, we get a new array containing titles in ascending order.

A filter invoked programmatically expects the same parameters as when it is used in a template. However, for a collection filter, as in this case, we must also pass as the first parameter the array on which the filter will apply.

For comparison, we show the **titles** array before and after sorting in Figure 3.12.

Figure 3.12: The console output of the sorted array

Summary

- You can sort a collection such as an array with the **orderBy** filter.
- The **filter** filter is a collection filter and comes with the template associated with the **ngRepeat** directive.
- Used in a template:
  `ng_repeat_expression | orderBy:predicate[:reverse]`
- Invoked programmatically using the **$filter** service:
  `$filter('orderBy')(array, predicate [, reverse])`
- As a predicate you can define a function, a string or an array to sort according to the options described above.
- You can reverse the sorting order by passing **true** to the second parameter. The second parameter is optional.

Filtering Data

After looking at the **orderBy** filter in the previous section, we will now go one step further and implement a function to filter entries for our List view. We will use another **filter** filter. With the **filter** filter, we can restrict the output of the underlying array based on certain criteria.

However, before we write the actual implementation, we will implement the test cases that specify the expected behavior for our filter function. For this purpose, we extend the E2E test suite for our List view and write three more test cases. This extension is shown in Listing 3.23.

Listing 3.23: The E2E tests for the search function

```
describe("E2E: book list view", function () {

    [...]

    it('should allow filtering by book title', function() {
        // Coffee
        var searchText = orderedTitles[0].substr(0, 6);
        input('searchText').enter(searchText);
        expect(
            repeater(selector).column('book.title')
        ).toEqual([orderedTitles[0]]);
    });

    it('should allow filtering by author', function() {
        // Andreas
        var searchText = expectedBooks[0].author.substr(0, 7);
        input('searchText').enter(searchText);
        expect(
            repeater(selector).column('book.title')
        ).toEqual([orderedTitles[0]]);
    });

    it('should allow filtering by isbn', function() {
        // 050-1
        var searchText = expectedBooks[0].isbn.substr(-5, 5);
        input('searchText').enter(searchText);
        expect(
            repeater(selector).column('book.title')
        ).toEqual([orderedTitles[0]]);
```

```
    });
});
```

In order to formulate the actual expectation, in the three test cases we use the same mechanism that we have seen in the previous sections, namely a repeater. However, unlike the previous test cases, in the new test cases we use the **input()** function of **ngScenario**. Using this function you can reference a DOM element that is defined in the template using an **<input>** tag. This means you can use the **input()** function to interact with, say, input fields, radio buttons and checkboxes. Therefore, the **input()** function expects as a parameter the name of a scope variable to which the **<input>** element is bound. In the implementation of the filter function we can bind the **<input>** tag to a scope variable using the **ngModel** directive. So using the **input()** function we specify that in our List view that there must be a listbox bound to the scope variable **searchText** by the **ngModel** directive. This input field is used to enter a search string, based on which the entries are to be filtered in the List view.

You can use **enter()** to enter a string into this box programmatically. You pass the string as the first parameter to the **enter()** function. If you take a closer look at the three new test cases, you will see that they all follow the same pattern. We let the execution environment enter a string in the input field and then inspect if the book list contains only the correct entries. It should be possible to do a full text search on all properties of a book. In each test case we have randomly defined a filter for a book title, an author and an ISBN, respectively. Thus, the filtered List view after the input "Coffee" in Test Case 1, "Andreas" in Test Case 2 and "050-1" in Test Case 3" should always lead to the same result, that is, only one entry should be displayed: the "CoffeeScript" book by Andreas Schubert.

Naturally, the execution of our E2E Test Suite for the List view should now lead to three unsuccessful tests.

```
Chrome 30.0.1599: Executed 7 of 7 (3 FAILED)
                                    (1.479 secs / 1.186 secs)
```

So we can now work to meet the test case expectations. We begin by expanding the template for the List view to the input field we just mentioned for the search function (See Listing 3.24).

Listing 3.24: The definition of the input field for the search function

```
<input type="text" placeholder="Search..." ng-model="searchText">
<table class="bm-book-list">
  <tbody>
    <tr ng-repeat="book in books | orderBy: getBookOrder">
      <td ng-bind="book.title"></td>
      <td ng-bind="book.author"></td>
      <td ng-bind="book.isbn"></td>
    </tr>
  </tbody>
</table>
```

The interesting thing here is the **ngModel** directive used with the **<input>** tag. It ensures that two-way data binding is established between the box and the **searchText** scope variable. We reference the **searchText** variable in the scope that is valid for the DOM section of the List view. That is to be the scope of our **BookListCtrl** controller. We have not chosen the name for the scope variable **searchText** arbitrarily. We know that in our test cases, we have specified that the input field should be bound to a scope variable named **searchText**.

We have seen the **ngModel** directive in action in Chapter 1, "AngularJS Quick Start." With two-way data binding AngularJS automatically updates the **searchText** scope variable when the input field's value changes. The same applies in the opposite direction. Therefore, a change in the value of the scope variable **searchText** will be visible immediately in the input field. For our filter function only the first aspect of the two-way data binding is relevant.

If we have not made a mistake, the search box should now appear on our book list (See Figure 3.13). However, the entries are not yet restricted to the list because we have not installed the **filter** filter.

We can now introduce the **filter** filter, as shown in Listing 3.25.

Figure 3.13: The search field in the List view

Listing 3.25: The search function with the filter filter

```
<input type="text" placeholder="Search..." ng-model="searchText">
<table class="bm-book-list">
  <tbody>
    <tr ng-repeat="book in books | orderBy: getBookOrder
     | filter: searchText">
      <td ng-bind="book.title"></td>
      <td ng-bind="book.author"></td>
      <td ng-bind="book.isbn"></td>
    </tr>
  </tbody>
</table>
```

Since the **filter** filter is a collection filter, just like the **orderBy** filter, we use it with the **ngRepeat** directive. For this purpose, we extend the **ng-repeat** expression with the pipe notation.

As mentioned previously, the **searchText** scope variable serves as a filter predicate for the filter. Therefore, we pass the value of this variable as the first parameter to the filter. This way, the **searchText** variable created has a connection from the box to the **filter** filter. As a result, the filter restricts the book list based on the input. AngularJS performs the filter logic so that every time the value of **searchText** changes, you immediately get a filtered list that represents a full text search result on the array of **Book** objects.

If you run the example in the browser and enter, for instance, the string "coffee" in the input field, you will get the expected effect immediately, as shown in Figure 3.14. Our List view should contain only the entry with the

"CoffeeScript" book by Andreas Schubert, because this is the only book that contains the string "Coffee" in one of its properties. We should emphasize at this point that we implemented the search function without writing a single line of JavaScript code.

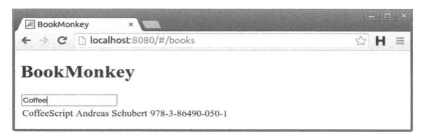

Figure 3.14: The filtered List view

The tests we created must now run successfully. The result from Karma with our configuration for the E2E tests is as follows.

```
Chrome 30.0.1599: Executed 7 of 7 SUCCESS (1.763 secs / 1.474 secs)
```

Before we discuss the operation of the **filter** filter in more detail, we can see in Figure 3.15 the relationship between the **ngModel** directive, the **filter** filter and the input() function in the E2E test.

```
<!-- book_list.html -->
<input type="text" placeholder="Suchen..." ng-model="searchText">
<table class="bm-book-list">
 <tbody>
  <tr ng-repeat="book in books | orderBy: getBookOrder | filter: searchText">
   <td ng-bind="book.title"></td>
   <td ng-bind="book.author"></td>
   <td ng-bind="book.isbn"></td>
  </tr>
 </tbody>
</table>
-------------------------------------------------------------------
// book_list.spec.js
var selector = 'table.bm-book-list tr';

it('[…]', function() {
    // Coffee
    var searchText = orderedTitles[0].substr(0, 6);


    input('searchText').enter(searchText);
    expect(repeater(selector).column('book.title')).toEqual([orderedTitles[0]]);
});
```

Figure 3.15: The relationship between ngModel, filter and input()

In Listing 3.25 the **filter** filter filters the array with respect to any property of the **Book** object that contains a string or can be converted to a string. A match is therefore determined based on the comparison of substrings without case distinction. This means this type of filter use is equivalent to a full-text search.

Like the **orderBy** filter, you can configure the **filter** filter further by passing a filter predicate instead of a string or a function. Thus, there are the following possibilities.

- If you pass a string as a filter predicate (as in Listing 3.25), then the filter will filter the underlying array by comparing each array element with the filter predicate. An element is included in the resulting array if it matches the string or any of its substrings when it is compared to the string without case sensitivity. If the array elements are objects (such as in the case of the **books** array), all the string properties of the objects and all properties that can be converted to string are compared. In addition, you can negate the filter predicate by prefixing it with the exclamation mark ("!").

- If the elements of the underlying array are objects (such as our **books** array), you can use the filter predicate to determine which object properties should be checked for a match. You can also specify a separate search string for each object property. Example:
  ```
  book in books | filter: {title: 'Coffee', author: 'Andreas'}
  ```
  In this case, only books that meet the two conditions will be included in the result, books whose title contains the string "coffee" and whose author contains the string "Andreas". Since the comparison is made without regard to case-sensitivity, the values "coffee" and "andreas" would also be a match.

- If you pass a function as the filter predicate, you can specify any filtering logic in the function. AngularJS calls this function for each element in the array when the filter is being evaluated. The framework passes the corresponding element to the function as the first parameter. The convention is that this function must return **true** if the element is to be included in the resulting array. Otherwise, it must return **false**. Example:
  ```
  book in books | filter: getCoffeeBook
  ```

In the controller's constructor function, we now have to ensure that the **getCoffeeBook()** function is defined in scope and contains the appropriate filtering logic.

```
$scope.getCoffeeBook = function(book) {
    return book.title.indexOf('Coffee') !== -1;
};
```

In this case, only books that contain the string "Coffee" will be included in the result. Since we are using **indexOf()**, the string "coffee" will no longer produce a match.

In addition to the filter predicate that passed as the first parameter, you can pass an optional second parameter to the **filter** filter. Using the second parameter you can specify a comparator. As the name suggests, a comparator is a function that defines logic to compare the filter predicate with the values from the array. It means you can use the comparator to determine whether or not string comparison should be case sensitive or define a different rule entirely. With regard to the comparator, you have a couple of options:

- If you pass a comparator function, the framework always calls this function when a comparison between a value from the array and the filter predicate needs to be performed. You obtain the filter predicate as the first parameter and the array value as the second parameter. The rule is that the function must return **true** if there is a match and **false** if no match was found.
- You can simply pass **true** to indicate comparison will be based on **angular.equals()**. This means case sensitivity is taken into account in comparison and an exact match, not just a substring match, is required for a match.

Calling the filter Filter Programmatically

Just like other AngularJS filters, the **filter** filter can be invoked programmatically in any application component (such as a controller, service and directive). For this you use the **$filter** service, which the framework can pass to you through dependency injection. The actual call would look like this.

```
$filter('filter')(array, predicate[, comparator]);
```

Again, you need to pass the array to be filtered as the first parameter, before you pass the filter predicate and a comparator as the second and optional third parameter.

Summary

- Using the **filter** filter you can filter an array based on certain criteria. For example, you can implement a client-side search feature.
- In addition to supporting full text search, you can control thoroughly how a data collection will be filtered.
- With an optional comparator you can define filtering logic for the compare operation.
- Used in a template:

  ```
  ng_repeat_expression | filter:predicate[:comparator]
  ```

- Invoked programmatically with the **$filter** service:

  ```
  $filter('filter')(array, predicate[, comparator]);
  ```

Navigating within the Application

We now have a rudimentary Details view and an implementation of a List view. However, so far there is no link between these two views. It means you currently can only navigate between these two views using the browser address bar. In this step we want to change that and show how we can implement navigation in AngularJS. For this purpose, we formulate this user story.

> As user Michael, I want to be able to navigate within the application and interact with the application.

> **Using the Downloaded Project**
> To test the code in this section, you can use the accompanying project
> that you downloaded from the publisher's website. To do this, change
> directory to **ch03_04_navigation/app** and start http-server from there.

The Default Route with $routeProvider.otherwise()

Recall that in the **app.js** file we configured a route for the two views.
Before we establish the link between them, we first want to optimize
something in our route configuration. With an **otherwise()** block we can
specify what should happen when the user navigates to a URL that is not
covered by the **when()** blocks. Using the **redirectTo** property we state that
such a call should be redirected to the **/books** route, which ultimately brings
the user to our List view. The extension is printed in Listing 3.26.

**Listing 3.26: Extending the route configuration (app.js) with an
otherwise() block**

```
[...]

bmApp.config(function ($routeProvider) {
  $routeProvider.when('/books/:isbn', {
    templateUrl: 'templates/book_details.html',
    controller: 'BookDetailsCtrl'
  })
  .when('/books', {
    templateUrl: 'templates/book_list.html',
    controller: 'BookListCtrl'
  })
  .otherwise({
    redirectTo: '/books'
  });
});
```

Now we want to establish a link between the List view and the Details view
by implementing a mechanism to call the Details view of a particular book
from the List view. Of course, there should also be a way to navigate from
the Details view back to the List view.

First, the Test

Before we start the actual implementation, we would like to specify the required behavior in the form of test cases. To do this, we need to extend the test suite for the List view (**book_list.spec.js**) as well as the test suite for the Details view (**book_details.spec.js**) by one test case.

Listing 3.27: The test case for navigating from the List view to the Details view

```
describe("E2E: book list view", function () {

    [...]

    it('should appropriately navigate to details view', function() {
        var i = 0,
            detailsLink = selector + ':nth-child('+ (i+1) +') a';
        element(detailsLink).click();

        expect(
            browser().location().path()
        ).toEqual('/books/' + expectedBooks[i].isbn);
    });

});
```

Listing 3.27 shows a test case for the List view. This test case shows some aspects of **ngScenario** that you have not encountered before. First, here we use the **element()** function to reference a DOM element using a CSS selector. Second, it shows that you can obtain certain information of the current status of the address bar using **browser().location()**.

We extend our original **selector** CSS selector so that we reference the <a> tag in the nth line that contains the hyperlink to the corresponding Details view. Next, we store the resulting selector in a local variable called **detailsLink**, which in this test case is restricted to the <a> tag in the first line (**var i = 0**). We have therefore specified that the link from the List view to the Details view should be created through a hyperlink. By calling the **click()** function of the referenced DOM element, we tell Karma to click on the corresponding DOM element upon the execution of the test case. Our application should respond to that click by opening the corresponding Details view. We can check this behavior easily by examining the content of the address bar. In line with our route configuration, the path component of the URL must match **/books/:*isbn*.** The ***isbn*** part of course corresponds to the ISBN of the book whose details we want to view. We formulate this expectation using **expect()**. We can access the path component of the current URL using **browser().location()**.

We now have a link from the List view to the Details view with the test case in Listing 3.27. Now we need a test case that specifies a way back from the Details view to the List view. We define this test case in Listing 3.28.

Listing 3.28: The test case to navigate from the Details view to the List view

```
describe("E2E: book details view", function() {

    [...]

    it('should appropriately navigate to list view',
    function() {
        browser().navigateTo('#/books/978-3-89864-728-1');

        element('.bm-list-view-btn').click();
        expect(
            browser().location().path()
        ).toEqual('/books');
    });
});
```

As shown in Listing 3.28, the test case for navigating back from the Details view to the List view has the same structure as the previous test case. We navigate to the detailed description of the book with the ISBN 978-3-89864-728-1 and let karma click on the DOM element, which we refer to using the **.bm-list-view-btn** CSS selector. Then, we expect our application to display the List view. We examine this aspect by comparing the value of the browser's address bar with the path component of the URL.

After we extended the two test suites, we can run our E2E tests with the E2E configuration and make sure they fail. We can then go ahead and implement the required features to eventually meet the user story.

Navigating with Hashbang URLs

To add a link to the Details view, we can easily expand the template for the List view by leveraging the **ngHref** directive. We used this directive at the beginning of the BookMonkey project to place a hyperlink to the publisher website in the Details view.

We need to use the **ngHref** directive with an **<a>** tag to define a hyperlink that contains one or more expressions. The reason for this is AngularJS uses this directive to make sure that the link is only set when the expression has been evaluated. If we do not use this directive, the user may see a link that is invalid because the framework has not yet evaluated the expression. Since AngularJS usually evaluates expressions pretty fast, the probability of displaying an invalid link is quite small, but not zero.

Therefore, we use the **ngHref** directive and an **<a>** tag to link the book title in the List view with the corresponding Details view. We do this by setting the **ng-href** directive with the relative path to the Details view (see Listing 3.29). Using the expression **{{book.isbn}}** we ensure that we use the correct ISBN for each book. However, we need a hash key (#) before the relative path, so that older browsers will not reload the web page completely with this URL.

We will now talk about hashbang URLs. we practically use the HTML anchor mechanism to display a different part of our application. AngularJS continuously monitors the content of the address bar and loads any change in the corresponding view.

To make various areas (List view, Details view, and other views later) available in our application by deep linking, we use hashbang URLs here. These are URLs where we code to invoke an application state mainly in the hash portion of the URL (the part after the hash). In essence, we use hashbang URLs to prevent older browsers to reload the page when the user clicks on a link that should load another part of the application.

In addition to the hashbang approach, which admittedly feels like an interim solution and also makes deep links look ugly, we can use the HTML5 History API. Using this API, it is possible to work with regular URLs and still prevent a complete reload of the web application. In

AngularJS you can activate the so-called HTML5 mode for your application.

By activating the HTML5 mode, the framework will use hashbang URLs for navigation in older browsers and regular URLs with the HTML5 History API in modern browsers. To accomplish this, AngularJS rewrite all links accordingly at runtime.

However, there is a drawback when using the HTML5 mode, which is why by default it is disabled. If you enable HTML5 mode for your application, you also need to describe any deep links on the web server that delivers your application. Finally, you have to ensure that every deep link used to invoke the application will produce the requested client-side application state as soon as it arrives at the browser for execution.

You can enable the HTML5 mode by using the **$locationProvider** component within a configuration block (**config()**). Here is the actual call:

```
$locationProvider.html5Mode(true)
```

Search Engine Optimization
The crawler program of a search engine is designed for static web pages and cannot index single-page applications easily. Since current development moves more and more in the direction of dynamic web pages and applications, there are now specifications for Ajax crawlers and HTML snapshots. Using the specifications that the major search engines have agreed to, it is possible for a dynamic page to be included in the search index. A good article on this can be found on the ng-newsletter website:

```
http://www.ng-newsletter.com/posts/serious-angular-seo.html#
.Ut6K6GSIUnV
```

Listing 3.29: The template for the List view with a hyperlink to call the Details view

```
<input type="text" placeholder="Search..."
       ng-model="searchText">
<table class="bm-book-list">
    <tbody>
        <tr ng-repeat="book in books | orderBy: getBookOrder
                | filter: searchText">
```

```
        <td><a ng-href="#/books/{{ book.isbn }}"
            ng-bind="book.title"></a></td>
        <td ng-bind="book.author"></td>
        <td ng-bind="book.isbn"></td>
    </tr>
  </tbody>
</table>
```

With the expansion in Listing 3.29 we have a link from the List view to the Details view. Executing the code in the browser should show the expected result and our book titles should be rendered as links (see Figure 3.16). As such, one of the tests we defined should now pass.

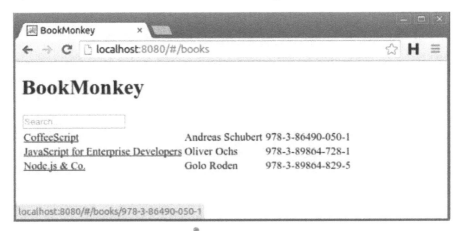

Figure 3.16: The List view with book titles as links

What is still missing is a link on the Details view to go back to the List view. To add the link, we need an **<a>** tag. However, we do not need the **ngHref** directive, because the relative path to the List view contains no expression. It is sufficient to provide the link with the ordinary **href** attribute.

However, there is one aspect that we have to consider. In the E2E test we reference the DOM element to be clicked using the **.bm-list-view-btn** CSS selector. This means that we need to annotate our Back link with a **bm-list-view-btn** CSS class so that Karma can reference the DOM element in the E2E test. The necessary changes can be seen in Listing 30.3.

Listing 3.30: The template for the Details view with a Back link to the List view

```
<h2 ng-bind="book.title" class="bm-book-title"></h2>
<h3 ng-bind="book.subtitle" class="bm-book-subtitle"></h3>

[...]

<a href="#/books" class="bm-list-view-btn">Back</a>
```

We have now implemented the required navigation. If we run our E2E test suites again, the two test cases created earlier should no longer fail. Also, the manual test in the browser should reflect the required behavior. Clicking on a book title on the List view should bring us to the Details view. To go back to the List view, we can click on the "Back" link.

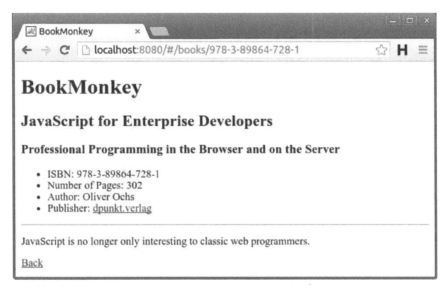

Figure 3.17: The Details view with a Back link

Of course in the Details view you still only see the details of the book "JavaScript for Enterprise Developers," because we do not use the ISBN that was passed via the URL in the **BookDetailsCtrl** controller (See Figure 3.17). We will take care of this in the next section when we introduce our first service.

The ngClick Directive: Responding to the Click Event

So far, so good. Nevertheless, we want to handle the implementation of the Back link in the Details view again to introduce two more interesting features of AngularJS, the **ngClick** directive and the **$location** service.

With the **ngClick** directive we can determine which function to call when the user clicks on a DOM element. Thus, it seems logical to implement the Back link using this directive, even though doing so will not bring any advantage other than for educational purposes.

Listing 3.31: Using the ngClick directive to call a function from the controller scope

```
<h2 ng-bind="book.title" class="bm-book-title"></h2>
<h3 ng-bind="book.subtitle" class="bm-book-subtitle"></h3>

[...]

<a ng-click="goToListView()" href=""
  class="bm-list-view-btn">Back</a>
```

As can be seen in Listing 3.31, we use the **ngClick** directive to specify that the **goToListView()** function be called when the user clicks on the **<a>** element. AngularJS therefore expects the **goToListView()** function to be defined in the currently valid scope of the Details view or a parent scope. The currently valid scope for the Details view is still the scope of the **BookDetailsCtrl** controller. Therefore, we will implement this feature in the same scope as this controller.

You may have noticed that our **<a>** tag contains an **href** attribute that is assigned an empty string. The only reason for this is that most browsers only format a link if the **<a>** tag contains a **href** attribute. Therefore, we simply define an empty **href** attribute to get around the CSS rule.

The $location Service: Interacting with the Address Bar

We can now proceed and implement the **goToListView()** function in the scope of the **BookDetailsCtrl** controller. See Listing 3.32.

Listing 3.32: The goToListView() function in the BookDetailsCtrl controller

```
bmApp.controller('BookDetailsCtrl',
function ($scope, $location) {

    [...]

    $scope.goToListView = function() {
        $location.path('/books');
    };
});
```

As you can see in Listing 3.32, the implementation of **goToListView()** is simple and consists of exactly one line of JavaScript code. The important thing to note is that we can get AngularJS to pass us the **$location** service through dependency injection. We do this by adding a parameter in the controller's anonymous constructor.

The **$location** service allows you to interact with the browser address bar easily. Internally, this service uses the **window.location** object of the DOM API and provides a kind of two-way data binding. This means any changes that you make with the **$location** service have a direct impact on the address line and vice versa. Thus, you can programmatically change the content of the address bar and navigate to another view within the application using this service easily.

That's what we do in the **goToListView()** function. Using the **path()** function we manipulate the path component of the current URL and assign **/books** to it. This means that when you click on the Back link in the Details view, the **/books** route is called, which causes the List view to be displayed. This behavior corresponds exactly to our first choice. Thus, the corresponding E2E test should still pass.

In addition to the **path()** function, the **$location** service provides a few more functions to interact with the address bar. A complete listing and description can be found here:

```
http://docs.angularjs.org/api/ng.$location
```

We should point out that the service API is structured so that you can use the functions to write to as well as read from the various components of the

URL. Thus, the call to **$location.path()** (without a parameter) would return the path component of the currently loaded URL.

Summary

- You can use **$routeProvider.otherwise()** in the route configuration to specify a default route that will be used when there is no match with any of the defined **when()** routes.
- You can use **element ()** to access a DOM element in an E2E test, by passing a CSS selector to the function. You can use **click()** to programmatically perform a mouse click on this element.
- You can use the **browser().location()** object and its numerous functions such as **path()** or **hash()** in an E2E test to collect certain information about the current status of the address bar.
- Within our AngularJS application we usually navigate between different parts of the application to which we have defined a route using hashbang URLs.
- Hashbang URLs also allows routes to be specified as deep links.
- For ordinary link, you use the **<a>** tag and the **href** attribute. If a link contains an expression, resort to the **ngHref** directive.
- You can switch to another application part programmatically. You can use the **$location** service of AngularJS to easily interact with the browser address bar.
- You can also use the HTML5 mode to force AngularJS to establish internal linking to the application with regular URLs. However, this mode requires an adjustment to the web server that delivers the application.
- Using the **ngClick** directive you can define in a template which function should be executed when the user clicks on the annotated DOM element.

The First Service

After implementing two views for the BookMonkey application and having shown in the previous chapter that you can establish a link between individual parts of the application, we now want to create the first service in this section. We want to fix the problem with the Details view always showing the information about the "JavaScript for Enterprise Developers" book because the passed ISBN is not being evaluated in the **BookDetailsCtrl** controller. The service we will create is called **BookDataService**.

As you have learned in Chapter 2, "Basic Principles and Concepts," you can use a service within an AngularJS application to perform a number of tasks, including accessing application data. Therefore, we can use a service to create a data access object, which is what our **BookDataService** will be designed to do.

An essential characteristic of services is that it provides a clear and stable API. It is important because with a clear and stable API you can replace the internal implementation of a service and offer overall flexibility.

For the feature we will implement in this section, we write this user story:

> As user Michael I want to be able to select a book from the list and retrieve the details of the book.

> **Using the Downloaded Project**
> To test the code in this section, you can use the accompanying project that you downloaded from the publisher's website. To do this, change directory to **ch03_05_first_service/app** and start http-server from there.

First, the Test

Like before, we start with the tests and we will write unit tests for the first time. At the beginning of the BookMonkey project, we created a directory named **unit** under the **test** directory. Now in the **unit** directory we need create a directory called **services**, and in this directory we will create a **book_data.spec.js** file that will contain the unit tests for **BookDataService**.

As already mentioned, AngularJS is fundamentally designed for testability. Thus, all application components can be tested with unit tests. So far we have only tested the user interaction with the views and thus more or less considered our application a black box. Our E2E tests are also made for this purpose. However, for the first time it makes sense to write unit tests to test **BookDataService**.

In Listing 3.33, you can see that the basic structure for unit testing looks the same as the structure for the E2E testing. However, we should make it clear from the beginning that we will use another testing framework for unit testing and therefore have to employ a different test API. For our E2E tests we have used ngScenario that is part of AngularJS. For unit testing, however, we will use Jasmine. Purely syntactically, the two frameworks are similar, but functionally they are designed for different purposes. As with ngScenario, where you can write E2E tests and practically define specific user behavior and then check rather superficial expectations based on the DOM, with Jasmine you can call and unit test all features of a component and make precise statements about the component state. Because of this, you can formulate very precise expectations.

AngularJS comes with the **ngMock** module to help you write Jasmine unit tests. This module offers an API that allows you to download and reference your application modules and components. Thus, you have full access to all functions that are provided by the components. Another great advantage is that the dependency injection mechanism of AngularJS can also be used in unit tests. This means that you can replace dependencies with predefined mock objects in tests. The **ngMock** module even comes with some mock implementations to simplify the creation of isolated unit tests.

Listing 3.33: The beforeEach() block of the unit tests for BookDataService

```
describe('Service: BookDataService', function () {
  var BookDataService;

  // load the application module
  beforeEach(module('bmApp'));
  // get a reference to the service

  beforeEach(inject(function (_BookDataService_) {
    BookDataService = _BookDataService_;
  }));
```

```
    [...]

});
```

Listing 3.33 shows the first steps of our unit tests for **BookDataService**. As with our E2E tests, we use the **describe()** function to define a test suite for the unit tests. This test suite contains two **beforeEach()** calls that define the functions to be performed before each unit test. In these **beforeEach()** calls we can even see two main functions, **module()** and **inject()**, in action. These functions are provided by the **ngMock** module.

With the **module()** function we will load our **bmApp** application module for the test. This ensures that we can access all components (services, directives, controllers etc) that have been implemented within this module.

The **inject()** function is largely responsible for making sure you can access the components of a module after you load the module. As the name implies, you can use this function to tell AngularJS to inject application components through dependency injection. This basically works by following the same pattern as the anonymous constructor of our components. The **inject()** function takes a function as a parameter, and within that function you can specify in the parameters which application modules should be provided by the framework. As you can see in Listing 3.33, these are still a small feature.

We want AngularJS to inject **BookDataService** because we want to test the functions in this service in the test. It is good practice to store the reference to the service object in a local variable that has the same name, so you can easily access the service in the unit tests. Here we save the passed reference in a local variable named **BookDataService**. We declare this variable at the beginning of our test suite (**var BookDataService**). Now, however, we have a problem.

According to dependency injection rules, dependency resolution is based on parameter names. Unfortunately, we cannot call the parameter in the second **beforeEach()** call **BookDataService**, because we would overshadow our local **BookDataService** variable. Fortunately, the **inject()** function allows us to enclose the variable name with underscores (**_BookDataService_**). The AngularJS injector, the internal component that resolves dependencies, knows that in tests it should ignore underscores when resolving dependencies. Consequently, we can assign our local variable **BookDataservice** the reference to the service object, to make it available for the following unit tests.

> ## Dependency Injection in Tests
> It is good practice to name the local variable that will reference a service the same name as the service. Therefore, the AngularJS injector can resolve dependencies that are enclosed with underscores.
>
> However, if you have to name a local variable differently, you can follow the usual specification of the dependencies without underscores in the **inject()** call.

Now that we have created the basic structure of the test suite, we can continue with the first unit tests for **BookDataService**.

As shown in Listing 3.34, it is entirely possible to nest **describe()** blocks and thus structure test suites a bit finer. The **beforeEach()** calls that we define in the outer **describe()** block to get a reference to our **BookDataService**, apply equally to all test cases defined within the inner **describe()** block. We should mention at this point that **describe()** blocks can nest to any arbitrary depth and that they may also contain **beforeEach()** and **afterEach()** blocks, which are executed before and after each inner test case.

Listing 3.34: Unit tests for verifying the public API definition

```
describe('Service: BookDataService', function () {

    [...]

    describe('Public API', function() {
        it('should include a getBookByIsbn() function', function ()
        {
            expect(BookDataService.getBookByIsbn).toBeDefined();
        });

        it('should include a getBooks() function', function () {
            expect(BookDataService.getBooks).toBeDefined();
        });
    });
```

```
    [...]
});
```

First, we verify the definition of the public interface of our
BookDataService. In the first step, we demand that the service provide two
functions, **getBookByIsbn()** and **getBooks()**. To this end, we define the
corresponding test cases with **it()** in a separate sub-suite.

Just like ngScenario, Jasmine ships with a beautiful collection of
matchers you can use to conveniently express expectations. In Listing 3.34
we use **toBeDefined()**, a matcher, to ensure the presence of the two API
functions (**getBookByIsbn()** and **getBooks()**).

Structural Tests

JavaScript is an interpreted programming language with a dynamic
type system. This means that you have to live with all the advantages
and disadvantages of such a language. One aspect that many critics feel
a big disadvantage is the fact that there is no compiler that can warn of
type mismatch. To address this issue, we write structural tests in
Listing 3.34 in JavaScript. Make sure that the so called duck typing is
maintained. In the context of software engineering, this term was first
coined by Alex Martelli in 2000 in the
newsgroup comp.lang.python: "In other words, don't check whether it
IS-a duck: check whether it QUACKS-like-a duck, WALKS-like-a
duck, etc. depending on exactly what subset of duck-like behavior you
need to play your language-games with."

Since we have ensured that the public API of our service is offering the
getBookByIsbn() and **getBooks()** functions, we can now go ahead and
write the implementations of these functions. For this we define a separate
suite (See Listing 3.35), which in turn has two sub-suites, each for each
function. From this example we can see how easily we can structure our
unit tests within a file.

**Listing 3.35: The unit tests for checking the functionality of the public
API**

```
describe('Service: BookDataService', function () {
```

```
[...]

describe('Public API usage', function() {
    describe('getBookByIsbn()', function() {
        it('should return the proper book object (valid isbn)',
        function() {
            var isbn = '978-3-86490-050-1',
                book = BookDataService.getBookByIsbn(isbn);
            expect(book.title).toBe('CoffeeScript');
        });

        it('should return null (invalid isbn)',
        function() {
            var isbn = 'test',
                book = BookDataService.getBookByIsbn(isbn);
            expect(book).toBeNull();
        });
    });

    describe('getBooks()', function() {
        it('should return a proper array of book objects',
        function() {
            var books = BookDataService.getBooks();
            expect(books.length).toBe(3);
        });
    });
});

});
```

What the two API functions should do is already apparent from the names. The **getBookByIsbn()** function returns the **Book** object that matches the passed ISBN, whereas **getBooks()** returns an array of all existing books.

The corresponding unit tests are implemented in Listing 3.35. We expect the **getBookByIsbn()** function to return a **Book** object with the title "CoffeeScript" when we call it by passing the ISBN 978-3-86490-050-1. We check it with the **toBe()** matcher. If no book is associated with the passed ISBN, the function should return null, which we test in the second test case using the **toBeNull()** matcher.

The third test case verifies that the **getBooks()** function returns an array with three elements. We have not entered more books in BookMonkey. In this test case, we could certainly implement more logic to check whether the returned object is actually an array, and if the corresponding elements have the structure of a **Book** object (keyword duck typing). We have kept the tests simple because we just want to explain the basic idea and not dive into the details.

We have therefore formulated our expectations of **BookDataService** in the form of unit tests. We can run the newly created test suite once, to ensure that the test cases fail. After all, we have not implemented the **BookDataService** service.

We also have to note that we are now using our Karma configuration for unit testing. This configuration is in the **karma.conf.js** file and should also be in the root directory of our project. If you have not done so, you should copy this configuration from the root directory of the downloaded zip file.

Here is the command to invoke Karma to run the unit tests with the configuration file.

```
karma start karma.conf.js
```

If you have not made a mistake, Karma should give you information about the failed unit tests.

```
Chrome 30.0.1599: Executed 5 of 5 (5 FAILED) ERROR
                                    (0.727 secs / 0.022 secs)
```

In addition to the summarized output, for each test case we get a detailed stack trace and an explanation of why the test case failed. It may be because we formulated an expectation incorrectly or because of an actual error in the program flow. In our case, each of the five test cases should fail for the same reason.

```
Error: Unknown provider: BookDataServiceProvider <- BookDataService
```

This error message means that the AngularJS injector could not find our **BookDataService** and thus the **inject()** function could not resolve the dependency. This is quite logical, because we have not yet implemented the service.

BookDataService: Encapsulating Data Access

We can now go ahead and write the first implementation of
BookDataService. We first create a directory called **services** in the
/app/scripts directory. We then create a **book_data.js** file in this directory
and implement **BookDataService**.

Listing 3.36: The public API of BookDataService

```
bmApp.factory('BookDataService', function() {

    [...]

    // Public API
    return {
        getBookByIsbn: function(isbn) {
            [...]
        },
        getBooks: function() {
            [...]
        }
    };
});
```

As you have learned in Chapter 2, "Basic Principles and Concepts,"
AngularJS comes with several services. In Listing 3.36, you can see that
you use the service factory (the **factory()** function) for **BookDataService**.
A service provider has the advantage over the factory, which can be
configured in a **config()** block. However, our **BookDataService** does not
need configuration and we can save time writing a provider. Another
possible alternative would be to use the **service()** function to register a class
instance as a service. In addition, we have decided not to make the example
unnecessarily complex. The service factory is the most common way to
create a service.

Listing 3.36 shows that in the first step we set the public interface of
BookDataService according to our unit tests. We usually return a so-called
API object in the anonymous function that defines the service. We define all
functions that belong to the public API of the service in this object. These
are all the features that we want to provide to other components. As

specified in the unit tests before, the first step should be in both **getBookByIsbn()** and **getBooks()** functions.

Having defined the object that the API will return, we can now take care of the implementation. In the first step we will store the static book data within the service. Before we tackle this step, we should create a local namespace for our implementation. To this end, we create a new object and assign it to a local variable named **srv**.

It is good practice to write the complete internal implementation in a namespace, so you do not accidentally pollute the global namespace with internal functions, which can lead to hard to identify errors if other parts of the application call these functions by mistake.

ECMAScriptECMAScript is the name of the standard behind the JavaScript language. At the time of writing this book, the most recent version is version 5.1, even though version 6 is currently in the works.

Strict Mode

In addition to the intermediate solution with the namespace object, there are other ways to counter the lack of namespaces in ECMAScript 5. These include the so-called Module design pattern and the activation of the strict mode. If you run a script in the strict mode, the JavaScript interpreter examines the source code for potential sources of error and stops the execution in case of such an error. The assignment of a value to a variable that has not been previously declared, for example, is considered a potential source of error in the strict mode. In principle it is always useful to enable the strict mode for the complete JavaScript code base.

After we have created our local namespace object **srv**, we define within this object an array named **_books**. This array will eventually contain **Book** objects (see Listing 3.37). Because the variable name is prefixed with an underscore, the array is only intended for internal use and is therefore not published externally. The **srv._books** array is therefore the first step in our internal data structure used for managing **Book** objects.

Listing 3.37: The internal data structure of BookDataService

```
bmApp.factory('BookDataService', function() {
    var srv = {};

    srv._books = [
        {
            title: 'JavaScript for Enterprise Developers',
            [...]
        },
        {
            title: 'Node.js & Co.',
            [...]
        },
        {
            title: 'CoffeeScript',
            [...]
        }
    ];

    // Public API
    return {
        [...]
    };
});
```

We can now implement the **getBookByIsbn()** function (See Listing 3.38). We declare **srv** in our namespace again. The implementation is relatively simple. We iterate over all books in the **srv._books** array and compare the ISBN of each book with the function parameter. If the book with the given ISBN is found, we return a copy of the corresponding object. We return a copy so that any reference to objects in our internal data structure is not exposed to the outside. Finally, we want to have control over the changes to the data structure in our service.

If no book with the given ISBN was found, we return null. Recall that we have specified this in the unit test. Finally, we need to establish a connection between our API object and the internal implementation. For this purpose, we delegate calls to our API (**getBookByIsbn()**) to our internal implementation (**srv.getBookByIsbn()**). JavaScript expert will notice immediately that this connection causes the **getBookByIsbn()** API function to turn to a closure and the references to the **srv.getBookByIsbn()**

function to "includes" so **srv.getBookByIsbn()** will not be cleared after the return of the API object from the runtime environment.

Listing 3.38: The internal implementation of the getBookByIsbn() function

```
bmApp.factory('BookDataService', function() {
    var srv = {};

    [...]

    // Service implementation
    srv.getBookByIsbn = function(isbn) {
        for (var i = 0, n = srv._books.length; i < n; i++) {
            if (isbn === srv._books[i].isbn) {
                return angular.copy(srv._books[i]);
            }
        }
        return null;
    };

    [...]

    // Public API
    return {
        getBookByIsbn: function(isbn) {
            return srv.getBookByIsbn(isbn);
        },
        [...]
    };
});
```

Next, we implement **getBooks()**, the second API function, also within our **srv** namespace (See Listing 3.39). The implementation is quite simple. Since we do not want to expose references to our internal data structure **srv._books**, we copy the array before returning it. Thus, we do not have to worry that a potential caller might obtain the reference to our data structure and manipulate it. As before, we have to delegate calls to the API **getBooks()** to the **srv.getBooks()** internal implementation function. In this case, the JavaScript runtime environment will not clear **srv.getBooks()** after returning the API object, because the **getBooks()** closure includes a reference to this implementation function.

Listing 3.39: The internal implementation of the getBooks() function

```
bmApp.factory('BookDataService', function() {
    var srv = {};

    [...]

    // Service implementation
    [...]

    srv.getBooks = function() {
        // Copy the array in order not to expose
        // the internal data structure
        return angular.copy(srv._books);
    };

    // Public API
    return {
        [...]
        getBooks: function() {
            return srv.getBooks();
        }
    };
});
```

So at this point we have implemented the first version of our
BookDataService. Consequently, the previously defined unit tests should
pass. To prove this, call karma again with our configuration for unit testing.

```
karma start karma.conf.js
```

You should get the following feedback.

```
Chrome 31.0.1650: Executed 5 of 5 SUCCESS (0.892 secs / 0.016 secs)
```

Integrating BookDataService

Now we can integrate **BookDataService** in our two controllers
BookListCtrl and **BookDetailsCtrl**. First, we take the **BookListCtrl**
controller (See Listing 3.40). For this purpose, we tell AngularJS to pass us
BookDataService via dependency injection, by specifying it as the third
parameter to the controller's anonymous constructor. Afterward, we can use
it inside the controller service.

Instead of the scope variable **books** that references the locally defined array of **Book** objects, we use the **getBooks()** API function of our **BookDataService** to access the information. Semantically, nothing is changed in our **BookListCtrl** controller.

Listing 3.40: Calling getBooks in the BookListCtrl controller

```
bmApp.controller('BookListCtrl', function (
      $scope, $filter, BookDataService) {
    $scope.getBookOrder = function(book) {
        return book.title;
    };

    $scope.books = BookDataService.getBooks();

    // This is just to demonstrate the programmatic
    // usage of a filter
    var orderBy = $filter('orderBy');

    var titles = $scope.books.map(function(book) {
        return {title: book.title};
    });

    console.log('titles before ordering', titles);

    // This is the actual invocation of the filter
    titles = orderBy(titles, 'title');

    console.log('titles after ordering', titles);
});
```

While we are editing the **BookListCtrl** controller, we can also remove the unnecessary artifacts for programmatic invocation of filters. After all, they add zero value to our application.

The result is shown in Listing 3.41. Since our **BookListCtrl** controller looks much better now, we can take care of the **BookDetailsCtrl** controller.

Listing 3.41: The BookListCtrl controller after some clean-up

```
bmApp.controller('BookListCtrl',
function ($scope, BookDataService) {
    $scope.getBookOrder = function(book) {
        return book.title;
    };
```

```
    $scope.books = BookDataService.getBooks();
});
```

The $routeParams Service: Selecting the URL parameter

An important aspect for fulfilling our user story is reading the ISBN passed in the URL path parameter. We need the ISBN to get the details of the right book using **BookDataService**. We implement the **getBookByIsbn()** function in **BookDataService**.

Listing 3.42: Reading a URL path parameter in the BookDetailsCtrl controller using the $routeParams service

```
bmApp.controller('BookDetailsCtrl',
function ($scope, $location, $routeParams, BookDataService) {
    var isbn = $routeParams.isbn;

    [...]
});
```

As apparent in Listing 3.42, we use the AngularJS **$routeParams** service to read the URL path parameter. As usual, we let dependency injection pass it by specifying it as a parameter in the controller's anonymous constructor. The **$routeParams** service contains the values of all URL path parameters that we have set for our route configuration. As you can see in the following code snippet, we only have the ISBN (**:isbn**) passed as the path parameter in the corresponding route.

```
$routeProvider.when('/books/:isbn', {
templateUrl: 'templates/book_details.html',
controller: 'BookDetailsCtrl'
})
```

We can access a value by accessing the matching property of the **$routeParams** service. In this case, the access looks like this:

```
var isbn = $routeParams.isbn;
```

We store the ISBN in the local variable **isbn**. We can now use this variable to invoke the **getBookByIsbn()** function of **BookDataService** and obtain the **Book** object whose Details view is called. Before we can do that, we have to get **BookDataService** by dependency injection. The resulting version of the **BookDetailsCtrl** controller is given in Listing 3.43.

Listing 3.43: Calling the getBookByIsbn() function in the BookDetailsCtrl controller

```
bmApp.controller('BookDetailsCtrl',
function ($scope, $location, $routeParams, BookDataService) {
    var isbn = $routeParams.isbn;
    $scope.book = BookDataService.getBookByIsbn(isbn);

    $scope.goToListView = function() {
        $location.path('/books');
    };
});
```

After we expanded **BookDetailsCtrl** to use **BookDataService**, we can run our application in a browser and see if we can now get every book's details. To do this we call the URL to our List view.

```
http://localhost:8080/#/books
```

Something seems wrong, because there is only one entry in the List view. If we examine the browser console closer, we notice that there is an error message.

```
Error: Unknown provider: BookDataServiceProvider <- BookDataService
```

This error looks familiar. We have seen the same message when running our unit tests before we created **BookDataService**.

The AngularJS injector was not able to find our **BookDataService** so it could not resolve the dependency in the **BookListCtrl** controller. This is logical because we have not imported the **book_data.js** file in our **index.html**.

Listing 3.44: Including BookDataService in index.html

```
<!DOCTYPE html>
<html ng-app="bmApp">
<head>
    [...]
</head>
<body>
    [...]
```

```
<!-- Scripts -->
<script src="lib/angular/angular.js"></script>
<script src="lib/angular-route/angular-route.js"></script>
<script src="scripts/app.js"></script>
<script src="scripts/controllers/book_details.js"></script>
<script src="scripts/controllers/book_list.js"></script>
<script src="scripts/services/book_data.js"></script>
</body>
</html>
```

After we imported the **book_data.js** file (See Listing 3.44), our BookMonkey application should run correctly and our List view should contain the correct entries.

In addition, we can now obtain each book's details by clicking on the corresponding entry. Figure 3.18 shows the Details view for the "CoffeeScript" book.

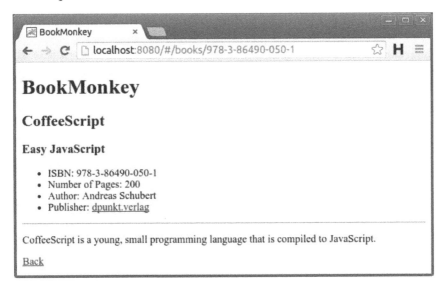

Figure 3.18: The Details view for the CoffeeScript book

We can also tell if our application is functioning correctly by running our E2E testing. These tests should confirm that the introduction of **BookDataService** has not adversely affected our application.

Summary

- In addition to the ngScenario DSL for creating E2E tests, AngularJS also comes with the **ngMock** module, which you can use to include AngularJS modules and allow your application components to be passed through dependency injection and allow you to write unit tests for the components.
- To create unit tests we chose Jasmine. Other framework we could have used included Mocha and QUnit.
- The main functions of ngMock are **module()** and **inject()**.
- We implemented our **BookDataService** using a service factory (**factory()**).
- **BookDataService** has a clear public API and an initial rudimentary implementation.
- We can pass **BookDataService** by dependency injection to other components. We currently use it in the **BookListCtrl** and **BookDetailsCtrl** controllers.
- We can read a URL path parameter using the **$routeParams** service.

Chapter 4
Extending the Application

In the previous chapter, we implemented basic functions to display book data. In this chapter we will address book creation, editing and deletion and build a small administration area to perform these actions. In addition, in the second part of this chapter we will work on tags for categorizing books by designing special directives.

Finally, to allow more clients to use BookMonkey, we will connect our application to a REST web service so that we can perform the administration of the book data centrally on the server.

The Administration Area

In this section we will build the administration area. In particular, we will write functions to address three aspects. We will start by implementing the remaining CRUD operations for creating, editing and deleting books in our **BookDataService**. We will ultimately need these functions to implement the corresponding features in the administration area.

After we extend the service, we will take a look at how easily we can process and validate input in an AngularJS form. The **FormController** and **NgModelController** controllers are part of the AngularJS core components.

Finally, we will familiarize ourselves with a few new directives that will allow us to reuse the existing templates in other views.

For these features we will write the following user story.

> As administrator Stefan, I want to be able to create, edit and delete books in order to always present up to date information on the unrestricted home page to the application user.

Using the Downloaded Project
To test the code in this section, you can use the accompanying project that you downloaded from the publisher's website. To do this, change directory to **ch04_01_admin/app** and start http-server from there.

First, the Test

In the first step, we extend our **BookDataService** to include the remaining CRUD operations for creating, editing and deleting a book. As usual, we specify the required behavior of the API functions with the aid of unit tests. This way, we extend the test suite for the **BookDataService** with the test cases in Listing 4.1.

Listing 4.1: Unit tests for the BookDataService's public API

```
describe('Service: BookDataService', function () {
    var BookDataService;

    // load the application module
    [...]

    // get a reference to the service
    [...]

    describe('Public API', function() {
        [...]

        it('should include a storeBook() function', function () {
            expect(BookDataService.storeBook).toBeDefined();
        });

        it('should include a updateBook() function', function () {
            expect(BookDataService.updateBook).toBeDefined();
        });
```

```
            it('should include a deleteBookByIsbn() function',
            function () {
                expect(BookDataService.deleteBookByIsbn).toBeDefined();
            });
        });
});
```

Listing 4.1 defines unit tests for the remaining functions. We specify that the create function should be called **storeBook**, the update function **updateBook** and the delete function **deleteBookByIsbn**.

There is more to the unit test for the **storeBook** function. As usual, we simultaneously create a separate suite for the new functions (See Listing 4.2).

Listing 4.2: The unit test for storeBook

```
describe('Service: BookDataService', function () {
    var BookDataService;

    [...]

    describe('Public API usage', function() {
        [...]

        describe('storeBook()', function() {
            it('should properly store the passed book object',
            function() {
                var beforeCount = BookDataService.getBooks().length;

                // store an example book
                var book = storeExampleBook();

                expect(BookDataService.getBooks().length).toBe(
                        beforeCount + 1);
                expect(BookDataService.getBookByIsbn(
                        book.isbn)).not.toBeNull();
            });
        });

        [...]
    });

    [...]
});
```

The implementation of the test is very clear. We store the current number of books in the local variable **beforeCount**. We obtain this information from the **length** property of the array that **getBooks()** returns. Subsequently, we create a new book with the help from the function **storeExampleBook()**. As shown in Listing 4.3, we use the API function **storeBook()** inside this function, which should be tested. Other test cases will need a sample book as well. As such, we can outsource the logic that creates a **Book** object to an external function. It should be noted that the **storeExampleBook()** function returns a sample book.

If the implementation is successful, the number of books has to increase by one. We check this with an **expect()** function in conjunction with a **toBe()** matcher. The resulting number should equal **beforeCount + 1**. In addition, using the API function **getBookByIsbn()** we make sure that our service really recognizes the newly created book. According to the **getBookByIsbn()** function specification, this function cannot return null. A **toBeNull()** matcher is negated if you chain the call to **expect()** with **not**.

Listing 4.3: The helper function storeExampleBook()

```
describe('Service: BookDataService', function () {
    var BookDataService;

    [...]

    // Helper functions
    var storeExampleBook = function() {
      var isbn = '978-3-86490-127-0',
        book = {
          title : 'Effective JavaScript (German edition)',
          subtitle : '68 Specific Ways to Harness the Power of'
              + ' JavaScript',
          isbn : isbn,
          abstract :'Do you realy want to master JavaScript?',
          numPages : 240,
          author : 'David Herman',
          publisher : {
              name: 'dpunkt.verlag',
              url : 'http://dpunkt.de/'
          }
      };

    BookDataService.storeBook(book);
```

```
    return book;
    };
});
```

In principle, the test case for the API function **updateBook()** follows the same pattern (See Listing 4.4). Next, we create our example book by calling **storeExampleBook()**. Subsequently, we change the example book's short description (**book.abstract**) by setting it to "TEST". We update the changed object by calling the API function **updateBook()** that we are testing. Consequently, **BookDataService**'s **getBookByIsbn()** should now return the object with an updated short description. Finally, we can write the test case for deleting a book.

Listing 4.4: The unit test for the API function updateBook in BookDataService

```
describe('Service: BookDataService', function () {
    var BookDataService;

    [...]

    describe('Public API usage', function() {
        [...]

        describe('updateBook()', function() {
            it('should properly update the book object',
            function() {
                // store an example book
                var book = storeExampleBook();

                // change it
                book.abstract = 'TEST';

                // update the example book
                BookDataService.updateBook(book);

                expect(BookDataService.getBookByIsbn(
                book.isbn).abstract).toBe(book.abstract);
            });
        });

        [...]
    });

    [...]
```

```
});
```

As you can see in Listing 4.5, the unit test for the API function **deleteBookByIsbn()** is clearer than the previous two test cases. Here we use **storeExampleBook()** to provide an example. We will immediately delete this book when we call the **deleteBookByIsbn()** function that we are testing. With the correct result, the **getBookByIsbn()** function should return null.

Listing 4.5: The unit test for the API function deleteBookByIsbn() in BookDataService

```
describe('Service: BookDataService', function () {
    var BookDataService;

    [...]

    describe('Public API usage', function() {
        [...]

        describe('deleteBookByIsbn()', function() {
            it('should properly delete the book object with
               the passed isbn', function() {
                // store an example book
                var book = storeExampleBook();

                // delete the example book
                BookDataService.deleteBookByIsbn(book.isbn);
                expect(BookDataService.getBookByIsbn(
                        book.isbn)).toBeNull();
            });
        });
    });

    [...]

});
```

At this point, as always, we will execute our unit tests once to ensure that the new test cases fail. If we have not made a mistake, all the newly created test cases will fail. Now we can take care of the implementation of the remaining API functions.

The CRUD Operations of BookDataService

Since we have specified the behaviors of the new API functions **storeBook()**, **updateBook()** and **deleteBookByIsbn()** by using some unit tests, we can continue with the implementation.

First we will discuss the **storeBook()** function. Along those lines, we will expand on the API object returned by the specified function and delegate the call to our internal implementation function **srv.storeBook()**. Because until now our **BookDataService** is still not able to communicate with a backend system, the implementation of the **srv.storeBook()** function consists of a "one-liner," with which we insert the new **Book** object into the internal array **srv._books** (See Listing 4.6).

Listing 4.6: The implementation of the API function storeBook() in BookDataService

```
bmApp.factory('BookDataService', function() {
    var srv = {};

    srv._books = [
        ...
    ];

    // Service implementation
    [...]

    srv.storeBook = function(book) {
        srv._books.push(book);
    };

    [...]

    // Public API
    return {
        [...]
        storeBook: function(book) {
            srv.storeBook(book);
        },
        [...]
    };
});
```

Basically, we will proceed in the same way with the other two API functions. We will further expand the API object for **updateBook()** and delegate the call to **srv.updateBook()**. The implementation of the function **srv.updateBook()** is therefore somewhat more complex than the implementation of **srv.storeBook()**. We iterate over our **srv._books** array in a for loop and look for a **Book** object whose ISBN matches the passed ISBN. When we find the right object, we call the function **angular.extend()** from AngularJS to copy the properties of the **Book** object passed to the function to the **Book** object found (See Listing 4.7). After calling the **extend()** function, we let the function terminate early with a return statement. That is a small optimization to prevent us from iterating over more books unnecessarily.

As the name implies, the helper function **angular.extend()** extends the first object with the properties of the second object. In the case of the same property name, the property of the first object will be overwritten with that of the second object.

Listing 4.7: The implementation of the API function updateBook() in BookDataService

```
bmApp.factory('BookDataService', function() {
    var srv = {};

    srv._books = [
        ...
    ];

    // Service implementation
    [...]

    srv.updateBook = function(book) {
        for (var i = 0, n = srv._books.length; i < n; i++) {
            if (book.isbn === srv._books[i].isbn) {
                angular.extend(srv._books[i], book);
                return;
            }
        }
    };

    [...]

    // Public API
```

```
        return {
            [...]
            updateBook: function(book) {
                srv.updateBook(book);
            },
            [...]
        };
    });
```

The API function **deleteBookByIsbn()** is yet to be discussed. We extend our API object and further delegate the call to the internal implementation function **srv.deleteBookByIsbn()**. Inside this function we once again iterate over all **Book** objects and search for the book having the same ISBN as the passed ISBN. Using the array function **splice()**, we separate the **Book** object found from the array and again prematurely terminate the function to optimize our code.

It should be noted at this point that we iterate over the **Book** objects using a while loop that decrements an index. This type of iteration is more appropriate in this case, because we need to delete an element from the array during the iteration using the **splice** function.

Listing 4.8: The implementation of the API function deleteBookByIsbn() in BookDataService

```
bmApp.factory('BookDataService', function() {
    var srv = {};

    srv._books = [
        ...
    ];

    // Service implementation
    [...]

    srv.deleteBookByIsbn = function(isbn) {
        var i = srv._books.length;
        while (i--) {
            if (isbn === srv._books[i].isbn) {
                srv._books.splice(i, 1);
                return;
            }
        }
    };
```

```
    // Public API
    return {
        [...]
        deleteBookByIsbn: function(isbn) {
            srv.deleteBookByIsbn(isbn);
        }
    };
});
```

With this, we have implemented all the CRUD operations in
BookDataService. If we have not made a mistake, our new test cases
should now pass. This means the operating methods of our service meet the
specification. We will incorporate the new API functions when we
implement the corresponding features in the administration area.

The ngShow and ngHide directives: Showing and hiding content

After we extended our **BookDataService** to include create, update and
delete functions in the previous section, we are now ready to lay the
cornerstone for the administration area.

As the first step, we want to create a special List view for the admin to
display an overview of all books. In addition, it should allow a new book to
be created and existing books to be deleted (See Figure 4.1). This special
List view will become the fundamental view of the administration area,
because an admin can use it as a view for creating a new book and editing
and deleting a book.

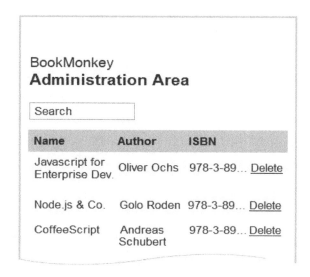

Figure 4.1: The wireframe for the Admin List view

Please note that at this stage we will not go into detail on the corresponding E2E tests for the new views because they do not contain any significant new aspects of the test, and it would only make this chapter longer than necessary. Interested readers can have a look at the corresponding test cases by checking out the project in the accompanying zip file and look in the directory for the current project status.

Listing 4.9: The route configuration for the Admin List view

```
var bmApp = angular.module('bmApp', ['ngRoute']);

bmApp.config(function ($routeProvider) {

    [...]

    /* Admin routes */
    .when('/admin/books', {
        // we reuse the template from the list view
        templateUrl: 'templates/book_list.html',
        controller: 'AdminBookListCtrl'
    })

    [...]
});
```

As shown in Listing 4.9, we need a route for the Admin List view. By using **when()**, we construct the corresponding route configurations in both the **/admin/books** route in the **book_list.html** template and the **AdminBookListCtrl** controller. The comment indicates that we want to reuse the template for the List view. That means we now have two routes that lead to the same template. The only difference is the controller behind the template. For this reuse to be successful, we have to slightly adjust the template for the List view and extend a few aspects. The corresponding extension is shown in Listing 4.10.

Listing 4.10: Extending the template for the List view to make it reusable

```
<h2 ng-show="isAdmin">Administration Area</h2>
    [...]
        <tr ng-repeat="[...]">
            <td ng-hide="isAdmin">
                <a class="bm-details-link"
                    ng-href="#/books/{{ book.isbn }}"
                    ng-bind="book.title">
                </a>
            </td>

            <td ng-show="isAdmin">
                <a class="bm-edit-link"
                    ng-href="#/admin/books/{{ book.isbn }}/edit"
                    ng-bind="book.title">
                </a>
            </td>
            <td ng-bind="book.author"></td>
            <td ng-bind="book.isbn"></td>
            <td ng-show="isAdmin">
                <a class="bm-delete-link"
                    ng-href="#/admin/books/{{ book.isbn }}/delete">
                    Löschen
                </a>
            </td>
        </tr>
    [...]
<p ng-show="isAdmin">
    <a class="bm-new-book-link" ng-href="#/admin/books/new">
        Create new book
    </a>
</p>
```

Essentially, we have extended the template so that now several HTML elements can be shown and hidden using **ngShow** and **ngHide** directives, respectively. The showing and hiding depend on the scope variable **isAdmin**. We set this variable to **true** in the **AdminBookListCtrl** controller, and we assign no value to it in the **BookListCtrl** controller. That in effect makes the value **false**. That means we want to show only those particular HTML elements when our application is displaying the Admin List view. We want to hide these elements, however, in the unrestricted List view.

The **<h2>** heading "Administration Area," the hyperlink to edit a book (**<a class="bm-edit-link">**), the hyperlink to delete a book (**<a class="bm-delete-link">**) and the hyperlink to create a new book (**<a class="bm-new-book-link">**) are HTML elements that should be displayed in the admin variant. By contrast, the hyperlink to open the Details view in the Admin List view should be hidden. Therefore, the resulting mutual exclusion that is based on **ngShow** and **ngHide** directives means that the book title is linked with the Edit view in the admin variant, whereas in the unrestricted variant it is linked to the book's Details view.

Now we can continue with the construction of the **AdminBookListCtrl** controller. For this, we will create the file **admin_book_list.js** in the **app/scripts/controllers/** directory.

Listing 4.11: The AdminBookListCtrl controller

```
bmApp.controller('AdminBookListCtrl',
function ($scope, BookDataService) {
    $scope.isAdmin = true;

    $scope.getBookOrder = function(book) {
        return book.title;
    };

    $scope.books = BookDataService.getBooks();
});
```

Listing 4.11 presents the **AdminBookListCtrl** controller that defines the scope of the Admin List view. Except for the fact that it assigns the value **true** to the scope variable **isAdmin**, its implementation of the **BookListCtrl** controller defines the same scope as that for the unrestricted variant.

That's everything that needs to be covered about the admin variant of the List view. At this point, we can call the view in the browser. The Admin List view should look like that in Figure 4.2.

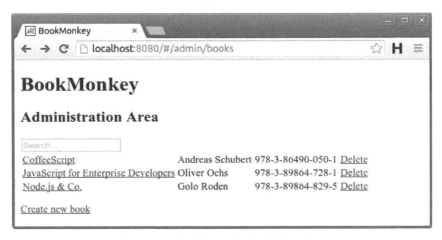

Figure 4.2: The Admin List view

Form Processing and Validation with FormController and NgModelController

Most web applications need user input. The HTML standard already defines a form and fields such as the text field, check box and radio button for that purpose. HTML5 extends the repertoire with a variety of other widgets, such as the slider control and input fields for numbers and URLs. Internally, browsers that support HTML 5 validate user input to make sure the user enters valid data.

In this section we will address form processing and validation. Despite the internal validation by the browser, AngularJS brings with it its own mechanism to easily validate form input. The reason for this is that you need a way to influence how validation works. The default mechanisms of HTML5 go in the right direction. However, it is quite limited. For example, with it you cannot format an error message with CSS or display a conditional error message. Thus, many requirements with respect to error handling cannot be implemented. Using the mechanisms that AngularJS provides, you can easily intervene with the validation behavior and easily implement specific requirements.

In terms of form processing, the framework additionally provides a mechanism for integrating user input into the two-way data binding cycle. That means you, for example, can bind specific input fields to scope variables and can thereby perform automatic updates in both directions.

In order to better clarify form processing, we will now use a form to create a new book in our BookMonkey project (See Figure 4.3). You will learn that AngularJS's validation mechanism is so powerful that you can define any validation for a form completely declaratively in a template, without writing a single line of JavaScript code. In addition, you can expect to use this feature for editing a book using the same template.

In the Admin List view (See Listing 4.10), we have provided a "Create new book" link and connects to the **/admin/books/new** route. As expected, we have to create this route now. To this end, we once again extend the route configuration with the **app.js** file (See Listing 4.12).

Figure 4.3: The wireframe of the view for creating a new book

Listing 4.12: The route configuration for the form for creating a new book

```
var bmApp = angular.module('bmApp', ['ngRoute']);

bmApp.config(function ($routeProvider) {

    [...]

    /* Admin routes */
    [...]

    .when('/admin/books/new', {
        templateUrl: 'templates/admin/book_form.html',
        controller: 'AdminNewBookCtrl'
    })

    [...]

});
```

As shown in Listing 4.12, the **/admin/books/new** route, the template in the **book_form.html** file and the **AdminNewBookCtrl** controller are cited in the code. That means we still have to create two more files. First, we need a **book_form.html** file in the **/app/templates/admin** directory. To do so, we need to create a subdirectory named **admin** in the **templates** directory. We will implement the **AdminNewBookCtrl** controller in an **admin_new_book.js** file located in the **/app/scripts/controllers** directory.

Next, we look at the template for creating and editing a book (**book_form.html**). As shown in Listing 4.13, this template will be designed to be as reusable as the template for the List view. Using the scope variable **isEditMode** as a switch, we can show or hide some elements. We will eventually set this scope variable to **true** in the **AdminEditBookCtrl** controller and set it to **false** in the **AdminNewBookCtrl** controller.

As expected, you will find the most interesting aspects of form processing and validation within the **<form>** element. In AngularJS the **<form>** element has special semantics. When you use the **<form>** tag in AngularJS, you don't just define an HTML form. In AngularJS, the **<form>** tag represents the **form** directive. The **form** directive gets executed and an instance of **FormController** gets created when a **<form>** tag is processed. The internal states of this **FormController** store information about the form, such as whether the form has been altered by the user and whether or not it is valid. You should not implement its logic as it is already covered by the **form** directive.

The crucial point that makes validation so convenient is the fact that you can set the instance of this controller in the current, valid scope. And you know that you can use a template to output all variables and functions defined within a scope or use them to "feed" the directives. That means you can use the **FormController**'s internal state properties in a template to specifically show certain content with the **ngShow** directive.

The questions that spring to mind are: How can you tell AngularJS to pass you the **FormController** instance in the scope? Which scope variable references the instance? The answer to these questions lie behind the **name** attribute of the **<form>** element. The **name** attribute also has a special meaning within the framework. Using this attribute, you can tell AngularJS to set the instance of the **FormController** in the scope. The scope variable, through which you can access the instance, is determined by the attribute value. In this case, it is the scope variable **bookForm**. With that, you can now use the internal properties in the template to conditionally show the specified content. The properties of a **FormController** include:

- **$pristine** – A boolean value that indicates whether or not the user has already interacted with the form.
- **$dirty** – Contains the negated value of **$pristine**.
- **$valid** – A boolean value that indicates whether or not the form's current condition is valid. Its value is determined by each of the respective form components' validators.
- **$invalid** – Contains the negated value of **$valid**.
- **$error** – Refers to an error object that specifies the reason why the form in its current state is invalid.

Listing 4.13: The submit and cancel buttons

```
<h2>Administration Area</h2>
<div>
    <h3 ng-hide="isEditMode">Create new book</h3>
    <h3 ng-show="isEditMode">Edit book</h3>

    <form name="bookForm" novalidate>
```

```
        [...]

        <button class="bm-cancel-btn"
               ng-click="cancelAction()">Cancel</button>
        <button class="bm-submit-btn"
               ng-click="submitAction()"
               ng-disabled="bookForm.$invalid">{{ submitBtnLabel }}
        </button>
    </form>
</div>
```

As shown in Listing 4.13, we use the **FormController**'s **$invalid** property
to disable the submit button when the form is invalid. The actual
deactivation happens when the **ngDisabled** directive, which depends on the
passed scope variable, either activates or deactivates the form component.
As we have told AngularJS to provide us with the instance of
FormController in the scope variable **bookForm**, we can use the
expression **bookForm.$invalid** to find out whether or not the form is valid.

> ### Note on Listing 4.13
> We have also annotated the **<form>** element with the **novalidate**
> attribute to turn off the browser's default validation because we are
> using AngularJS's validation mechanism.

We may now ask this question: Based on which **FormController** properties
is a form considered valid or invalid? In the descriptions of the **$invalid** and
$error properties above, we mention that the individual validators of the
respective form components are the deciding factor. Listing 4.14 shows how
you can provide a form component with a validator. The **required** attribute
used in the **<input>** field for the book title is responsible for that. Those
familiar with HTML 5 know that you can achieve this with the **required**
validator, which tells the browser that the user must enter a value in the
corresponding input field. If you use the **novalidate** attribute in the **<form>**
tag to turn off the default browser validation, the browser will ignore the
required validator and other validators in that form. However, the
AngularJS **required** directive gets executed at this point and then, if the
necessary precautions have been taken, it activates the corresponding
validation for the input field.

Note though that the prerequisite for using the **required** validator in AngularJS is that the **ngModel** directive must also be used in the annotated **<input>** tag. With the help from the **ngModel** directive, you produce two-way data binding between a form component (e.g., input field) and a scope variable. That means the framework automatically ensures that each input is bound to the scope variable and it also updates the input every time the variable is manipulated.

The critical aspect at this stage is that AngularJS instantiates the **ngModel** controller with each use of the **ngModel** directive for the specified form component. The **ngModelController**, like the **FormController**, includes data-binding logic as well as the necessary mechanisms to perform the validation of the specified form components. Validator directives like **required** use this mechanism to feed the necessary validation logic. Therefore, it is imperative that all available validators be used in conjunction with the **ngModel** directive.

Just as the **FormController** make the five properties (**$pristine**, **$dirty**, **$valid**, **$invalid**, and **$error**) available to assess the overall state of a form, the **NgModelController** includes these five properties in order to obtain this information for a single form component. That means you can display, for example, error messages that depend on the validation state of a single form component. Listing 4.14 shows that you can display a specific error message for the "title" field. However, here too we pose the question again as to how we can access the five properties of the **NgModelController** in the template.

Listing 4.14: The form template for creating and editing a book with the required validator

```
<h2>Administration Area</h2>
<div>
    <h3 ng-hide="isEditMode">Create new book</h3>
    <h3 ng-show="isEditMode">Edit book</h3>

    <form name="bookForm" novalidate>
        <input type="text" placeholder="Title..."
            ng-model="book.title" name="title" required>
        <span ng-show="bookForm.title.$dirty
                && bookForm.title.$invalid">
            Please enter a book title.
        </span>
```

```
        <br>

        [...]

    </form>
</div>
```

As with the **FormController**, the answer for the **ngModelController** also lies in the **name** attribute. There is a slight difference with the **NgModelController**, however. While AngularJS provides you with the **FormController** instance through the variable specified as a value in the currently valid scope (here, **bookForm**), the mechanism in the **NgModelController** works by publishing the instance as a property within the parent **FormController**. Again, you can specify the name of the property using the attribute value (here, **title**). That means you can access the **NgModelController** instance for the "title" field with the expression **bookForm.title**. Thus, you can use, say, **bookForm.title.$dirty** or **bookForm.title.$invalid**. Using both these properties, you can display an error message conditionally. For that, once again you use the **ngShow** directive. The command in this case would be: If the user has interacted with the "title" field (**bookForm.title.$dirty**) and one of the validators returned states that the input is considered invalid (**bookForm.title. $invalid**), then display the appropriate error message.

If you look at Listing 4.15, you can see that the input field for ISBN has been annotated with the **required** validator. In this case, we tell AngularJS to publish the **NgModelController** instance within the **FormController** instance. As such, you can display a conditional error message with the expression **bookForm.isbn.$dirty && bookForm.isbn.$invalid**.

Listing 4.15: Using the ngDisabled directive

```
<h2>Administration Area</h2>
<div>
    <h3 ng-hide="isEditMode">Create new book</h3>
    <h3 ng-show="isEditMode">Edit book</h3>

    <form name="bookForm" novalidate>

        [...]

        <input type="text" placeholder="ISBN..."
               ng-model="book.isbn" name="isbn"
```

```
            ng-disabled="isEditMode" required>
      <span ng-show="bookForm.isbn.$dirty
            && bookForm.isbn.$invalid">
         Please enter an ISBN.
      </span>
      <br>

      [...]

   </form>
</div>
```

FormController and NgModelController

Equivalent to the five conditional properties **$pristine**, **$dirty**, **$valid**, **$invalid**, and **$error**, the **FormController** and the **NgModelController** will ensure that the specified CSS classes will be set for the form and its components. For example, if **$dirty** and **$valid** are both **true**, then the **NgModelController** annotates the corresponding **<input>** element with the CSS classes **ng-dirty** and **ng-valid**.

That means you can define specific rules for these CSS classes to give the user visual feedback with the error message during validation. We won't say anything more about that. If you have downloaded the BookMonkey project from the publisher's website, you will learn that we have defined CSS rules for many examples in the **main.css** file. These rules will display a green background for valid input and a red background for invalid input.

In addition, we use the **ngDisabled** directive in Listing 4.15 to make the ISBN uneditable in edit mode.

In addition to the **required** directive, AngularJS internally includes more validator directives that are intentionally named after the native validators of the corresponding HTML5 attributes to make seamless conversion possible. Specifically, there are validator directives for the following attributes:

- **required**. Defines an obligatory input.
- **pattern**. Checks of the input against a regular expression.
- **min**. Sets a minimum value for a numeric value.

- **max**. Sets a maximum value for a numeric value
- **minlength**. Sets a minimum length for input.
- **maxlength**. Sets a maximum length for input.

In addition, the framework also provides validator directives for HTML5 new input fields.

- **<input type="number"/>**. Checks for numeric value.
- **<input type="url"/>**. Checks if the input specifies a valid URL
- **<input type="email"/>**. Checks if the input specifies an email address

Listing 4.16 shows a partial template that defines the **numPages** input field. From this you know that you are using two extra validators in addition to the **required** validator. The first is the validator brought by **<input type="number"/>**, the other is the **min** validator, which specifies a minimum value for the input field. That means the result of the expression **bookForm.numPages.$invalid** depends on these three validators.

Listing 4.16: The min validator in the input fields for numbers

```
<h2>Administration Area</h2>
<div>
    <h3 ng-hide="isEditMode">Create new book</h3>
    <h3 ng-show="isEditMode">Edit book</h3>

    <form name="bookForm" novalidate>

        [...]

      <input type="number" min="1" placeholder="Number of pages..."
             ng-model="book.numPages" name="numPages" required>
      <span ng-show="bookForm.numPages.$dirty
            && bookForm.numPages.$invalid">
          <span ng-show="bookForm.numPages.$error.min">
             The book must have a minimum number of pages.
          </span>
          <span ng-hide="bookForm.numPages.$error.min">
             Please enter a valid number of pages.
          </span>
      </span>
      <br>
```

```
    [...]

  </form>
</div>
```

We want only one aggregate error message displayed when the **required** or number validator failed. In addition, if the **min** validator failed, we want to display instead a special error message that instructs the user to enter a higher number of pages. For that, we use the **$error** property of the **NgModelController**.

As just mentioned, the **$error** property references an error object whose properties are the string representations of the validators that determine that the current input is invalid. In the case of the **NgModelController**, the values of these properties are certainly not arrays of form components, but rather boolean values that each indicates whether the corresponding validator thinks the input is valid or invalid. Therefore, you can show or hide your special error message using the expression **bookForm.numPages.$error.min**. Here, you are using the well-known pattern of mutual exclusion as when you employed the **ngShow** and **ngHide** directives.

Listing 4.17: The URL validator in URL input fields

```
<h2>Administration Area</h2>
<div>
    <h3 ng-hide="isEditMode">Create new book</h3>
    <h3 ng-show="isEditMode">Edit book</h3>

    <form name="bookForm" novalidate>

      [...]

      <input type="url" placeholder="Publisher's website..."
             ng-model="book.publisher.url" name="publisherUrl"
             required>
      <span ng-show="bookForm.publisherUrl.$dirty
            && bookForm.publisherUrl.$invalid">
        <span ng-show="bookForm.publisherUrl.$error.url">
            Please enter a valid URL.
        </span>
        <span ng-hide="bookForm.publisherUrl.$error.url">
            Please enter the publisher's website.
        </span>
```

```
        </span>
        <br>

        [...]

    </form>
</div>
```

Now, take a look at the code in Listing 4.17. The input field looks the same as the one in Listing 4.16, except we input a URL instead of the number of pages. In this case, we certainly want to display a special error message that depends on the **url** validator.

The only thing missing in order to complete the feature for creating a book is an **AdminNewBookCtrl** controller that we will be writing in the **admin_new_book.js** file. In Listing 4.18 you can see that we are using dependency injection to pass the **BookDataService**. We will be using this service in the **submitAction()** function to save the new **Book** object when the user clicks on the "Create new book" button. In addition, in this function we call the **goToAdminListView()** function to go from the save operation back to the Admin List view. We use the already known **$location** service in the **goToAdminListView()** function.

Listing 4.18: The AdminNewBookCtrl controller

```
bmApp.controller('AdminNewBookCtrl',
function ($scope, $location, BookDataService) {
    $scope.book = {};
    $scope.submitBtnLabel = 'Create book';

    $scope.submitAction = function() {
        BookDataService.storeBook($scope.book);
        goToAdminListView();
    };

    $scope.cancelAction = function() {
        goToAdminListView();
    };

    var goToAdminListView = function() {
        $location.path('/admin/books');
    };
});
```

The important reason that we can implement the **submitAction()** function with so little source code is the fact that we use two-way data binding between the **Book** object properties and the form definition in the **ngModel** directives. That causes the **Book** object to continue to be populated with the necessary information while the user fills out the form. Finally, all the book information is found in the **Book** object, and thus the object can be passed directly to the **storeBook()** function of **BookDataService**. Actually, we still don't have to initialize the **Book** object in the scope (**$scope.book = {}**). AngularJS will take care of this as soon as the user interacts with the first form component. Certainly there are many third-party directives that cannot handle uninitialized objects. In that case, you should do the initializing yourself.

> ### Using Data Binding with the ngModel Directive
> The value of the **ngModel** directive should have a period separator (e.g., **ng-model="book.title"**). This way, you can easily populate an object with the appropriate data. In addition, you can use it to avoid unpleasant side effects due to the prototypical changing of scope.

If we have not made an error up to this point, then it should be possible to create a new book. The form should look like that in Figure 4.4.

When you interact with the form, you will learn that even validators we defined are taking effect, and thus the error messages received are displayed in the invalid state.

Binding Templates with the ngInclude Directive

After constructing the form for creating and editing a book, we now want to address the preview. When entering book information, the user will be receiving immediate feedback, as shown in Figure 4.5.

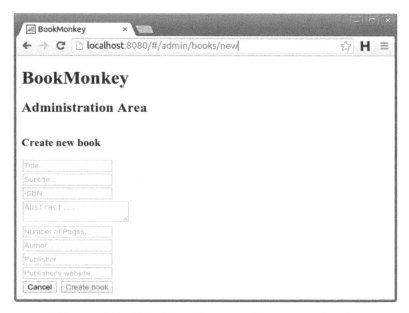

Figure 4.4: The form for creating a new book

Figure 4.5: The view for adding a new book with preview

Using two-way data binding, you can easily implement a preview, by which you establish data binding with the **ngModel** directive that will be displayed on the template at some point.

At this point, we can certainly save a lot of template coding if we reuse the template for the Details view. The important element for this type of reuse is the **ngInclude** directive.

Listing 4.19: Using the ngInclude directive

```
<h2>Administration Area</h2>
<div class="split-screen">
    <h3 ng-hide="isEditMode">Create new book</h3>
    <h3 ng-show="isEditMode">Edit book</h3>

    <form name="bookForm" novalidate>

        [...]

    </form>
</div>
<div class="split-screen">
    <h3>Preview</h3>
    <div class="simple-border padded"
        ng-include="'templates/book_details.html'">
    </div>
</div>
```

As you can see in Listing 4.19, you can include a template in another template by using the **ngInclude** directive. To do this, you have to provide the relative path to the template. Note that the **ngInclude** directive expects the relative path to be provided by a scope variable. Therefore, static paths must be entered with single quotation marks.

Instructions for the Preview Feature

To make sure the preview is rendered in a frame just to the right of the form, we have annotated the corresponding HTML elements with some CSS classes (**split-screen**, **simple-border**, and **padded**). We will not cover the exact CSS rules again here. Those interested will find the corresponding stylesheet in the downloadable zip file that accompanies this book.

If we have not made any errors at this step, the browser should look similar to that in Figure 4.6.

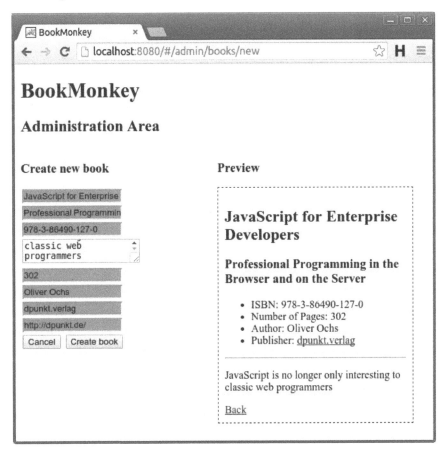

Figure 4.6: The view with the form for creating a new book that includes live preview

When entering data in the form, you should notice that what you enter immediately appears at the right in the preview. To implement this feature, we have made sure that all object properties (**title**, **subtitle**, etc.) have the same names as the input fields.

The Function for Editing A Book

Our BookMonkey application should allow the admin to edit an existing book. We have already added in the Admin List view the appropriate hyperlink for that, which navigates to the Edit Book form. Therefore, we once again have to update our route configuration in **app.js** and enter the route **/admin/books/:isbn/edit** (See Listing 4.20). When we open this route in our application, the template from the **book_form.html** file as well as the **AdminEditBookCtrl** controller should load. That means we are reusing the template for the Create New Book form in the edit function. You should already be familiar with the necessary changes that need to be done in the template.

Listing 4.20: The route configuration for the Edit Book form

```
var bmApp = angular.module('bmApp', ['ngRoute']);

bmApp.config(function ($routeProvider) {

    [...]

    /* Admin routes */
    [...]

    .when('/admin/books/:isbn/edit', {
        templateUrl: 'templates/admin/book_form.html',
        controller: 'AdminEditBookCtrl'
    })

    [...]

});
```

For the **AdminEditBookCtrl** controller we still have to save the **admin_edit_book.js** file in the **/app/scripts/controllers/** directory. You can see the implementation in Listing 4.21.

Listing 4.21: The AdminEditBookCtrl controller

```
bmApp.controller('AdminEditBookCtrl',
function ($scope, $routeParams, $location, BookDataService) {
    $scope.isEditMode = true;
```

```
    $scope.submitBtnLabel = 'Buch editieren';

    var isbn = $routeParams.isbn;
    $scope.book = BookDataService.getBookByIsbn(isbn);
    $scope.submitAction = function() {
        BookDataService.updateBook($scope.book);
        goToAdminListView();
    };

    $scope.cancelAction = function() {
        goToAdminListView();
    };

    var goToAdminListView = function() {
        $location.path('/admin/books');
    };
});
```

For the most part, the **AdminEditBookCtrl** controller is designed using the same pattern as the **AdminNewBookCtrl** controller. One of the main differences between the two controllers is the definition of the scope variable **isEditMode**. We change the value of this variable to show or hide the necessary HTML elements in the template and to disable the ISBN field. Furthermore, we assign the scope variable **submitBtnLabel** the string "Edit book" to be displayed on the button that will call the **submitAction()** function when it is clicked. We should also know which book will be edited. For that, we once again access the ISBN, which is presented as a URL path parameter, with the **$routeParams** service. Using the ISBN, we can get the corresponding **Book** object with **BookDataService.getBookByIsbn()** and reference it with the scope variable **book**. Finally, we update the **Book** object using **BookDataService.updateBook()** by calling the **submitAction()** function. That's all we need at this point to implement the edit feature. The result is shown in Figure 4.7.

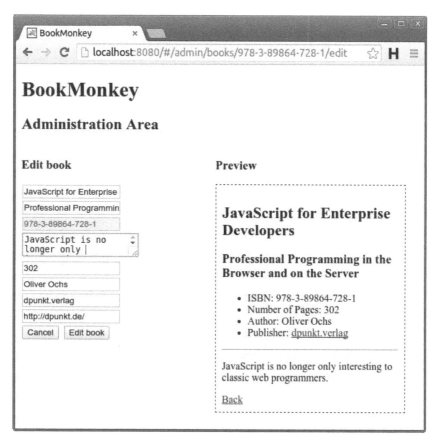

Figure 4.7: The Edit Book form with live preview

The Function for Deleting A Book

Similar to creating and editing a book, deletion is naturally an important function for an admin. The actual view is very simple because it consists of a question and two buttons, one for confirming and one for canceling the operation (See Figure 4.8).

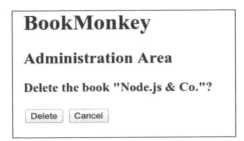

Figure 4.8: The wireframe of the view for deleting a book

We have already added a hyperlink for the delete function in the Admin List view. We just have to edit **app.js** to update the route configuration, so that when the route **/admin/books/:isbn/delete** is called, the **book_delete.html** template and the **AdminDeleteBookCtrl** controller will be loaded (See Listing 4.22).

Listing 4.22: The route configuration for the Delete Book dialog

```
var bmApp = angular.module('bmApp', ['ngRoute']);

bmApp.config(function ($routeProvider) {
    [...]

    /* Admin routes */
    [...]

    .when('/admin/books/:isbn/delete', {
        templateUrl: 'templates/admin/book_delete.html',
        controller: 'AdminDeleteBookCtrl'
    })

    [...]
});
```

As before, we have to create files for it. For the template, we create a **book_delete.html** file in the **/app/templates/admin/** directory. The content of the file is shown in Listing 4.23.

Listing 4.23: The template for the Delete Book dialog

```
<h2>Administration Area</h2>
<h3>
    Delete the book
    &quot;{{ book.title }}&quot;
```

```
       ?
</h3>
<button class="bm-delete-btn"
        ng-click="deleteBook(book.isbn)">Delete</button>
<button class="bm-cancel-btn"
        ng-click="cancel()">Cancel</button>
```

We only use functions in the template that we have already discussed. We ask the admin whether the book should really be deleted and let him or her confirm or cancel the operation. For both actions we have defined a button. If the admin confirms the deletion, we call the **deleteBook()** function and pass the ISBN. Otherwise, if the admin cancels the operation, the **cancel()** function is called.

The **AdminDeleteBookCtrl** controller also consists of a minimum number of lines of code. We create an **admin_delete_book.js** file for the controller in the **/app/scripts/controllers/** directory. As with all other Java script files we use, we must also include **admin_delete_book.js** in our **index.html** using a **<script>** tag.

Listing 4.24: The AdminDeleteBookCtrl controller

```
bmApp.controller('AdminDeleteBookCtrl',
    function ($scope, $routeParams, $location, BookDataService) {
    var isbn = $routeParams.isbn;
    $scope.book = BookDataService.getBookByIsbn(isbn);

    $scope.deleteBook = function(isbn) {
        BookDataService.deleteBookByIsbn(isbn);
        goToAdminListView();
    };

    $scope.cancel = function() {
        goToAdminListView();
    };

    var goToAdminListView = function() {
        $location.path('/admin/books');
    };
});
```

Listing 4.24 shows the implementation of the **AdminDeleteBookCtrl** controller. Like the **AdminEditBookCtrl** controller, we obtain the ISBN of the book to be deleted with the **$routeParams** service. We then pass the

ISBN to the service function **BookDataService.getBookByIsbn()** and assign the returned **Book** object to the scope variable **book**, so we can access the book title and ISBN in the template. Finally, we define the two functions **deleteBook()** and **cancel()** that will be called when the user clicks one of the buttons. The **deleteBook()** function internally calls the **BookDataService.deleteBookByIsbn()** function, which actually deletes the book when the admin has confirmed the deletion. Subsequently, we will be forwarded to the Admin List view using the **$location** service. The forwarding also occurs in the event the user cancels the delete operation.

Figure 4.9 shows how the Delete Book dialog looks like. To view it, you have to click on the Delete hyperlink in the Admin List view. Clicking on "Delete" deletes the book and takes you to the Admin List view. Clicking on "Cancel" takes you back to the Admin List view, though in this case, no book has been deleted.

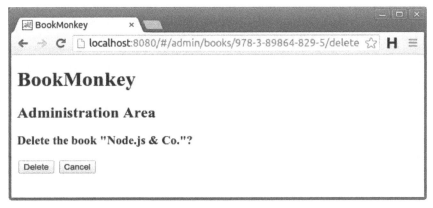

Figure 4.9: The Delete Book dialog

Summary

- You can use the **ngShow** and **ngHide** directive to either show or hide the content of a template.
- AngularJS includes a validation mechanism.
- For every HTML form AngularJS instantiates, you will immediately find the overall state of the form and a **FormController** in five object properties (**$pristine**, **$dirty**, **$valid**, **$invalid**, and **$error**).

- The overall state is an aggregate of the individual state of the relevant **NgModel**Controller instance.
- For every form component, an **NgModelController** will be created with the help of the five previously discussed properties, depending on the states of the form components.
- Validators play an important role in validation. AngularJS includes the corresponding validators for all HTML5 attributes and form components.
- You can use the **ngInclude** directive to bind one template with another and thereby making the template easy to reuse.

Creating Categories with Tags

In the previous section, we set up a basic administration area in which we can create, edit and delete a book. Now we want to introduce a way to separate our books into categories. Many modern web applications use tags to annotate a book, and a tag may represent a category to which the book belongs (See Figure 4.10). We can also use these tags, for example, to restrict search results or to search for books in a particular category. However, for now we will only create a list of tags for a book.

Tags usually have a particular form. They are mostly lowercase and do not contain a space. Therefore, in our application, typical tags may look like this: **javascript**, **web**, **browser** or **realtime**.

As usual, we define a user story for this command.

> As user Michael, I want to be able to see information on the state of tags in a form and to know to which categories the book belongs.

> **Using the Downloaded Project**
> To test the code in this section, you can use the accompanying project that you downloaded from the publisher's website. To do this, change directory to **ch04_02_tags/app** and start http-server from there.

Figure 4.10: The diagram of the view for creating a book with a tag input option

Extending the Data Model with Tags

In order to be able to categorize our books with tags, obviously we need to extend our data model. To that end, open the **book_data.js** file that contains the implementation of our **BookDataService** and extend every **Book** object in the **srv.books** array with matching tags (See Listing 4.25).

Listing 4.25: Extending our data model with tags

```
bmApp.factory('BookDataService', function() {
    var srv = {};

    srv._books = [
        {
            title : 'JavaScript for Enterprise Developers',
            [...]
```

```
                tags : [
                    'javascript', 'enterprise',
                    'nodejs', 'web', 'browser'
                ]
        },
        {
            title : 'Node.js & Co.',
            [...]
            tags : [
                'javascript', 'nodejs', 'web',
                'realtime', 'socketio'
            ]
        },
        {
            title : 'CoffeeScript',
            [...]
            tags : [
                'coffeescript', 'web'
            ]
        }
    ];

    [...]
});
```

As you can see in Listing 4.25, the book *JavaScript for Enterprise Developers* are decorated with tags **javascript**, **enterprise**, **nodejs**, **web** and **browser**. We also assign tags **javascript**, **nodejs**, **web**, **realtime** and **societio** to the book *Node.js & Co*. In addition, we annotate the book *CoffeeScript* with **coffeescript** and **web**.

On top of that, we have to extend the **BookDataService** with the **getTags()** function (See Listing 4.26). We will use this function in the **tokenfield** directive in order to be able to provide an auto-complete feature for the **token** input field. At this point, we are only writing the implementation of the **getTags()** function. The defining of the appropriate test cases is left as an exercise for those interested in it.

Listing 4.26: Extending BookDataService with getTags()

```
bmApp.factory('BookDataService', function() {
    var srv = {};

    [...]
```

```
srv.getTags = function() {
    var obj = {},
        tag;

    for (var i = 0, n = srv._books.length; i < n; i++) {
        for (var j = 0, m = srv._books[i].tags.length;
                j < m; j++)
        {
            tag = srv._books[i].tags[j];
            if (!obj.hasOwnProperty(tag)) {
                obj[tag] = true;
            }
        }
    }

    return Object.keys(obj);
};

// Public API
return {
    [...]
    getTags: function() {
        return srv.getTags();
    },
    [...]
};
});
```

Essentially, in Listing 4.26 we use a pair of for loops to iterate over all the tags in a book and use them as keys in the **obj** object. Because each key can only be used once in an object, the object is practically a set. In other words, it does not allow duplicate tags. We then use **Object.keys()** to return an array that contains all the keys. That is the data structure the **tokenfield** plugin expects as a source.

First, the Test

The jQuery plugin "Tokenfield for Bootstrap"

When we discussed tags in the previous section, the central focus was on the construction of special directives. At this point, we want to specify a few unit tests for our **tokenfield** directive.

The **tokenfield** directive will simplify input tags in the HTML form for creating/editing a book, because it converts an ordinary **<input>** field into a so-called **token** input field. This **token** input field is provided by a jQuery plugin named "Tokenfield for Bootstrap," which you can download from this website:

```
http://sliptree.github.io/bootstrap-tokenfield
```

To take advantage of the features offered by this jQuery plugin, you have to connect it using our **tokenfield** directive so that it integrates seamlesssly with two-way data binding. The binding of a jQuery plugin in AngularJS is a use that can be useful in many applications. We also want the enormous ecosystem of jQuery to also be useable from inside AngularJS.

Before we can write unit tests for our future **tokenfield** directive, we first need to clarify how the **tokenfield** plugin works. As it is customary for a jQuery plugin, the **tokenfield** plugin extends a jQuery base object with a **tokenfield()** function. Thereby we can convert every **<input>** element into a **token** input field that allows us to select and ultimately call the **tokenfield()** function using jQuery. At the same time, we can pass a configuration object to this function to set the method of operation for the **token** input field. A possible call may look like this:

```
$('input').tokenfield({
  autocomplete: {
    source: ['javascript','web','browser'],
    delay: 100
  },
  showAutocompleteOnFocus: false,
  allowDuplicates: false,
  createTokensOnBlur: true
});
```

You can set the token source (by using **source**) for auto-complete with a delay (**delay**) the completion should work. The **showAutocompleteOnFocus** property controls whether auto-complete should be showing when the input field is having focus. In addition, you can use the **allowDuplicates** property to determine whether or not duplicate tokens should be allowed in the input. The most-recently used property, **createTokensOnBlur**, controls whether or not the input text should be automatically converted into a token when the input field loses focus.

So when you use the **tokenfield()** function with the fore-mentioned configuration object, the tokenfiled plugin will render an **<input>** element as the following DOM structure:

```
<div class="tokenfield form-control">
  <input type="text" tabindex="-1"
         style="position: absolute; left: -10000px;">
  <span role="status"
        aria-live="polite"
        class="ui-helper-hidden-accessible"></span>
  <input type="text" class="token-input ui-autocomplete-input"
         placeholder=""
         id="1385909441234157-tokenfield"
         style="min-width: 60px; width: 431px;"
         autocomplete="off">
</div>
```

The original **<input>** element will be hidden thanks to the CSS properties **position: absolute** and **left: -10000px**, and instead the plugin will show other HTML elements to establish the token functionality. Especially at this stage, we should mention the second **<input>** element with the CSS class **token-input**, namely the input field in which we enter input data before it is finally converted into a token. In addition, it is worth mentioning that the original **<input>** element is now a child element of the **<div>** element generated by the plugin.

Further, we should also look more closely at the DOM elements the plugin generates when we have entered some tokens. With the input **javascript**, **web** and **browser**, the following DOM elements are generated:

```
<div class="tokenfield form-control">
  [...]
  <div class="token" data-value="javascript">
    <span class="token-label" style="max-width: 419px;">
      javascript
    </span>
    <a href="#" class="close" tabindex="-1">×</a>
  </div>

  <div class="token" data-value="web">
    <span class="token-label" style="max-width: 419px;">
      web
    </span>
    <a href="#" class="close" tabindex="-1">×</a>
```

```
  </div>

  <div class="token" data-value="browser">
    <span class="token-label" style="max-width: 419px;">
      browser
    </span>
    <a href="#" class="close" tabindex="-1">×</a>
  </div>

  [...]
</div>
```

As can be seen in the code above, the plugin generates a **<div>** element with the CSS class **token** for every token. Within this element is a **<span>** element that contains the token text. In addition, there is an **<a>** tag with CSS class **close** inside the **<div>** element. This is the hyperlink for extracting the appropriate token.

The unit tests for the tokenfield directive

We can now write our unit tests. We need to create a directory named **directives** in the **/test/unit/** directory. In the **directives** directory we will create a file named **tokenfield.spec.js** that will contain the test suite for our **tokenfield** directive.

Listing 4.27: The beforeEach() blocks of the test suite for the tokenfield directive

```
describe('Directive: tokenfield', function () {

    var $compile,
        $rootScope,
        element,
        scope;

    var testTags = ['test1', 'test2', 'test3'];

    // load the application module
    beforeEach(module('bmApp'));

    // get a reference to all needed AngularJS components
    beforeEach(inject(function (_$compile_, _$rootScope_) {
        $compile = _$compile_;
        $rootScope = _$rootScope_;
```

```
    }));

    // init logic for every test case
    beforeEach(function() {
        scope = $rootScope.$new();

        scope.book = {
            tags: angular.copy(testTags)
        };

        element = $compile('<input tokenfield="book">')(scope);
    });

    [...]
});
```

As you can see in Listing 4.27, we define three **beforeEach()** blocks in our test suite. We put our application module **bmApp** in the first block. The second block assigns the **$compile** and **$rootScope** services to class-level variables using dependency injection. We need both components in the third **beforeEach()** block to implement the actual initialization logic for every test case.

If the AngularJS automatisms do not work during the execution of the unit tests, you have to finish some directive test tasks manually in order to offer the developer full control over the test sequence. This means you need to create a part of the scope hierarchy that your directive needs for smooth operation.

In our case, that means we have to create a new scope for every test case using the scope function **$new()**. We define in this scope a rudimentary **Book** object (**scope.book**) that only has a **tags** property. Using this property, we reference an array of test tags by copying the **testTags** array. We have previously defined the test suite with three test tags, **test1**, **test2**, and **test3**, as local variables.

The last line of the third **beforeEach()** block is the most important part of the directive testing. We use the **$compile** service to compile the simple template **<input tokenfield="book">**. This effectively executes the **tokenfield** directive specified as an attribute. We assign to the variable **element** the processed template, which in this case only consists of the

<input> element affected by the **tokenfield** directive. We can then use the variable **element** to access the individual test cases.

We can start the first test case after we have made the necessary preparation using the **beforeEach()** blocks to easily implement the test cases.

Listing 4.28: The test case for ensuring a proper initialization

```
describe('Directive: tokenfield', function () {

    [...]

    it('should properly create available tokens on initialization',
    function () {
        var tokens = element.parent().find('div.token');
        expect(tokens.length).toBe(testTags.length);
        tokens.each(function(index, token) {
            expect(
                angular.element(token).data('value')
            ).toEqual(testTags[index]);
        });
    });
    [...]
});
```

Listing 4.28 shows the first test case for our forthcoming **tokenfield** directive. In the first step, we want to test in this test case if an appropriate token would be generated for each of the three tags from the **Book** object. We know that for each token the **tokenfield** plugin creates a **<div>** element that contains other elements.

However, since we only have a reference to the original **<input>** element that will still be inserted as a child node in the parent **<div>** element, we have to do something to reference the parent **<div>** element.

After a successful execution of our directive, the element will contain exactly three **<div>** elements with a CSS class token. We obtain a jQuery object using the statement **find('div.token')** that is contained in the found **<div>** element with the CSS class tokens. We assign this jQuery object to the local variable **tokens**. Finally, we can use the **length** property to expect there must be as many **<div>** elements with the CSS class token as there are tags in the **testTags** array.

In addition, we can use **each()** to iterate over the individual **div.token** elements and expect for each element that the token content must match the corresponding tag in the **testTags** array. We must be careful in doing that, so that we also obtain the corresponding DOM element within the callback function in addition to the index. To create a jQuery object from the DOM element and to be able to call the **data()** function, we have to use the **angular.element()** function.

Instructions for using jQuery in AngularJS

AngularJS includes its own jQuery implementation called jqLite. You can access the jqLite implementation using the AngularJS function **angular.element()**, which takes a CSS selector as a parameter. As the name implies, jqLite implements only a subset of the functions that can be found in jQuery.

Basically, if possible, you should familiarize yourself with this feature subset so that you do not have to rely on external dependencies. However, most big projects, including BookMonkey, still need one or several jQuery plugins, which means you still need the correct jQuery library as a dependency. In this case, you have to make sure that you include jQuery before AngularJS in your **index.html**. This way, AngularJS will ensure the correct jQuery library is included and continue to delegate all calls from **angular.element()** to jQuery. In other words, you should always use **angular.element()**, including when you are using the full jQuery library. The output from **angular.element()** will always contain a complete jQuery object.

Our second test case deals with creating new tokens. To do this, we first determine the current number of input tokens using the same call we used before, and then assign it to the local variable **tokenCount** (See Listing 4.29). In addition, we get a reference to the **input.token-input** input field and store it in the local variable **tokenInput**. Recall that it is the input field the user will instantiate and whose content will eventually be converted into tokens.

Listing 4.29: The test case for adding new tokens

```
describe('Directive: tokenfield', function () {
```

```
    [...]

    it('should properly add new tokens', function () {
        var tokenCount = element.parent().find('div.token').length,
            tokenInput = element.parent().find('input.token-input'),
            testToken = 'test4';

        tokenInput.focus();
        tokenInput.val(testToken);
        tokenInput.blur();
        var tokenCountAfter
            = element.parent().find('div.token').length;
        expect(tokenCountAfter).toBe(tokenCount + 1);
        expect(scope.book.tags.length).toBe(tokenCountAfter);
        expect(element.parent().html()).toContain(testToken);
    });
    [...]
});
```

We set focus on the **input.token-input** input field (using
tokenInput.focus()), set its value to "test4" (**tokenInput.val(testToken)**),
and remove focus from it (**tokenInput.blur()**). As a result, the **tokenfield**
plugin will create a new token for the given input once the input field loses
focus. Accordingly, we develop the expectation that another **div.token**
element should now be present.

Because we will seamlessly connect the **tokenfield** plugin to
AngularJS's two-way data binding using the **tokenfield** directive, the array
should now contain another element as well. Finally, the last expectation
tests whether the returned string actually was converted to a token and not
something else.

Listing 4.30: The test case for token removal

```
describe('Directive: tokenfield', function () {

  [...]

  it('should properly remove new tokens', function () {
    var indexToRemove = 0;

    angular.element(
      element.parent().find('div.token')[indexToRemove]
    ).find('a.close').click();
```

```
    expect(
      element.parent().find('div.token').length
    ).toBe(testTags.length - 1);
    expect(
      scope.book.tags.length
    ).toBe(testTags.length - 1);
    expect(
      element.parent().html()
    ).not.toContain(testTags[indexToRemove]);
  });
});
```

Listing 4.30 presents the last unit test for our forthcoming **tokenfield** directive. In this test case, we want to ensure the proper removal of existing tokens. To do that, we assign zero to the local variable **indexToRemove** to indicate that we want to delete the first token. Subsequently, we reference the **a.close** hyperlink under the **div.token** element and trigger the **click** event. As a result, the **tokenfield** plugin will remove the corresponding token. At the same time, the number of elements in the **scope.book.tags** array should have been reduced by one, and the string of the deleted token should no longer appear in the **tokenfield** input field.

Before we run the recently created test suite to make sure that the unit tests for the **tokenfield** directive actually fail, we should extend the Karma configuration for unit testing the dependencies we will need to implement the **tokenfield** directive. Therefore, the **files** property should now have the following value:

```
// list of files / patterns to load in the browser
files: [
    'app/lib/jquery/jquery-1.10.2.min.js',
    'app/lib/jquery-ui/jquery-ui.min.js',
    'app/lib/bootstrap-tokenfield/bootstrap-tokenfield.min.js',
    'app/lib/angular/angular.js',
    'app/lib/angular-route/angular-route.js',
    'app/lib/angular-mocks/angular-mocks.js',
    'app/scripts/app.js',
    'app/scripts/**/*.js',
    'test/unit/**/*.js'
],
```

Alternatively, you can copy the new configuration from the corresponding project folder in the accompanying zip file for the book.

Next, you can use the known console command to run the unit test to ensure that the three new test cases fail.

The tokenfield Directive: Creating the Tag

Have presented the jQuery plugin "Tokenfield for Bootstrap" and defined the corresponding test cases in the previous section, we now need to deal with the implementation of the **tokenfield** directive. To do that, we set two goals with regard to the creation of this directive: First, we want to use a more complex example to show how powerful this AngularJS feature is. Second, we want to use an actual example of a tokenfield plugin to show how a jQuery plugin can be integrated into AngularJS such that the plugin can work seamlessly in two-way data binding.

We will extend the form for creating/editing a book to use the **tokenfield** directive. This jQuery plugin also provides an auto-complete feature in addition to the token allocation feature. That means the admin has less writing to do to incorporate the tags for a book.

Unfortunately, the tokenfield plugin requires some dependencies. In particular, we now have to include the following third-party libraries in our index.**html** to be able to use the tokenfield plugin.

jQuery (http://jquery.com/)
jQuery UI (http://jqueryui.com/)
Twitter Bootstrap (only the style sheet at http://getbootstrap.com/)
Tokenfield for Bootstrap (http://sliptree.github.io/bootstrap-tokenfield/)

accompanying zip file for the book, we have prepared the project along with all of the dependencies so that you don't have to search for them. In addition, in Chapter 5, "Project Management and Automation" we will explain further how you can easily manage our frontend dependencies with Bower.

Next, we create a subdirectory named **directives** in the **/app/scripts/** directory for our directive. We will create a file named **tokenfield.js** in the **directives** directory, which will contain the implementation of our **tokenfield** directive.

In Chapter 2, "Basic Principles and Concepts" we have used the AngularJS feature for defining a directive. As we can observe in Listing 4.31, we decided on the definition in the **tokenfield** directive using a directive definition object (DDO).

We specified in our unit tests that we wanted to use the **tokenfield** directive as an HTML attribute. To do that, we entered "A" (for attribute) in the **restrict** property of the DDO. Actually, we could also skip this step, because the framework by default assumes that we want to create new HTML attributes with directives.

Furthermore, we have defined the requirement in the unit tests that the directive should contain a **Book** object as input. That means we have to enter the **scope** property of the corresponding DDO. When we assign an object to the **scope** property of the DDO, AngularJS will create its own isolated scope for every instance of our **tokenfield** directive. Since we need to access the given **Book** object within the directive, we define two-way data binding to the parent scope by assigning the equal sign ("=") to the **tokenfield** property's object. That means now we can access the given **Book** object in the link function using **scope.tokenfield**. With the two-way data binding we defined with the equal sign, all the changes that we make to the **Book** object within the directive are immediately shown in the parent scope as well. You will learn that this property is crucial in being able to see the given tags directly in the preview.

Note on Directives
In the **tokenfield** directive definition, we use a typical pattern for creating custom HTML attributes. The directive is given the same name as its parameter. That means you can use the directive in the template as an HTML attribute, and the value of the HTML attribute simultaneously supplies the input of the directive.

Listing 4.31: The tokenfield directive

```
bmApp.directive('tokenfield', function(BookDataService) {
    return {
        restrict: 'A',
        scope: {
            // tokenfield holds a two-way bounded
            // reference to the book object
```

```
        tokenfield: '='
    },
    link: function(scope, elem) {
        [...]
    }
  }
})
```

In Chapter 2, "Basic Principles and Concepts" you learned that a directive is characterized by its link function. You define a link function by assigning a function to the DDO's **link** property. AngularJS calls the link function just once for each directive instance. That means you can initialize the instance within the link function. Typically, you register specific event handlers in the link function and carry out the DOM manipulations.

In Listing 4.32 we register two event handlers so that we can respond to certain events within the **tokenfield** plugin. Before we do that, however, we initialize the plugin by calling the **tokenfield()** function. Since the **elem** object is a jQuery object that wraps the DOM element on which the directive acts and we have decided in the unit tests that our **tokenfield** directive is primarily intended to act on **<input>** elements, we can call this function directly on the **elem** object.

Thus, we use the same configuration object as the one we used in the previous section when we introduced plugins. However, here we use a different source for the auto-completion. We allow the corresponding **source** array to receive output from the **BookDataService** by calling **getTags()**. This requires that **BookDataService** be integrated via dependency injection. Specifically, it is important that we set the **createTokensOnBlur** property to true in the configuration object in order to automatically convert all text in a token when the tokenfield field loses focus. Recall that we defined a unit test we could only satisfy using this property.

Listing 4.32: The tokenfield directive

```
bmApp.directive('tokenfield', function(BookDataService) {
  return {
    [...]
    link: function(scope, elem) {
        elem.tokenfield({
            autocomplete: {
                source: BookDataService.getTags(),
```

```
                    delay: 100
                },
                showAutocompleteOnFocus: false,
            allowDuplicates: false,
            createTokensOnBlur: true
        }).on('afterCreateToken', function (e) {
            addToken(e.token.value);
        }).on('removeToken', function (e) {
            removeToken(e.token.value);
        });

        [...]
        }
    }
});
```

As mentioned before, we registered two event handlers after the initialization. First, we want our local function **addToken()** to be invoked when the event **afterCreateToken** occurs. Second, the occurrence of the **removeToken** event should call the local function **removeToken()**. In both cases we pass the created or removed token that we can access with **e.token.value**.

Listing 4.33: The tokenfield directive

```
bmApp.directive('tokenfield', function(BookDataService) {
    return {
        [...]
        link: function(scope, elem) {
            [...]

            // only call $apply when directive is initialized
            // to avoid 'digest already in progress'
            var initialized = false;

            function addToken(token) {
                if (initialized) {
                    // $apply() to trigger dirty checking
                    // because of 3rd-party callback
                    scope.$apply(function() {
                        scope.tokenfield.tags.push(token);
                    });
                }
            }
        }
```

```
    }
});
```

Now we can deal with the implementation of the local functions **addToken()** and **removeToken()**. Both functions are responsible for integrating the tokenfield plugin into the two-way data binding cycle.

Let's now look at the **addToken()** function in Listing 4.33. This function is actually quite simply designed, because it does nothing more than inserting a new token into the **tags** array of our **Book** object (**scope.tokenfield**). The key point is that we implement this logic in a callback function passed to the **scope.$apply()** function. This means that immediately after the insertion logic is executed, AngularJS's dirty checking is triggered, which eventually ensures that the newly entered change is visible in all other components within AngularJS. We have to do it this way, because we perform scope manipulations within a callback function that come from a third-party library. Thus, we must be informed of any changes using **scope.$apply()**. If we did not do that, the other components within the framework would not register the changes until the next dirty checking cycle.

Dirty Checking in AngularJS

After the scope manipulations you perform outside of AngularJS in a callback function, you have to call the **$apply()** function on the corresponding scope, so that dirty checking is triggered for this scope. When dirty checking is active, AngularJS will notice that certain data in this scope have changed and ensure that all affected components will be updated automatically according to two-way data binding. The principle relates to any changes made by third-party libraries (e.g., the tokenfield plugin) in the callback functions. However, even with a scope manipulation in the callback function **setTimeout()** or **setInterval()**, you have to trigger dirty checking with **$apply()**. As such, AngularJS also includes the equivalent services **$timeout** and **$interval**. These services can also work internally with **$apply()**.

In addition, we introduced a flag named **initialized** and would only execute the logic we just discussed if the flag was set to **true**. You will learn that this flag is needed to get the so-called "Digest already in progress" errors out of the way. AngularJS raises these errors if you try to trigger dirty checking when you are already in a dirty checking cycle. Since the link function is carried out in a dirty-checking cycle, under a certain condition you may get a "Digest already in progress" error when you call **scope. $apply()** . We will discuss this condition in more detail later

Let's take another look at the **removeToken()** function in Listing 4.34.

Listing 4.34: The tokenfield directive

```
bmApp.directive('tokenfield', function(BookDataService) {
    return {
        [...]
        link: function(scope, elem) {
            [...]

            function removeToken(token) {
                if (initialized) {
                    // $apply() to trigger dirty checking
                    // because of 3rd-party callback
                    scope.$apply(function() {
                        var tags = scope.tokenfield.tags,
                            i = tags.length;
                        while(i--) {
                            if (token === tags[i]) {
                                tags.splice(i, 1);
                                break;
                            }
                        }
                    });
                }
            }

            [...]
        }
    }
});
```

The same rules naturally apply to the **removeToken()** function as well. However, in this function we manipulate the scope in a callback function called by the plugin and must manually trigger dirty checking with **scope. $apply()**. The actual logic for removing a token that was returned by the tokenfield plugin is once again very simple. We iterate over the book tags and delete the corresponding tag once we find a match.

Finally, we discuss the **init()** function that we will immediately call after defining it (See Listing 4.35). At this point, it is also clear how much the flag **initialized** helps us get rid of the "Digest already in progress" error.

Listing 4.35: The tokenfield directive

```
bmApp.directive('tokenfield', function(BookDataService) {
    return {
        [...]
        link: function(scope, elem) {
            [...]
            function init() {
                if (angular.isDefined(scope.tokenfield.tags)) {
                    if (scope.tokenfield.tags.length > 0) {
                        // this call emits an 'afterCreateToken'
                        // event and this would imply a 'digest
                        // already in progress' without the
                        // initialized flag
                        elem.tokenfield('setTokens',
                                        scope.tokenfield.tags);
                    }
                }
                else {
                    scope.tokenfield.tags = [];
                }

                initialized = true;
            }

            init();
        }
    }
});
```

Our tokenfield directive has to deal with two potential call scenarios, when we edit a book and when we create a new book. In the first case, it is very likely that the **Book** object has already been annotated with the specified tags. This means that, in this case, we must ensure that the tokenfield plugin has been populated with the existing tags so that it can generate the corresponding tokens. The call looks like this:

```
elem.tokenfield('setTokens', scope.tokenfield.tags);
```

The effect of this call is why we would get the "Digest already in progress" error, if we had not been using the **initialized** flag. With this call, the default for the tokenfield plugin also means that the plugin will raise the **afterCreateToken** event for every token created. Recall that we call the **addToken()** function in response to this event, which means it internally initiates dirty checking using **scope.$apply()**. That means we would make the mentioned error by initiating another dirty checking during a dirty checking cycle. If we first set the **initialized** flag to **true** after we have initiated the potential default, this error will now be excluded.

Listing 4.36: Using the tokenfield directive in the template with the form for creating/editing a book

```
<h2>Administration Area</h2>
<div class="split-screen">
    [...]

    <form name="bookForm" novalidate>
        [...]

        <input tokenfield="book">

        [...]
    </form>
</div>
<div class="split-screen">
    <h3>Preview</h3>
    <div class="simple-border padded"
         ng-include="'templates/book_details.html'">
    </div>
</div>
</div>
```

That's everything at this point for wrapping up the tokenfield plugin in AngularJS. If we now use our **tokenfield** directive according to our definition in the template with the form (**book_form.html**) for creating/editing a book (See Listing 4.36), then we should see a token input field (See Figure 4.11) that integrates seamlessly in the two-way data binding cycle. With this input field, we can now easily group our books into categories by giving each one of them appropriate tags. Additionally, the defined unit test should now pass.

The result will be even clearer once we have implemented the directive tags for outputting the tag in the next section.

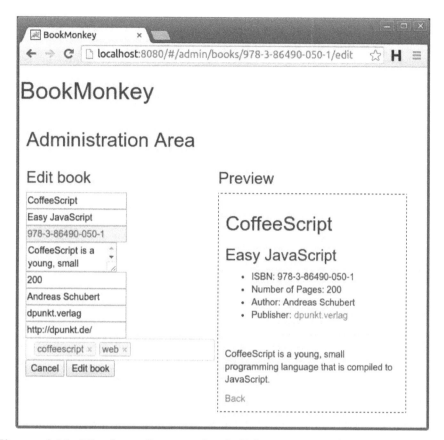

Figure 4.11: The form for creating/editing a book with the tokenfield directive

The tags Directive: Showing the tags

In addition to an input option for tags, naturally we also have to create a mechanism that can display the tags. As already mentioned, we also want to once again implement a directive that addresses that.

The **tags** directive should define a new HTML element **<tags>**. Furthermore, we should be able to specify a data source for the tag output using an HTML attribute (**tag-data**). We want to specify a string array as the data source. Listing 4.37 shows the template for the book Details view (**book_details.html**) using our **tags** directive. We set the **tag-data** attribute to **book.tags** to pass the array of book tags to the directive.

Listing 4.37: Using the tags directive in the detailed view

```
<h2 ng-bind="book.title" class="bm-book-title"></h2>
<h3 ng-bind="book.subtitle" class="bm-book-subtitle"></h3>
<p>
    [...]
    <tags tag-data="book.tags"></tags>
</p>
<hr>
<p ng-bind="book.abstract" class="bm-book-abstract">
</p>
<a ng-click="goToListView()"
  href=""
  class="bm-list-view-btn">
  Zurück
</a>
```

The implementation of the **tags** directive is straightforward. Next we will create the **tags.js** file in the **/app/scripts/directives/** directory. The file will contain the directive implementation. Listing 4.38 shows the content of this file.

Listing 4.38 : The tags directive

```
bmApp.directive('tags', function() {
    return {
        restrict: 'E',
        templateUrl: 'component_templates/directives/tags.html',
        scope: {
            tagData: '='
        }
    }
});
```

In Listing 4.38 we define the directive using a directive definition object (DDO). We set the **restrict** property to "E" to notify AngularJS that we want to define an HTML element with this definition. Additionally, we give our directive its own template using the **templateUrl** property. Also, we assign to the **scope** property an object containing a **tagData** property. With this property, we provide our directive with access to the **tag-data** attribute. All of these comply with the naming conventions discussed in Chapter 2,

"Basic Principles and Concepts." Since we want to maintain a two-way bound reference, we assign the value "=" to the **tagData** property. You will learn that this two-way binding is crucial to automatically updating our directive's tag output when the content of the array changes.

Now we still have to define the template. For that, we create a directory named **component_templates** in the **app** directory of our application. In this directory we will also create a subdirectory named **directives**, which will be the location of the **tags.html** file that we assigned to the **templateUrl** property in Listing 4.38. The **tags** directive is shown in Listing 4.39. For the output of the two-way data binding, we use the **ngRepeat** directive to iterate over the **tagData** array and display the value of the tag variable we use in the loop. The CSS class **bm-tag** in the **<span>** element gives our tags a blue background and rounded corners. We won't go into detail about how the CSS class works here.

Listing 4.39: The template of the tags directive

```
<span class="bm-tag" ng-repeat="tag in tagData">
    {{ tag }}
</span>
```

Since the **ngRepeat** directive automatically generates a **<span>** element for every element in the array and also automatically updates the output in the event of a data change in the array, we will now get direct feedback in the preview of the form for creating/editing a book when we populate or remove a tag using the **tokenfield** directive. Recall that we reuse the template for the Details view in the template for the book creation/editing form to create the live preview.

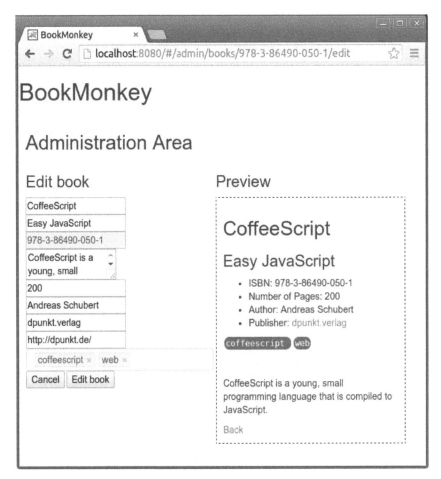

**Figure 4.12: The live preview of the form for creating/editing a book
with tags directive**

Summary

- The internal mechanisms of AngularJS in unit tests are not
  automatically executed in order to give the developer full control over
  the test procedure.
- That means that you have to manually handle some aspect of the test
  when testing directives that the framework would normally execute
  automatically under normal operation.

- In particular, this means you have to manually compile the template used in the directive using the **$compile** service. When compiling, AngularJS will recognize the tested directive and thereby execute its link function.
- You always compile a template against a scope. You can generate a new scope in unit tests, passing the **$rootScope** from AngularJS via dependency injection and calling the **$new()** function on the **$rootScope**.
- You should often review the state of the DOM in unit tests for directives using jqLite over **angular.element()**. That is the only jQuery implementation that AngularJS provides. However, the tradeoff is that jqLite only provides a subset of the functions in jQuery.
- If you include the correct jQuery implementation before including AngularJS in your **index.html**, AngularJS will set and delegate every call from **angular.element()** to the jQuery implementation.
- In AngularJS it seems simple to use directives to connect to existing jQuery plugins and other third-party libraries.
- However, you should make sure that you integrate a plugin in the two-way data binding cycle correctly. Therefore, you should ensure that you manually initiate dirty checking using **scope.$apply()** with every scope manipulation executed within a callback function that is executed within a third-party library.

Connecting to A REST Web Service

To be honest with you, our application is still pretty boring because each user has his or her own data in the browser, and there is no data management. This means it is not possible to synchronize the book data between two active applications. In this section we would like to lift this restriction by managing our application data centrally on a server. Communication with a backend is one of the typical application cases for single-page applications.

As we already mentioned at the beginning of this project that we would be using a backend implementation that is based on Node.js, we will use

Express Frameworks (http://expressjs.com) to set up an endpoint that will allow our AngularJS application to send HTTP requests. We have tried as much as possible to design the backend interface "RESTfully." Thus, our backend is a REST web service.

At this point, we define the command using a user story.

> As user Michael, I want to be able to save my data on a central server so that it can be retrieved from multiple terminals.

Using the Downloaded Project
To test the code in this section, you can use the accompanying project that you downloaded from the publisher's website. To do this, change directory to **ch04_03_http/app** and start http-server from there.

The BookMonkey Backend

At this point, we want to briefly present the backend. The REST endpoint enables calls on both the books and tags resources and uses JSON as its data format. In particular, we allow HTTP requests to these resources:

```
// books resource
GET /api/books // get all books
POST /api/books // create a new book
GET /api/books/:isbn // get a book by isbn
PUT /api/books/:isbn // update the book with the specified isbn
DELETE /api/books/:isbn // delete the book with the specified isbn

// tags resource
GET /api/tags // get all tags
```

Thanks to this interface definition we can describe the basic CRUD operations offered by our **BookDataService**. For example, with a **GET /api/books**, we get an array of **Book** objects. On the other hand, **POST /api/books/:isbn** returns a single book object. With a **POST /api/books** and a **PUT /api/books/:isbn**, the backend expects a **Book** object. The request for deleting a book, **DELETE /api/books/:isbn**, proceeds without user data. We get all the system tags with **GET /api/tags**. The success or failure of a request is indicated by an HTTP status code.

That is everything we need to know about the backend to be able to connect our BookMonkey application. However, we should still look briefly at what is left to do to connect to the server.

Next you have to make sure you have installed the current version of Node.js on your machine. That should have happened already when you began designing your BookMonkey project (See Chapter 3). Now you have to install Express Framework for the server. To do that, change directory to the **04_00_backend** project directory of the extracted zip file you downloaded from the publisher's website. Here, you will find a **package.json** file. Then, type this to download all the dependencies defined in **package.json** from the npm registry

```
npm install
```

Once you have downloaded the dependencies, you can start the server by entering the following command:

```
node server.js
```

If the environment variable **PORT** is not defined, or if it contains an invalid value, the server starts on the default port 4730. Otherwise, the server will connect to the port specified by the environment variable.

You can test the connection by visiting this URL from your browser (assuming the server is running on port 4730):

```
http://localhost:4730/api/books
```

You should see a JSON array containing all our **Book** objects in the response as shown in Figure 4.13.

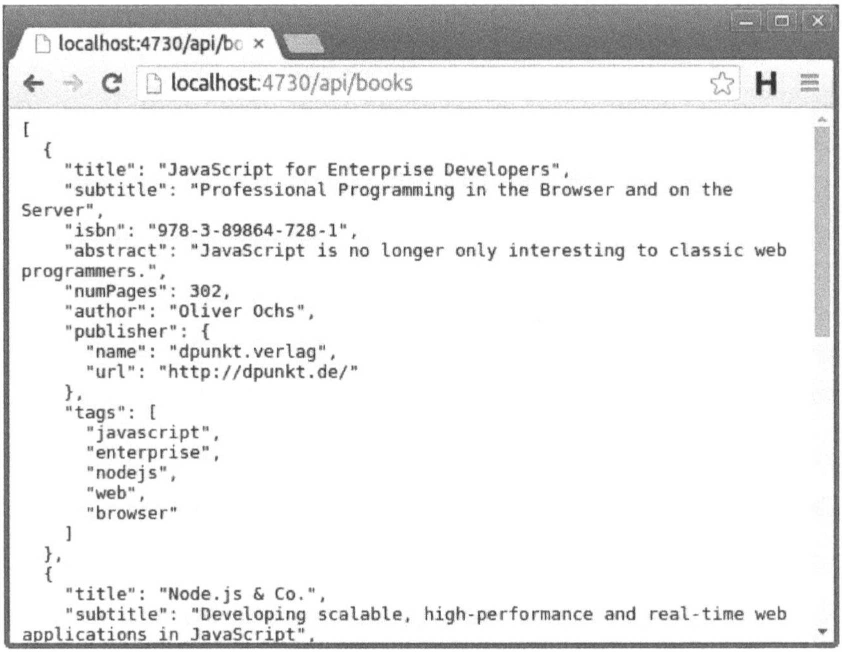

Figure 4.13: Response from calling GET /api/books

HTTP Communication with the $http Service

In order to reload single-page application data asynchronously using HTTP when the application is running, the browser needs to use the so-called **XMLHttpRequest** object. The underlying program model is known as AJAX (Asynchronous JavaScript and XML). Using the **XMLHttpRequest** object directly is not recommended as you still have to write some code and address cross-browser issues. The best way to use AJAX is by using a library like jQuery that provides a wrapper for **XMLHttpRequest**.

AngularJS also includes a component that greatly simplifies the sending of HTTP requests: the **$http** service. It is the best you've got for working with AJAX as it ensures that after receiving an HTTP response any scope manipulation will trigger dirty checking. The **$http** service API is based on the so-called promises.

A promise represents the eventually arriving result of an asynchronous operation and is largely responsible for your ability to comfortably work with asynchronous APIs. It is especially responsible for your not losing yourself in the whole "callback bustle" and avoiding the so-called "pyramid of doom." We will provide the relevant background information in Chapter 7, "Frequently Asked Questions."

If the **$http** service only consists of a function, you can specify an HTTP request that will call this **$http()** function. The function would then expect as a parameter a configuration object that describes how the HTTP request should be constructed. The following properties are among the most important properties of this configuration object:

- **method** – specifies the HTTP method as a string (e.g., "GET" or "POST")
- **url** – specifies the absolute or relative URL to be requested
- **data** – the user data that should be sent with the request. The service automatically takes care of the deserialization from and serialization to JSON.
- **headers** – an object that describe which HTTP headers should be sent.

In addition to the core properties, there are other properties that you can use to configure certain aspects of the HTTP request. You can find the complete overview in the official API documentation of the **$http** service at http://docs.angularjs.org/api/ng.$http.

In order to call, for example, the books resource of our backend, the corresponding **$http()** call would look like this:

```
$http({
  method: 'GET',
  url: 'http://localhost:4730/api/books'
});
```

The output of an **$http** call is always a promise. That means that in our complete application we can pass around this promise and register a callback function with all components interested in this HTTP request. We will see later how to do that after we design the **BookDataService**.

The framework offers the following help functions:

- $http.get()
- $http.head()

- $http.post()
- $http.put()
- $http.delete()
- $http.jsonp()

For example, you can simplify the retrieval of the books resource with the following code:

```
$http.get('http://localhost:4730/api/books');
```

First, the Test

We already mentioned repeatedly that AngularJS has been designed from the ground up with testability in mind. In addition to ngScenario DSL for E2E tests and the ngMock module's **module()** and **inject()** base functions, the provided mock implementation for this property is also particularly important.

In this section we focus on one of these mock objects, namely the **$httpBackend** mock object. The background is that the **$http** service uses an **$httpBackend** object to execute the actual HTTP request. In the unit tests, you usually replace this **$httpBackend** object with the **$httpBackend** mock object to avoid sending actual requests to a server and make it possible to define your own responses. In addition, the **$httpBackend** mock object allows you to formulate expectations that ensure that a component will really execute certain requests when they are executed in production. These are the so-called request expectations. This way, you can easily test components that communicate with a backend.

Our **BookDataService** is one such component. Therefore, we will now modify the existing test suite in the file **book_data.spec.js** to specify which HTTP requests we expect and when the API functions of **BookDataService** will be called. To formulate the request expectations, we will use the **$httpBackend** mock object. We will not describe all the test cases in detail. Instead, we will pick a test case to show how we can easily set predefined responses with the **$httpBackend** mock object and formulate request expectations.

Next, we have to inject the **$httpBackend** mock object using dependency injection. We assign the mock object to the local variable **$httpBackend** so it can be accessed by all calls to **beforeEach()** and **afterEach()** as well as to **describe()** or **it()**. We do not have to do anything at this stage to actually get our hands on the mock object because we have included the files **angular-mocks.js** and **angular.js** in our Karma configuration for unit tests (**karma.conf.js**). For the unit tests, the **$httpBackend** object will be overwritten by the **$httpBackend** mock object.

Listing 4.40: The beforeEach blocks of the new version of the BookDataService's test suite

```
describe('Service: BookDataService', function () {
    // just to match the baseUrl in the service
    var baseUrl = 'http://localhost:4730';

    var BookDataService, $httpBackend;

    // load the application module
    beforeEach(module('bmApp'));

    // get a reference to all used services
    beforeEach(inject(function (_BookDataService_, _$httpBackend_) {
        BookDataService = _BookDataService_;
        $httpBackend = _$httpBackend_;
    }));
    [...]
});
```

In the last **beforeEach()** block, we set some predefined HTTP responses for the **$httpBackend** mock objects (See Listing 4.41). For that, we use the **when()** function of the **$httpBackend** mock object. Therefore, if the **$http** service sends an HTTP GET request to **baseUrl + '/api/books'** during the execution of our unit tests, the **$httpBackend** components will respond with our test array of Book objects (**testBooks**). This test array contains the three books we have often used.

This way, we set a predefined response for every HTTP request submitted during the execution of our unit tests. It is important that we perform this step at least for every HTTP request for which we will formulate a request expectation in the test cases. Otherwise, the test cases that have no predefined response will fail with the message "No response defined!"

Listing 4.41: Definition of the predefined HTTP responses

```
describe('Service: BookDataService', function () {
    [...]

    // define trained responses
    beforeEach(function() {
    $httpBackend.when(
        'GET', baseUrl + '/api/books'
    ).respond(testBooks);

    $httpBackend.when(
        'GET', baseUrl + '/api/books/' + csBook.isbn
    ).respond(csBook);

    $httpBackend.when(
        'GET', baseUrl + '/api/books/test'
    ).respond(404, '');

    $httpBackend.when(
        'POST', baseUrl + '/api/books'
    ).respond(true);

    $httpBackend.when(
        'PUT', baseUrl + '/api/books/' + csBook.isbn
    ).respond(true);

    $httpBackend.when(
        'DELETE', baseUrl + '/api/books/' + csBook.isbn
    ).respond(true);
    });

    [...]

});
```

In Listing 4.42 we use an **afterEach()** block for the first time. As you know, this block gets executed once after every test case. In this block we use **verifyNoOutstandingExpectation()** to check after every test case if there are still outstanding request expectations that have not been fulfilled. If that is the case, that means an expected HTTP request sent via the code being tested was not deleted. This would therefore cause the test case to fail.

Next, we use **verifyNoOutstandingRequest()** to test if there are still existing HTTP requests. This way, we check the opposite case. Are there still existing HTTP requests? If that is the case, then additional requests were submitted after the requests for which we had formulated an expectation. We don't generally allow that, so we also build a **verifyNoOutstandingRequest()** test after every test case.

Listing 4.42: The afterEach() block of BookDataService's test suite

```
describe('Service: BookDataService', function () {

[...]

    afterEach(function() {
        $httpBackend.verifyNoOutstandingExpectation();
        $httpBackend.verifyNoOutstandingRequest();
    });

[...]

});
```

Now we can finally show you a test case, which we print in Listing 4.43. This is a test case for saving a new book. Other test cases will follow the same pattern.

Listing 4.43: The test case for saving a new book

```
describe('Service: BookDataService', function () {

    [...]

    describe('Public API usage', function() {
        [...]

        describe('storeBook()', function() {
            it('should properly store the passed book object',
            function() {
                $httpBackend.expectPOST(
                    baseUrl + '/api/books', effectiveJsBook
                );
                BookDataService.storeBook(effectiveJsBook);
                $httpBackend.flush();
            });
        });
```

```
        [...]
    });

    [...]

    // Helper objects
    var effectiveJsBook = {
        title : 'Effective JavaScript (German Edition)',
        [...]
    };

});
```

The critical point when formulating a request expectation is calling the **expect()** function. As you can see in Listing 4.43, for every HTTP method (GET, POST, etc.) there is a corresponding help function that makes it easier for you to formulate a request expectation.

Therefore, in this case we expect that the function **BookDataService.storeBook()** internally uses the **$http** service to submit an HTTP POST request to the URL **baseUrl + '/api/books'**. In addition, we expect that with this request the user data that is defined in the local variable **effectiveJsBook** will be sent along.

We should not forget to call **$httpBackend.flush()** at the end of the function. Otherwise, the **verifyNoOutstandingRequest()** test in the **afterEach()** block would fail. The reason for this is that the actual **$httpBackend** object works asynchronously. Therefore, the **$httpBackend** mock object must also adhere to these rules to keep it from altering the code execution. Testing asynchronous code is not that simple and requires some extended Jasmine constructs like **runs()** and **waitsFor()**. Using **flush()**, we can make sure that our tests, despite being asynchronous, can be executed synchronously in the unit test. With this call we can set the point in the test where the corresponding HTTP response will be returned and thereby simulate a response from the server.

With the **$httpBackend** mock object you can test your AngularJS application with ease.

We leave the adaptation of the remaining test case as an exercise for you. Alternatively, you can open the new version of the file **book_data.spec.js** from the zip file accompanying this book.

Using $http in BookDataService

In the previous section, we adapted the unit tests for the **BookDataService** so that it would send HTTP requests to our backend when its API functions were called. Now we want to update the new implementation to fulfill these specifications.

We will therefore ensure that, at this point, we have to make an API break. It will become clear shortly why we have to do that.

As shown in Listing 4.44, we let the **$http** service pass via dependency injection so that we can send HTTP requests using this service. In addition, we have to adapt the returned API object a bit. In the new version, all the API functions essentially return something. This is also why our API breaks compared to the previous version. Previously the API calls directly returned the data available locally. By contrast, now every access is associated with an HTTP request and this process occurs asynchronously, so we handle it in the most elegant way by simply returning the promise that provides us with the corresponding **$http** call. Thus, a **BookDataService** caller (e.g., all controllers) can decide what should happen when the HTTP response arrives from the server. More importantly, the caller can decide what should happen if it receives an error in the response.

Listing 4.44: BookDataService's new API object

```
bmApp.factory('BookDataService', function($http) {
    [...]

    // Public API
    return {
        getBookByIsbn: function(isbn) {
            return srv.getBookByIsbn(isbn);
        },
        getBooks: function() {
            return srv.getBooks();
        },
        getTags: function() {
            return srv.getTags();
```

```
        },
        storeBook: function(book) {
            return srv.storeBook(book);
        },
        updateBook: function(book) {
            return srv.updateBook(book);
        },
        deleteBookByIsbn: function(isbn) {
            return srv.deleteBookByIsbn(isbn);
        }
    };
})
```

Listing 4.45 shows the implementations of the read operations. As expected, the implementations break, because we simply send a request to the server using **$http** and return the resulting promise. This way, we direct all API calls to the corresponding resources that are available to us in our REST web service.

Listing 4.45: Read accesses are converted using HTTP GET requests

```
bmApp.factory('BookDataService', function($http) {
    var srv = {};

    srv._baseUrl = 'http://localhost:4730';

    // Service implementation
    srv.getBookByIsbn = function(isbn) {
        return $http.get(
            srv._baseUrl + '/api/books/' + isbn
        );
    };

    srv.getBooks = function() {
        return $http.get(
            srv._baseUrl + '/api/books'
        );
    };

    srv.getTags = function() {
        return $http.get(
            srv._baseUrl + '/api/tags'
        );
    };

    [...]
```

```
});
```

What about the write operations? Naturally we also proceed with the write operations as shown in Listing 4.46. Here as well, an API call will simply be directed to the relevant REST endpoint. We return the resulting promise as before so that the caller can decide how to handle the HTTP response.

Listing 4.46: The write operations are handled using HTTP POST/PUT/DELETE requests

```
bmApp.factory('BookDataService', function($http) {
    var srv = {};

    srv._baseUrl = 'http://localhost:4730';

    // Service implementation
    srv.storeBook = function(book) {
        return $http.post(
            srv._baseUrl + '/api/books', book
        );
    };

    srv.updateBook = function(book) {
        return $http.put(
            srv._baseUrl + '/api/books/' + book.isbn, book
        );
    };

    srv.deleteBookByIsbn = function(isbn) {
        return $http.delete(
            srv._baseUrl + '/api/books/' + isbn
        );
    };

    [...]
});
```

After the revision, our **BookDataService** looks pretty slim, because we only design the API functions in the relevant HTTP requests. However, these changes have far-reaching effects on our application's functionality.

When we execute our unit tests, the modified test cases for the **BookDataService** should turn "green" now. However, the test cases for our **tokenfield** directive will fail because the directive–like all other users of **BookDataService**--does not expect that our service now returns promises

With this change we really shake up a large part of our E2E tests as well.

Fixing the Application

Through the changes we made in **BookDataService** in the previous section, our application, for the most part, no longer works. However, it is also clear that it is because all the **BookDataService** callers do not know yet how to deal with a returned promise.

In this section we want to show how the caller should handle the promise-based API of **BookDataService** to restore the functionality of the application. We will not discuss all the necessary changes in every single component. Rather, we will show two examples of how we bring the relevant components to life again.

In particular, we will not describe the failed test cases. In the accompanying zip file for the book we have naturally resolved all the existing problems in the project.

Based on the two examples we now present, you should know what changes to make to the calling components to get the entire application up and running again.

We assume that you have dealt with promises. If that is not the case, you can review the necessary information in Chapter 7, "Frequently Asked Questions."

Fixing the Edit Function

We have to make the necessary changes at the points where we call an API function of **BookDataService**. As an example, we have picked the **AdminEditBookCtrl** controller as shown in Listing 4.47, because that is where the most changes have to be carried out.

Specifically, it deals with calls to the **getBookByIsbn()** function. Previously, this function returned the relevant **Book** object directly. From now on, we can assign the data to the scope variable **book**. We can do this since this function now returns a promise. To be able to respond to the arrival of an HTTP response, the promise offers us the **then()** function. This function expects as the first parameter the so-called success function that will be executed when the promise is resolved. As such, we include a successful HTTP response from the server. This function includes as a parameter a **Response** object representing the HTTP response. Using the object we can especially include the user data we received to access to the **data** property. If the user data in this case comes from a **Book** object, we can directly assign **res.data** to the scope variable **book** in the success function.

We can pass a second parameter to the **then()** function. The second parameter is an error function that will be called when the promise is rejected or when an error occurs in the HTTP request. The error function includes as a parameter an **Error** object that tells us what has gone wrong. In this case, we simply show the error on the console. Of course, we could write a more intelligent error handler here.

> ## Promises in the $http service
> The **$http** service resolves the promise if the HTTP response includes a status code between 200 and 299. With HTTP redirection, the service transparently follows the redirection without resolving or rejecting the promise. In all other cases, the promise is rejected.

Listing 4.47: The necessary changes to the AdminEditBookCtrl controller when calling the getBookByIsbn() function

```
bmApp.controller('AdminEditBookCtrl',
function ($scope, $routeParams, $location, BookDataService) {
    $scope.isEditMode = true;
    $scope.submitBtnLabel = 'Buch editieren';

    var isbn = $routeParams.isbn;
    BookDataService.getBookByIsbn(isbn).then(function(res) {
        $scope.book = res.data;
    }, function(error) {
        console.log('An error occurred!', error);
    });

    [...]
});
```

When calling the **updateBook()** function in Listing 4.48, we have to do exactly this. We cannot directly call the **goToAdminListView()** function after calling **updateBook()**. Instead, we can first make this call when the server has successfully responded and the corresponding book was also updated in the server.

Listing 4.48: The necessary changes in the AdminEditBookCtrl controller when calling the updateBook() function

```
bmApp.controller('AdminEditBookCtrl',
function ($scope, $routeParams, $location, BookDataService) {
    [...]

    $scope.submitAction = function() {
        BookDataService.updateBook($scope.book).then(function() {
            goToAdminListView();
        }, function(error) {
            console.log('An error occurred!', error);
        });
     };

    $scope.cancelAction = function() {
        goToAdminListView();
    };

    var goToAdminListView = function() {
        $location.path('/admin/books');
    };
});
```

For now that is everything we have to do to make the Book Edit view work again.

Repairing the tokenfield directive

In addition to the **AdminEditBookCtrl** controller, we want to look at the **tokenfield** directive, because asynchrony has double impacts in this component.

As you know, the **tokenfield** directive relies on the **BookDataService** to access all the available tags in the system to fill the auto-completion of the tokenfield plugins. Since now the **getTags()** function returns a promise, we can only execute the actual initialization of the tokenfield plugins in the success function when we have populated the array with tags from the server, as shown in Listing 4.49. In order to structure the source code a bit better, we have defined the local function **initializeTokenfield** for the initialization routine. We call this function in the success function and pass to it the included user data from the server that only exists in the **tags** array.

Listing 4.49: The necessary changes in calling getTags() in the tokenfield directive

```
bmApp.directive('tokenfield', function(BookDataService) {
    return {
        [...]
        link: function(scope, elem) {
            var initialized = false;

            // Fetch the tags from the server
            // and initialize directive.
            BookDataService.getTags().then(function(res) {
                initializeTokenfield(res.data);
            }, function(error) {
                console.log('An error occurred!', error);
            });

            // Main initialization routine
            function initializeTokenfield(tokens) {
                elem.tokenfield({
                    autocomplete: {
                        source: tokens,
                        delay: 100
                    },
                    [...]
                }).on('afterCreateToken', function (e) {
                    addToken(e.token.value);
                }).on('removeToken', function (e) {
                    removeToken(e.token.value);
                });

                function addToken(token) { [...] }

                function removeToken(token) { [...] }

                [...]
            }
        }
    }
}
```

```
});
```

The actual initialization logic now looks like the previous version of the **tokenfield** directive. However, there is a difference and this difference is shown in Listing 4.50. The difference is the **initializeTagsArray()** function, which in the previous section was called **init()**.

Listing 4.50: The necessary changes in the tokenfield directive

```
bmApp.directive('tokenfield', function(BookDataService) {
    return {
        [...]
        link: function(scope, elem) {
            var initialized = false;

            [...]

            // Main initialization routine
            function initializeTokenfield(tokens) {
                [...]

                function initializeTagsArray() {
                    if (angular.isUndefined(scope.tokenfield)) {
                        scope.$watch('tokenfield', function(book) {
                            if (!initialized &&
                                angular.isDefined(book)) {
                                elem.tokenfield('setTokens',
                                    book.tags);
                                initialized = true;
                            }
                        });
                    }
                    else {
                        if (angular.isUndefined
                          (scope.tokenfield.tags))
                        {
                            scope.tokenfield.tags = [];
                        }
                        else {
                            elem.tokenfield('setTokens',
                                scope.tokenfield.tags);
                        }

                        initialized = true;
                    }
                }
```

```
                initializeTagsArray();
            }
        }
    }
});
```

The directive now has to deal with the fact that the **Book** object from the parent scope (e.g., the scope of the **AdminEditBookCtrl** controller) that we can obtain from the two-way bound reference **scope.tokenfield** is also asynchronously loaded from the server. For this reason, we have to register a one-time watcher in case the **Book** object is not yet available. Recall that we have also employed an observer in our color picker to be notified of changes in scope variables and to be able to respond to them. In case **scope.tokenfield** is still undefined, here we proceed almost exactly in this way: we register an observer using **scope.$watch()**. However, we do not want to listen to changes in **scope.tokenfield** all the time, only until the scope variable **book** has been assigned. Therefore, we call this pattern a one-time watcher. Using the **initialized** flags, we can make sure the token assignment is executed only once when the **Book** object is eventually available.

In case the **Book** object is already available, we have to check if the **tags** array already exists (e.g., editing) or still has to be created (e.g., creating a new book) before the **initializeTagsArray** function is called.

After completing these changes, we have made the **tokenfield** directive work again.

BookMonkey with Backend Communication

Since we have worked to make sure all components that call an API function of **BookDataService** work again, we can now execute the entire project. In order to do that, we have to start the server with the following console command:

```
node server.js
```

Additionally, we have to ensure that the correct server URL is used.

```
srv._baseUrl = 'http://localhost:4730';
```

Like before, we deliver our AngularJS application with the **http-server** module. That results in our application handling all data access with an HTTP request to the server. We know that by showing the execution in Chrome in the Network tab. The HTTP requests our application sends to the backend should be listed there (See Figure 4.14).

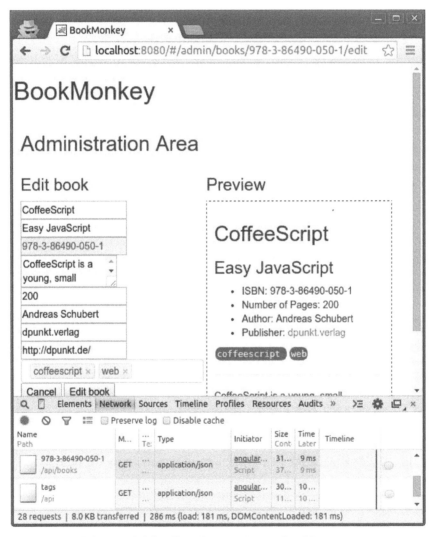

Figure 4.14: The Network tab in Chrome

Summary

- You can use the **$http** service to communicate with a REST web service easily.
- In addition to the **$http()** base function, the service offers help functions that correspond to specific HTTP methods (GET, POST, etc.). These help functions are **$http.get()**, **$http.post()** and so on.
- The **$http** service always returns a promise and a caller can use the **then()** function to register a success or error function as a callback function.
- Using a promise, you can deal with asynchrony elegantly.
- The application code that relies on the **$http** service is easy to test because AngularJS provides the **$httpBackend** mock object in the **ngMock** module.
- Using this mock object you can formulate request-expectations and set predefined HTTP responses.

Chapter 5
Project Management and Automation

Software development is not easy. There are many challenges that require the full concentration of a developer. Repetitive monotone tasks can lead to careless mistakes and slow down the development process. Therefore, it makes sense to utilize automation in order to be able to produce fast and, most importantly, stable results. Many tools have been developed recently to complete tasks and solve problems in the world of JavaScript development. Among others, these tools manage client-side dependencies, automate repetitive tasks, generate source code matrices and provide automatic test environments. In this chapter, we introduce the individual tools and look at Project Yeoman, a project that provides a pre-defined workflow for web development.

Node.js: The Runtime Environment for Tools

We will use Node.js again as the runtime environment for the tools introduced in this chapter. We have used Node.js for our BookMonkey application. The platform also provided the runtime environment for the **http-server** module and Karma.

Node.js is a platform based on Google's V8 JavaScript engine. It executes Java source code on the server side. One of its primary strengths is that it has a non-blocking event-driven IO model, allowing you to write lightweight and efficient applications. The Node.js installer can be downloaded from its official website here:

```
http://nodejs.org
```

Package Management with npm

A lot of very useful packages and tools have been developed in the realm of frontend web development and you can now write JavaScript applications on the Node.js platform. For managing these packages, the platform provides npm (Node.js package manager). Npm is a command line tool for searching, managing, installing and uninstalling packages. Currently, over 50,000 packages are available from its official register at https://npmjs.org.

> ### Note for Developers with Ruby Experience
> npm is very similar to the popular tool gem from the Ruby world. With gem you can choose from a very large selection of packages that are managed in the Ruby gems register. The website for Ruby gems is http://rubygems.org.

A Node.js module contains a data file named **package.json**. This file contains, among other things, information on package names, the version number and dependencies on other packages. Since an application can be defined as a Node.js module, you can define dependencies on other packages by using **package.json**. As shown in Listing 5.1, you can generate this data file with the **npm init** command. The script will ask a series of questions about the configuration.

Listing 5.1: Creating a package.json file

```
[app] $ npm init

This utility will walk you through
creating a package.json file.
It only covers the most common items,
and tries to guess sane defaults.

See 'npm help json' for definitive
documentation on these fields
and exactly what they do.

Use 'npm install <pkg> --save'
afterwards to install a package and
save it as a dependency in the package.json file.
```

```
Press ^C at any time to quit.
name: (app) bookMonkey
version: (0.0.0) 1.0.0
description: Example Application
git repository:
keywords: javascript angularjs
author: Robin Boehm, Philipp Tarasiewicz
license: (BSD-2-Clause) MIT
About to write [...]


{
  "name": "bookmonkey",
  "version": "1.0.0",
  "description": "Example Application",
  "main": "index.js",
  "scripts": {
    "test": "echo \"Error: no test specified\" && exit 1"
  },
  "author": "Robin Boehm, Philipp Tarasiewicz",
  "license": "MIT",
  "dependencies": {},
  "devDependencies": {},
  "keywords": [
    "javascript",
    "angularjs"
  ]
}
```

To add dependencies to your project, use the **npm install {packagename}** command. Using the additional parameter **--save**, you can automatically enter your application dependencies in **package.json**. With the help of **--save-dev**, you can do the same for development dependencies. The following example installs the Node.js package **http-server** and allows it to be entered in your **package.json** under **devDependencies**.

```
npm install http-server --save-dev
```

The resulting **package.json** file is shown in Listing 5.2. You can use npm to install the other tools in this chapter.

Listing 5.2: Automatic entry of the installed package

```
{
  "name": "bookmonkey",
  "version": "1.0.0",
```

```
[...]
"dependencies": {},
"devDependencies": {
  "http-server" : "0.6.1"
},

[...]
}
```

Node.js uses the Common JS module system to let you embed existing modules when creating a new module easily.

Summary

- Node.js is a platform that executes JavaScript source code on the server side. Installers for all platforms are available from http://nodejs.org.
- One of the primary strengths of this platform is that it has a non-blocking event-driven IO model.
- With npm, Node.js brings with it a package manager that simplifies package management. You have access to over 50, 000 packages in its official register.
- You have learned how to install Node.js modules and dependencies.
- All modern tools that aim to simplify the web development process use Node.js as the runtime environment.

Managing Frontend Dependencies with BowerBower (http://bower.io) is an open source tool for managing dependencies in web frontend applications. Project specific dependencies are easily defined in a JSON file named **bower.json**. With the help of an easy command in the command line, all defined packages can be loaded into the respective project. On the other hand, it is also possible to activate Bower using a JavaScript API within a Node.js process.

Packages that have not been configured are stored in a directory called **bower_components**. A package can contain any content and provides web components. With Bower, projects such as Twitter Bootstrap, jQuery as well as AngularJS can be easily embedded into your own project. Packages can be referenced in one of many different ways, including

- An officially registered package in the Bower register
- A Git repository
- A short form that directly refers to GitHub, e.g. angular/angular.js
- A URL to a file in .zip or .tar.gz format

Since Bower uses Node.js as its runtime environment, you install Bower using npm. You should install Bower as a global package so that you can use it from anywhere in the system. You can achieve this with the following command.

```
npm install -g bower
```

Defining the bower.json File

You can define Bower-specific information of your package in a **bower.json** file. In addition to the definition of dependencies, it contains information about project names, the version number and a description. You don't have to create this file yourself; you can use the **bower init** command to generate the file interactively. As shown in Listing 5.3, you can call this command in the command line. It will then ask a series of questions. Your answers will be used to create an initial **bower.json** file. After you answer all the questions, you will get an output in the form of generated configuration. If you reply **yes** to the last question ("Looks good?"), a **bower.json** file will be created in the current directory with the corresponding content.

Listing 5.3: Generating a bower.json file with bower init

```
[my-angular-project] $ bower init
[?] name: my-angular-project
[?] version: 1.0.0
[?] description: Sample project for the bower chapter
[?] main file: path/to/app.js
[?] keywords: angularjs, bower, book, example
[?] authors: Robin Böhm, Philipp Tarasiewicz
[?] license: MIT
[?] homepage: http://www.angularjs.de
[?] set currently installed components as dependencies? Yes
```

```
[?] add commonly ignored files to ignore list? Yes
[?] would you like to mark this package as private
    which prevents it from being accidentally
    published to the registry? No

{
  name: 'my-angular-project',
  version: '1.0.0',
  description: 'Sample project for the bower chapter',
  main: 'path/to/app.js',
  keywords: [
    'angularjs',
    'bower',
    'book',
    'example'
  ],
  authors: [
    'Robin Böhm',
    'Philipp Tarasiewicz'
  ],
  license: 'MIT',
  homepage: 'http://www.angularjs.de',
  ignore: [
    '**/.*',
    'node_modules',
    'bower_components',
    'test',
    'tests'
  ]
}

[?] Looks good? Yes
```

One of the most important properties in your configuration is the **main** property. With this property, you can define a subset of the delivered package, which can be embedded into other projects. This is necessary, because there often exist different versions—e.g. a development and a minimized version—in the same package. In such a case, an automatic processing would be impossible or very difficult. In addition, a lot of files in the project repository that Bower should not download can be listed in the **ignore** property. These include the definitions of the build process of the project.

Defining Dependencies

The actual primary task of this file is to define a project's external dependencies using the **dependencies** property. In addition, dependencies can be listed in the **devDependencies** property to indicate that they are only needed during development and are not part of the final artifact. Using the **bower install {packagename}** command, you can install individual packages. You can install AngularJS with **bower install angular**. As shown in Listing 5.4, you can add an installed package automatically into an existing **bower.json** configuration file with the **--save** or **–save-dev** parameter.

Listing 5.4: Installing external dependencies

```
bower install angular --save
bower install angular-route --save
bower install angular-mocks --save-dev
```

After executing this command, the resulting **bower.json** of our **my-angular-project** project will have dependencies on the **angular** and **angular-route** packages. In addition, the **angular-mocks** package will be provided as development dependency (**dev-dependencies**). With the **search** argument, you can do a full text search against the Bower register via the command line. Alternatively, you can search the register by going to its website at http://sindresorhus.com/bower-components. To delete a package from this project, you can use **bower uninstall angular**. A section of our current **bower.json** file is printed in Listing 5.5.

Listing 5.5: The structure of a bower.json file

```
{
  "name": "my-angular-project",
  "version": "1.0.0",
  "dependencies": {
    "angular": "1.2.3",
    "angula-router": "1.2.3",
  },
  "devDependencies": {
    "angular-mocks": "1.2.3"
  }

  [...]
```

}

> **Installing A Package from A Specific Version**
> If you want to use the command line to install a package from a
> specific version, you can suffix the package name with a hash followed
> by a version description. Therefore, to install AngularJS version 1.0.0,
> use the command **bower install angular#1.0.0 --save**. It will also be
> entered in your configuration. Sometimes, however, it is also desirable
> to always use the current version of a development of a repository. To
> do this, simply provide the desired package in the repository.

Including Installed Packages

If the project directory contains your configuration, you can download all
dependencies defined in the configuration with **bower install**. The
bower_components directory is generally not imported when using a
version management tool such as Git and the directory is listed in Git's
.gitignore file. After exporting a project, you can reload all the necessary
packages in the correct version by executing the **bower install** command.

After you have installed the dependencies, you can implement the
following as you desire. Listing 5.6 shows an **index.html** example that uses
the **<script>** tag to include dependencies.

Listing 5.6: Including packages that have been installed by Bower

```html
<!DOCTYPE html>
<html ng-app>
<head>
    <title>AngularJS.DE Bower Example</title>
</head>

<body>

<script src="bower_components/angular/angular.js"></script>
<script src="bower_components/angular-route/angular-route.js">
</script>
</body>
</html>
```

Configuring Bower

You can configure Bower with a **.bowerrc** file. You can do this specifically for a project by creating the file in your project directory and adding configuration to the file. In addition, you can create a global configuration for a user in the user's home directory. Project-specific configuration overwrites any global parameters. Within this file, you can set the following configuration parameters:

- **directory**. The install location for components
- **endpoint**. The definition of your own bower register
- **json**. The name of Bower's metadata file in the project
- **searchpath**. The list of additional Bower registers
- **shorthand_resolver**. The template for shorthands.

Listing 5.7 shows a sample **.bowerrc** file.

Listing 5.7: The structure of a .bowerrc file

```
{
  "directory": "bower_components",
  "endpoint": "https://bower.mycompany.com",
  "json": "myOwnBower.json",
  "searchpath": [
    "https://bower.herokuapp.com"
  ],
  "shorthand_resolver":
    "git://example.com/organization/package.git"
}
```

To register your own package in the official Bower register, you need a Git repository that is publicly available. This repository must contain a valid **bower.json** file in the main directory and the file must contain the required metadata for the package. In this case, you have to make sure that you describe the different versions of your package as Git tags and they comply with semantic versioning (http://semver.org). After meeting the requirements, you can register the package in the public register with the command in Listing 5.8.

Listing 5.8: Registering a package in the Bower register

```
bower register <my-package-name> <git-endpoint>
```

Currently it is not possible to delete a registered package from the public register independently. At present, this is being managed inelegantly via an entry in the Bower project's issue tracker in Github. However, it is likely that there will be a new mechanism for resolving this issue in the near future.

Creating A Private Register

It is not always desirable to publish a package in an external and publicly available repository. Fortunately, you can use the **endpoint** configuration parameter to register a package in a private register. To this end, you have to create your own register. This can be done with relatively little effort. The register application is a very simple Ruby program that can be downloaded from Github at this URL:

```
https://github.com/bower/registry
```

Other public and alternative registers can be defined using the **searchpath** configuration parameter. You can list multiple registers in an array (See Listing 5.9).

Listing 5.9: .bowerrc with its own endpoint

```
{
  "endpoint": "https://bower.mycompany.com",
  "searchpath": [
    "https://bower.herokuapp.com",
    "https://bower.anothercompany.com"
  ],
}
```

Potential Problems with Proxy Servers

If you need to operate Bower behind a proxy server, you can reroute network communication via the proxy server by using the **HTTP_PROXY** and **HTTPS_PROXY** environment variables. A problem that often appears in a company network is the company-wide firewall that blocks port 22 for SSH communication. Since many repositories work with SSH in the Bower register, problems arise relatively quickly. In order to get around these problems, you can configure Git so that all SSH communications will be automatically redirected over http or https. You can use this Git command:

```
git config url."http://".insteadOf git://
```

Summary

- Bower is a tool for managing front-end dependencies. Bower is based on Node.js.
- You can define project-specific dependencies in a JSON file named **bower.json**. You can have this file generated interactively using the **bower init** command. In addition, you can install new dependencies with the command **bower install {packagename}** in the command line. To uninstall a package, use the command **bower uninstall {packagename}**.
- Bower differentiates between project dependencies and development dependencies.
- You can define configuration in a **.bowerrc** file and thus use your own company register.
- Problems related to proxy servers may occur. You can resolve these by configuring Git.

Automating Tasks with GruntGrunt (http://gruntjs.com) is an open source tool to simplify and, in many cases, completely eliminate tiring completion of repetitive tasks. The tool automates the following tasks.

- compilation tasks
- minimizing
- executing tests
- executing tools for quality assurance, such as JSLint (http://www.jslint.com)

To use Grunt, you need Node.js version 0.8 or later and the npm package manager. A typical project construction with Grunt contains a **package.json** file, which defines a Node.js module. You use this file to define the dependency to the Node.js modules that your project requires. Since Grunt is also a Node.js module, you can install it in your project with the

following command and specify it as a development dependency in your
package.json file:

```
npm install grunt --save-dev
```

> **Initializing A package.json File**
> You can generate a **package.json** file for your project using the **npm
> init** command. A detailed description of this function can be found in
> the section "Node.js: The Runtime Environment for Tools."

Making Grunt Useful with the Command Line

A Node.js module named **grunt-cli** is available to make using Grunt easier.
This module allows you to use Grunt commands from the command line.
The script executed searches the respective local project directory for an
installed Grunt package and delegates the calls from the command line to
this location. This delegation is important, because you need different
versions from Grunt for different projects. A global installation of Grunt is
thus not recommended. You can install Grunt using this command.
(Sometimes administrator rights are required!)

```
npm install -g grunt-cli
```

After the installation, Grunt is available system-wide. If you run the Grunt
command now in a fresh project, you will get an error message as shown in
Listing 5.10. If you see this, do no panic. You have just forgotten to install
the Node.js module **Grunt** in your current project.

Listing 5.10: A potential error message when using Grunt-CLI

```
[app] $ grunt
grunt-cli: The grunt command line interface. (v0.1.9)

Fatal error: Unable to find local grunt.

If you're seeing this message, either a Gruntfile
wasn't found or grunt hasn't been installed
locally to your project. For more information about
installing and configuring grunt,
please see the Getting Started guide:
```

http://gruntjs.com/getting-started

Configuring Tasks

To configure the tasks that Grunt should execute for you, use the script in the **Gruntfile.js** file. Grunt expects you to export a function as a CommonJS module within this script. In this function, you can configure all the tasks that you want Grunt to automatically execute. When doing so, Grunt executes the exported function and delegates it to the so-called Grunt API, which you can access. At this point, you should make sure that the JavaScript source code is contained in the **Gruntfile.js** file and no configuration in JSON format such as in **package.json** is included.

Listing 5.11: The basic structure of a Gruntfile.js file

```
module.exports = function(grunt) {
  // do some stuff
};
```

> ### Note for CoffeeScript Developers
> It is also possible to create this definition in CoffeeScript. However, the extension of your configuration file must then be **.coffee**. For example, **Gruntfile.coffee** is a valid file name.

Registering Tasks

You can register JavaScript functions with Grunt. Such functions in Grunt's world are called tasks. You register a task using the **grunt.registerTask** function. This function expects three arguments. The first argument provides a name you can use to retrieve the function. The second argument contains a description that will be displayed when you type **grunt -help**. The third argument specifies a function that should be executed when this task is called. Listing 5.12 shows the definition of a very simple task.

Listing 5.12: Defining your own function within Grunt

```
module.exports = function(grunt) {

  // A very basic default task.
  grunt.registerTask('log', 'Log some stuff.', function() {
```

```
    grunt.log.write('Logging some stuff...');
  });

};
```

You can execute this task with the command line command **grunt**. You need to specify the name of the task that should be executed as a parameter to the **grunt** command. The result of the execution is shown in Listing 5.13.

Listing 5.13: Executing your own function using the command line

```
[app] $ grunt log
Running "log" task
Logging some stuff...

Done, without errors.
```

> **Determining A Default Task**
> There is a convention within Grunt that allows you to define a default task, which will be executed when Grunt is called without a parameter. You simply have to define a task named **default** using **grunt.registerTask**. Normally, this will be a delegation to one or more tasks.

You can also register multiple functions with the **grunt.registerTask** function. However, the functions should have a unique name, because they would otherwise overwrite each other. In the latter case, you could only access the most recently defined function.

You can pass arguments to a task. Two arguments should be separated with a colon. Listing 5.14 shows you how to pass arguments to a task.

Listing 5.14: Executing your own commands using the command line

```
[app (master)] $ grunt count
Running "count" task
Arguments: 0

Done, without errors.
[app (master)] $ grunt count:1:2:3
Running "count:1:2:3" (count) task
Arguments: 3
```

```
Done, without errors.

};
```

You can also use the **grunt.registerTask** function to link multiple tasks with a name. In this case, you need to provide two arguments. As before, the first argument specifies the name of the task. As a second argument, you specify an array containing the names of the desired tasks. The order in which you define the tasks in the array determines the order of execution. Listing 5.15 shows a **Gruntfile.js** file that defines three tasks. The last task is called **all** and is associated with the previous two tasks.

Listing 5.15: Defining your own functions in Grunt

```
module.exports = function(grunt) {

  // A very basic log task
  grunt.registerTask('log', 'Log some stuff.', function() {
    grunt.log.writeln('Logging some stuff...');
  });

  // A very basic task with arguments
  grunt.registerTask('count', 'Count given Arguments.', function()
  {
    grunt.log.writeln('Arguments: '+arguments.length);
  });

  // An aggregation task
  grunt.registerTask('all', ['log', 'count:a:b']);

};
```

In addition, you can pass as a parameter to a task a JavaScript object that contains project-specific configuration using the **grunt.initConfig()** function. Listing 5.16 shows an example of configuring the **log** task. You can access these configuration settings using the **grunt.config** method, passing a JavaScript expression. In this case, it is **grunt.config('log.prefix')**.

Listing 5.16: Configuring Grunt tasks

```
module.exports = function(grunt) {

  grunt.initConfig({
        log: {
```

```
            prefix: "LOG"
        }
    });

// A very basic log task with prefix
grunt.registerTask('log', 'Log some stuff.', function() {
    grunt.log.write('[' + grunt.config('log.prefix') + ']');
    grunt.log.writeln('Logging some stuff...');
});
};
```

Defining Multi-Tasks

In addition to registering simple tasks, you can also register multi-tasks with the **grunt.registerMultiTask()** function. A multi-task is a task that can receive a number of known configuration values called targets. If no target is defined when executing the task, all targets registered by this task will be executed.

In a multi-task function, you have access to the names of the targets being executed. You can access a target using **this.target**. Using **this.data**, you have access to the enclosed data. You can enclose the definition of these targets in the form of a configuration object by using the API function **grunt.initConfig()**. Listing 5.17 presents a **log** task that displays the number of enclosed arguments, the current target and the enclosed data.

Listing 5.17: Defining Multi-Tasks in Grunt

```
module.exports = function(grunt) {

  grunt.initConfig({
      log: {
        string: 'Logging some stuff...',
        array: [1, 2, 3],
        object: { x: 5 }
      }
  });

  // Register Multi Task
  grunt.registerMultiTask('log', 'Log stuff.', function() {
    grunt.log.writeln('args: '
                  + arguments.length
                  + '\n'
                  + this.target
```

```
                    + ': '
                    + this.data);
  });

};
```

The example shows configuration for the registered multi-task as well as the multi-task itself. For this, we use the familiar **grunt.initConfig()** method. You can define targets for a specific multi-task by using the name of the configuration object's property. The name of this target corresponds to the name of the selected object property, which in our case is **log**. A target definition can be any kind of JavaScript data structure. If you follow the naming convention, the data structure defined by **grunt.initConfig()** is connected to the property **this.data** in the multi-task function. Thus, you do not have to export this data by using **grunt.config**, because you have direct access to the data structure. In Listing 5.18, you can see the retrieval of the multi-task **log** with various targets that also can be specified using colons. It is also possible to enclose more arguments by using colons after the target selection.

Listing 5.18: Executing the log multi-task with different targets

```
[app] $ grunt log
Running "log:string" (log) task
args: 0
string: Logging some stuff...

Running "log:array" (log) task
args: 0
array: 1,2,3

Running "log:object" (log) task
args: 0
object: [object Object]

Done, without errors.
[app] $ grunt log:array
Running "log:array" (log) task
args: 0
array: 1,2,3

Done, without errors.
[app] $ grunt log:array:hello:world
Running "log:array:hello:world" (log) task
```

```
args: 2
array: 1,2,3
```

```
Done, without errors.
```

Normally, a multi-task expects a JavaScript object that defines a specific configuration which you can then use within your multi-task function. It is thus possible to define generic tasks.

> ### Grunt Alternative: Gulp
> In addition to Grunt, there are other build tools that use Node.js as a platform. One of these alternatives is Gulp (https://github.com/gulpjs/gulp). Gulp is impressive because of the simplicity of its configuration. This is because the latter can be very easily described in JavaScript code by using stream insertion. It is a very young project; Nevertheless, it is still worth looking into.

Outsourcing Tasks

With Grunt you can outsource tasks to different files. All you have to do is load the tasks in your Grunt file when needed. The command that facilitates this is called **grunt.loadTasks**. With this command, you can provide a path to a task directory that will be searched for the JavaScript files.

Let us transfer our multi-task function **log** to a directory named **log**. The name of the file is not important in this case, because Grunt will search the whole directory. The only requirement is that the file name has **.js** extension. The content of this file is given in Listing 5.19.

Listing 5.19: Transferring a log task to an external file

```
module.exports = function(grunt) {

  // Register Multi Task
  grunt.registerMultiTask('log', 'Log stuff.', function() {
    grunt.log.writeln('args: '
                + arguments.length
                + '\n'
                + this.target
                + ': '
                + this.data);
```

```
    });
};
```

Listing 5.20 shows a Grunt file that contains the statement
grunt.loadTasks('log'). With this, you can search the **log** directory and
load the definitions of the multi-task. By using **grunt.initConfig**, you can
define different tasks as usual. With this mechanism, you can build generic
reusable modules. In the world of Grunt, these special modules are called
plugins.

Listing 5.20: Loading a task from an external file

```
module.exports = function(grunt) {

  grunt.loadTasks('log');

  grunt.initConfig({
      log: {
        string: 'Logging some stuff...',
        array: [1, 2, 3],
        object: { x: 5 }
      }
  });

};
```

Loading Grunt Plugins

You can use npm to register Grunt plugins and make them publicly
available. You and other developers can also install these published plugins
and add them to a **package.json** file. This will allow you to define a Node.js
module and its dependencies. Just as you have installed Grunt as a module,
you can now install Grunt plugins by using npm.

Listing 5.21 shows a sample **package.json** file after the installation of
two Grunt plugins **contrib-copy** and **contrib-uglify**. Both are listed under
devDependencies.

**Listing 5.21: The structure of a package.json file with its own Grunt
plugins as dependencies**

```
{
  [...]
```

```
"devDependencies": {
  "grunt": "0.4.1",
  "grunt-contrib-copy": "0.4.1",
  "grunt-contrib-uglify": "0.2.7"
}

[...]
}
```

There are a lot of Grunt plugins available over npm. You can read the descriptions of these plugins through the "plugins" tab on the official project website at http://gruntjs.com/plugins.

You can load Grunt plugins that have been installed by using npm with the help of the function **grunt.loadNpmTasks**. As you can see in Listing 5.22, you just have to add the name of the installed plugin as an argument.

Listing 5.22: Loading Node.js Grunt Plugins

```
module.exports = function(grunt) {

  [...]

  grunt.loadNpmTasks('grunt-contrib-uglify');
  grunt.loadNpmTasks('grunt-contrib-clean');

  [...]
};
```

Just like with your own tasks, the configuration of this task occurs via a JavaScript object that you provide to the **grunt.initConfig** function. We will not discuss the configuration details of these two plugins here. However, you can see a small example configuration in Listing 5.23.

Listing 5.23: An example configuration of Grunt plugins

```
module.exports = function(grunt) {

  grunt.initConfig({
    uglify: {
      build: {
        src: 'src/app.js',
        dest: 'build/app.min.js'
      },

    clean: ['build/**/*'],
```

```
  }
});

  grunt.registerTask('build', ['clean' , 'uglify']);
};
```

At the end of this configuration, you have created a new task named **build** with the **grunt.registerTask** function. This will execute the tasks **clean** and **uglify** in the correct order. If you call Grunt with parameter **build** in the command line, you will get the result that is printed in Listing 5.24.

Listing 5.24: Executing an example configuration

```
[app] $ grunt build
Running "clean:dist" (clean) task

Running "uglify:build" (uglify) task
File "build/app.min.js" created.

Done, without errors.
```

Using Templates

You can work with a small template mechanism in Grunt. In the context of Grunt, a template is a character string that begins with **<%** and ends with **%>**. In between, you can use template variables that correspond to object access expressions to access the object properties. The latter is very dependent on the notation that you use in JavaScript. Let us expand our example and define a **pkg** property in our configuration object. This property allocates an object that holds some data from our application. Listing 5.25 shows the expanded configuration of our **uglify** task through templates.

Listing 5.25: Using templates

```
module.exports = function(grunt) {

  grunt.initConfig({
    pkg: {
            name: 'app',
            version: '0.0.1'
         }

    uglify: {
```

```
      build: {
        src: 'src/<%= pkg.name %>-<%= pkg.version %>.js',
        dest: 'build/<%= pkg.name %>-<%= pkg.version %>.min.js'
      },

     clean: ['build/**/*'],
     }
  });

  grunt.registerTask('build', ['clean' , 'uglify']);
};
```

To reduce redundancy, you can access the **package.json** file in Grunt and allocate the content of its property. This is shown in Listing 5.26. It is a good thing that Grunt offers a **grunt.file.readJSON** function to help you with this task.

Listing 5.26: Importing a file as a configuration object

```
module.exports = function(grunt) {

  grunt.initConfig({
    pkg: grunt.file.readJSON('package.json'),

    uglify: {
      build: {
        src: 'src/<%= pkg.name %>-<%= pkg.version %>.js',
        dest: 'build/<%= pkg.name %>-<%= pkg.version %>.min.js'
      },

    clean: ['build/**/*'],
    }
  });

  grunt.registerTask('build', ['clean' , 'uglify']);
};
```

As a result, you can define project specific information centrally in one place, namely in the **package.json** file, much easier than when all pieces of information were scattered around the project.

Appropriate Packages for Development

Next, we would like to discuss a couple of public Grunt plugins that are almost always essential in AngularJS development. In practice, there are a few Grunt plugins that can be inserted into almost every program.

load-grunt-tasks

Right after loading the first package, you quickly come to a point at which repeating lines, in addition to the **loadNpmTasks** statement, make configuration hard to understand. In order to get around this problem, you can use a Node.js module called **load-grunt-tasks** (https://npmjs.org/package/load-grunt-tasks). An example is given in Listing 5.27.

Listing 5.27: A sample configuration for load-grunt-tasks

```
module.exports = function(grunt) {
  require('load-grunt-tasks')(grunt);
};
```

This plugin uses the convention that all Node.js packages that have been specially created for Grunt have the prefix **grunt-**. Thus, this plugin can export your **node_modules** directory and load all modules that match the regular expression **grunt-***. You can use npm to install this plugin using this command.

```
npm install load-grunt-tasks --save-dev
```

If you need this functionality in a more generic version, you can use the alternative module matchdep (https://npmjs.org/package/matchdep).

ng-min

The package grunt-ngmin (https://npmjs.org/package/grunt-ngmin) is a pre-minifier for AngularJS applications. You need this package because the implementation of dependency injection uses the parameter names of your functions in AngularJS in order to cancel the dependencies at this point.

Since this is substituted when minimizing, the mechanism does not work after this process.

Listing 5.28: Example for the effects of ng-min

```
// before ng-min
angular.module('bmApp').controller('MyCtrl',
function ($scope, $http) {

    [...]

});

// after ng-min
angular.module('bmApp').controller('MyCtrl',
['$scope', '$http', function ($scope, $http) {

    [...]

}]);
```

In order to allow minification in AngularJS projects, there is a convention for function annotations within AngularJS. It states that the function should be given as the last element in an array and that all parameters before the dependencies are passed as strings. Since the strings are not affected by the minification, cancellation of the dependencies will work again after this point. As usual, the configuration must be added to your **Gruntfile.js** file. The parameters **src** and **dest** used here represent the source and target files. The exact directory of all parameters with explanation can be removed from the project documentation.

Listing 5.29: Example configuration for ng-min

```
module.exports = function(grunt) {
  grunt.initConfig({

  [...]

    ngmin: {
      files: {
        src: 'build/**/*.js',
        dest: 'build/'
      }
    },
```

```
  [...]

  });

  grunt.registerTask('build', [
    'clean',
    'copy:build',
    'ngmin',
    'uglify'
  ]);
};
```

You can use npm to install this plugin using this command.

```
npm install grunt-ngmin --save-dev
```

concat and uglify

With the help of the uglify package (https://github.com/gruntjs/grunt-contrib-uglify), it is possible to reduce the file size of an application. This can be achieved with smart substitutions of variable names. However, this will cause readability to suffer for human readers. It is unsurprisingly due to this fact that this project got its name. It is worthwhile to perform minification to make loading time as short as possible for the user.

Listing 5.30: Sample configuration for concat and uglify

```
module.exports = function(grunt) {

  grunt.initConfig({

    [...]


    concat: {
        src: ['src/module.js' , 'src/book.js', [...] ],
        dest: 'build/bookmonkey.js',
    },

    uglify: {
        files: {
          'build/bookmonkey.min.js':
              [
                build/bookmonkey.js'
              ]
```

```
        }
      }

      [...]

    });
};
```

In the configuration shown in Listing 5.30, the **bookmonkey.js** file is converted to a **bookmonkey.min.js** file. This task is usually done last in the building process. In this example, it comes after we concatenate our JavaScript files using Concat (https://github.com/gruntjs/grunt-contrib-concat) to a **bookmonkey.js** file.

You can use npm to install both plugins using these commands.

```
npm install grunt-contrib-concat --save-dev
npm install grunt-contrib-uglify --save-dev
```

Summary

- Grunt is an open source tool based on Node.js for automating the processing of repetitive tasks. You can use npm to install it.
- You can define your own tasks that can take parameters. In addition, there is a concept of multi-tasks, which allows you to use different targets from a configuration.
- There are a lot of public plugins that you can also install with npm.
- You can configure these tasks by using a file named **Gruntfile.js**.
- You have looked at a few plugins that are essential for AngularJS as well as their configurations. These include the ng-min plugin.

Executing Tests Automatically with KarmaKarma (http://karma-runner.github.io) is a runtime environment for testing JavaScript applications automatically. It is an open source project created for AngularJS and was developed by same team that developed AngularJS. Karma's main objective is to make testing an internet application as easy as possible. The defined test specifications are executed in real devices to minimize discrepancies in the end product. Karma starts its own web server and sends a page to any device that connects to it. A device to be tested must be able to handle HTTP and interpret JavaScript. The page contains an iframe used as the actual runtime environment. Higher-level data is guided by this. Every connected browser receives the commands directly from the running Karma process via a web socket connection or a corresponding fallback transport mechanism such as long polling.

Since Karma is executed on the Node.js platform like most of the previously discussed tools, you can use npm to install it with this command:

```
npm install -g karma
```

You can now start Karma directly by using the **karma start** command, as shown in Listing 5.31.

Listing 5.31: Starting Karma

```
[bookMonkey] $ karma start
INFO [karma]: Karma v0.10.4 server
started at http://localhost:9876/
```

Since you have not written any configuration, this phase is fairly uneventful. As such, let us look at the next section to find out how you can configure Karma.

Configuration

Karma configuration is done through a JSON file. If no explicit configuration file provided was found, Karma will search for a file named **karma.conf.js** in the directory in which you have executed it. If you want to use another file as a configuration file, you have to provide the path to this file as a second parameter to **karma**.

```
karma start myproject.unit.js
```

When executing the **karma** command, you can overwrite a parameter in the configuration file just for this session by using passing arguments to **karma**. This can be very useful in the case that you wish to overwrite individual values from the configuration in a CI (continuous integration) environment without creating a new file. More information about Karma's configuration file can be found on its official website at this address.

```
http://karma-runner.github.io/0.10/config/configuration-file.html
```

Listing 5.32 shows an excerpt from a Karma configuration file.

Listing 5.32: An example of Karma configuration

```javascript
'use strict';

module.exports = function(config) {
    config.set({
        basePath: 'src/main/webapp/app/',

        frameworks: ['jasmine'],

        files: [
            'components/angular/angular.js',
            'components/angular-mocks/angular-mocks.js',

            'scripts/module.js',
            'scripts/**/*.js',
        ],

        reporters: ['progress'],
        port: 9876,
        logLevel: config.LOG_WARN,
        singleRun: true,
        autoWatch: false,
        browsers: ['Chrome']
    });
};
```

Configuration in CoffeeScript

It is also possible to provide configuration in CoffeeScript. You can save your configuration for this in a file with extension **.coffee**. Karma recognizes the format and uses the corresponding CoffeeScript processor automatically.

The Most Important Parameters

At this point, we briefly explain the most important parameters for the configuration. A complete and always current list can be found online in the official Karma documentation at this URL:

```
http://karma-runner.github.io/0.10/config/configuration-file.html
```

basePath

To save significant typing chores, you can set the **basePath** property as the base path for other paths, including paths that are defined by the **files** and **exclude** properties.

files and exclude

You can use the **files** and **exclude** properties to specify a list of files that should be included or excluded when running Karma.

> ### Using GlobStar Paths
> You can use wildcard matchers in your definition. In this case, there are two wildcard constructs you can use, a single asterisk (*) or double asterisks (**). The single asterisk defines a wildcard that effects all files in the current directory. Double asterisks can be used recursively on all other subdirectories. You could thus create rules such as scripts/**/*.js that affect all files with extension .js in all subdirectories of the **scripts** directory. The selected implementation is called Glob and is available for free on GitHub (https://github.com/isaacs/node-glob).

frameworks

You use the **frameworks** property to embed different test frameworks in your environment. You can view the list of available framework adapters in the npm register here:

```
https://npmjs.org/browse/keyword/karma-adapter
```

To use this test framework, you first have to use npm to install it.

```
npm install karma-<test-framework> --save-dev
```

In addition, you have to specify the framework in your configuration. Listing 5.33 shows how you can specify the popular test framework Jasmine.

Listing 5.33: Embedding Jasmine as a test framework

```
'use strict';

module.exports = function(config) {
    config.set({
    [...]

        frameworks: ['jasmine'],

    [...]
    });
};
```

browsers

You can use the **browsers** property to select a variety of browsers that Karma should automatically start to execute your tests. Karma offers native support for the Chrome and PhantomJS browsers. However, you can use npm to install packages for Firefox, Opera, Internet Explorer and Safari.

Headless Browser PhantomJS
The headless browser PhantomJS (http://phantomjs.org) is a fully functional WebKit browser that has no graphic user interface. You can thus execute your tests with this browser on a platform that has no windowing system. Nevertheless, you have all the features offered by other browsers and can receive the current report of the tested website.

Generating an Initial Karma Configuration File

You do not have to create the initial Karma configuration file yourself. Karma comes with a generator that can create an initial configuration file when you run Karma with the **karma init** command. By answering some questions about your desired testing environment, the tool generates your specific **karma.conf.js** file and stores it in the directory in which you executed the command. For our BookMonkey project, the dialogue would look like the on in Listing 5.34.

Listing 5.34: Generating a Karma configuration file via the command line

```
[bookMonkey] $ karma init

Which testing framework do you want to use?
Press tab to list possible options.
Enter to move to the next question.
> jasmine

Do you want to use Require.js?
This will add Require.js plugin.
Press tab to list possible options.
Enter to move to the next question.
> no

Do you want to capture a browser automatically?
Press tab to list possible options.
Enter empty string to move to the next question.
> Chrome
>

What is the location of your source and test files?
You can use glob patterns, eg. "js/*.js"
or "test/**/*Spec.js".
Enter empty string to move to the next question.
> scripts/**/*.js
Should any of the files included
by the previous patterns be excluded?
You can use glob patterns, eg. "**/*.swp".
Enter empty string to move to the next question.
>

Do you want Karma to watch all the files
and run the tests on change?
Press tab to list possible options.
> no

Config file generated at
"/Users/AngularJS/bookMonkey/karma.conf.js".
```

You can now extend or modify the resulting file. The format and the essential parameters are already set so you can immediately run your test cases. Sources of errors such as forgetting some required parameters and deviating from a supported format are thus reduced to a minimum.

> **Automatic Execution of Changes**
> With Karma you can run tests automatically every time you change your source code. You can use the **singleRun** and **autoWatch** properties to activate this feature. In order to achieve this, you have to set **singleRun** to false and **autoWatch** to true in your configuration file. However, this may incur high system utilization in the case of a large amount of data. Thus, we recommend you check the rules that have been defined in the **files** property once more and exclude files with the **exclude** property if necessary.

Using Karma Extensions

You can extend Karma. There are already a lot of plugins available. You can search for and install them using the npm register at this URL.

```
https://npmjs.org/browse/keyword/karma-plugin
```

To achieve this, use the already familiar npm command.

```
npm install karma-<plugin name> --save-dev
```

In this case, the following convention applies: Karma automatically includes all npm modules with the prefix **karma-**. If you need a plugin that does not follow this convention, you can extend your Karma configuration with the **plugins** property.

Listing 5.35: Embeding plugins in Karma configuration

```
plugins: [
  'karma-*',
  'plugin-example'
]
```

Executing Tests Directly in WebStorm

Currently WebStorm IDE is one of the most popular JavaScript development environments. We will discuss it in Chapter 6, "Debugging." For this reason, we will discuss how to install Karma in this environment.

We start with a system that already has Node.js and Karma installed. Since WebStorm 7, you can use the official Karma plugin that makes WebStorm integration very easy. As shown in Figure 5.1, you can select a test type under the "Karma" node in the Run/Debug Configurations dialog.

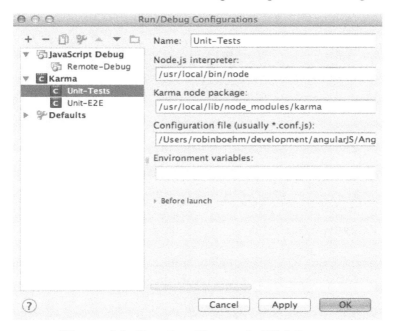

Figure 5.1: Starting Karma in WebStorm

You have to enter some path information in the dialog. First, you have to provide the install directory of Node.js. Subsequently, you have to type in the install directory of Karma, with which you want to execute the tests. In the case that WebStorm recognizes your Node.js and Karma installations, the two fields will be filled with the right paths automatically. If you want to execute your tests with another version of Node.js or Karma, you can configure it here. It should come as no surprise that you also have to provide the **karma.conf.js** file for the testing environment. If you have entered these parameters correctly, you can start the execution via "run". Execution in debug mode is also possible. Figure 5.2 shows the result of our test execution.

Figure 5.2: Result of a test execution

Test Frameworks

As already hinted at in the sample configuration, you can use testing frameworks other than Karma. Currently there are plugins for Jasmine (http://pivotal.github.io/jasmine/), Mocha (http://visionmedia.github.io/mocha) and Qunit (http://qunitjs.com). You can also create your own plugins for other test frameworks and embed them. Jasmine and Mocha are examples of behavior-driven development (BDD) frameworks. As shown in Listings 5.36 and 5.37, their syntax is also very similar.

Listing 5.36: A Jasmine test specification

```
describe("A suite", function() {
  it("contains spec with an expectation", function() {
    expect(true).toBe(true);
  });
});
```

Listing 5.37: A Mocha test specification

```
describe('A suite', function(){
  it('contains spec with an expectation', function(){
    ok(true);
  })
})
```

Listing 5.38: A QUnit test specification

```
test( "a basic test example", function() {
  var value = "hello";
  equal(value, "hello", "We expect value to be hello");
});
```

Regardless of which test framework you decide to use, you can use npm to install it and embed it in your Karma configuration by using the **frameworks** property.

```
npm install karma-jasmine --save-dev
```

As an example, Listing 5.39 shows how you can embed Jasmine.

Listing 5.39: Embedding the Jasmine framework

```
frameworks: ['jasmine'],
```

Continuous Integration

The theme continuous integration (CI) is also covered by Karma. Currently, there is an integration for the CI systems Jenkins, Travis and Teamcity. In this section, we primarily discuss using Jenkins and Maven together, because it is very popular configuration in corporate structures.

At this point, we assume that Node.js and Karma have already been installed. In your **pom.xml** file (the project file of Maven), you can now initiate the execution of the Karma process by using the Maven Antrun plugin (http://maven.apache.org/plugins/maven-antrun-plugin). Listing 5.40 shows a summary from the **pom.xml** file.

Listing 5.40: Starting Karma from Maven with the Maven Antrun plugin

```
<plugin>
    <artifactId>maven-antrun-plugin</artifactId>
    <version>1.7</version>
    <executions>
        <execution>
            <phase>generate-sources</phase>
            <configuration>
                <target name="building">
                    <exec
```

```
                    executable="cmd"
                    dir="\${project.basedir}"
                    osfamily="windows">
                    <arg line="/c karma start "/>
            </exec>
            <exec
                    executable="karma"
                    dir="\${project.basedir}"
                    osfamily="unix">
                    <arg line="start"/>
            </exec>
        </target>
    </configuration>
    <goals>
        <goal>run</goal>
    </goals>
</execution>
</executions>
</plugin>
```

You must now redirect the results of the test back to Jenkins. To this end, you can configure Karma so that it produces a test report in JUnit XML format after the execution of the test. For this, you first have to install the karma-junit-reporter plugin. As always, you can use npm to do this.

```
npm install karma-junit-reporter --save-dev
```

After you have successfully run the installation, you can activate and configure the plugin in your Karma configuration (See Listing 5.41).

Listing 5.41: Generating a JUnit report with Karma

```
reporters = [ 'junit'];
junitReporter = {
  outputFile: 'test-results.xml'
};
```

Finally, the xUnit plugin from Jenkins (https://wiki.jenkins-ci.org/display/JENKINS/xUnit+Plugin) allows you to embed the generated test results by using the JUnit report file. To this end, you have to install this plugin and select the option "publish JUnit test result report" under "post build action." You can now select your report file with the test results, which will be imported and added after each run. In addition, you can define threshold values that determine when a complete build can be regarded as failed.

Summary

- Karma is a tool that is based on the Node.js platform. It allows you to automatically execute tests.
- Karma starts its own web server, which the test devices can connect to. Every browser on every device that accesses this server on the network is a potential area for a test execution. In this way, the execution can also be easily done on mobile devices.
- Configuration occurs via a simple file in JSON format. This file is usually called **karma.conf.js**.
- Karma can be integrated into the WebStorm IDE.
- You can embed different test frameworks that you can use for your test cases. We have introduced the most popular JavaScript frameworks.
- Karma offers a mechanisms that allows easy integration in a CI system. You can initiate the system to export the results in an XML file. This file acts as an interface with other systems.
- By using the example, we have introduced the integration in an existing system with Maven and Jenkins.

Yeoman: A Defined Workflow

What is Yeoman?Yeoman (http://yeoman.io) is a workflow that has been proven to work. Used with Bower and Grunt, it helps you focus completely on the actual application development. You can let the tools complete the accompanying additional tasks such as determining an appropriate directory structure, managing dependencies or selecting the right syntax for application components. Yeoman also offers a solution for tasks which affect development infrastructure. The solution especially includes the provision of a web server and the creation of a build process.

Installing Yeoman

Since Yeoman is a Node.js module, you can use npm to install it.

```
npm install -g yo
```

The installation contains the tools Bower and Grunt as well as a generator called Yo. After a successful installation, you will be able to use the commands **yo**, **bower** and **grunt** on the command line. The official installation instructions are also available online at http://yeoman.io/gettingstarted.html. To actually use the Yo generator, you first need a generator for the framework you decided to use. These generators are also Node.js modules and can also be installed using npm. For instance, to install the generator for AngularJS, you would use this command.

```
npm install -g generator-angular
```

There are many other generators you can install. One way to find a generator is by searching for it with npm. Another way is to look at the generator list at the official Yeoman project at GitHub (https://github.com/yeoman). To start the corresponding search inquiry with npm, use this command:

```
npm search generator-%name%
```

Generating Application Modules

In every new project, you start by creating the underlying structures for the project. In the case of a web application, this includes primarily the creation of specific files such as an **index.html** file and often directories for images, CSS files and JavaScript files (the "assets"). That being said, there is no easy way to create these underlying structures. Quite the opposite: as a developer, you are often spoiled for choice. The final selection is often influenced by personal preference. Some developers introduce an in-between directory with assets. Others name this directory **res** or refrain completely from doing so. To be honest with you, these repetitive tasks are arduous, error-prone and often lead to many different project structures. Why can't we automate and homogenize these tasks?

Inspired by Rails, the project Yo (http://yeoman.io) was created. Yo deals with the completion of these tasks for client-side web development. Yo is a command line tool for generating the underlying structures for new projects automatically and consistently. The definitions for this tool are provided in generators. Yo also comes with generators for many currently relevant frameworks, including a generator for AngularJS (https://github.com/yeoman/generator-angular). The AngularJS generator is actually one of the first generators developed in this project. In addition to the generator for AngularJS, there are generators for the following frameworks:

- Ember.js
- Backbone.js
- jQuerry
- Jasmine
- Mocha
- Twitter Flight

The use of a generator has the positive side effect that the project structures are always unified and thus make it easier for new developers to adapt to already existing projects.

Yo for AngularJS Projects

The generator for AngularJS was one of the first generators created in the Yeoman project. The generator generates typical AngularJS application modules and automatically enters these settings in an **index.html** file. In addition, a test suite is provided right away for every created application module.

We discuss the different sub-generators in this chapter. We start by presenting in Listing 5.42 the underlying directory structure created by the AngularJS generator. On the first level, you have two directories, **app** and **test**, for the application and the tests, respectively. Within the **app** directory, you have directories for scripts, style sheets and template files. In the

scripts directory, the generator creates directories for different components of a typical AngularJS application (**controllers**, **services**, **directives**, etc.).

Listing 5.42: The directory structure generated with the AngularJS Generator

```
app/
  scripts/
    controllers/
    decorators/
    directives/
    filters/
    services/
  styles/
  views/
test/
  spec/
    controllers/
    decorators/
    directives/
    filters/
    services/
```

In the **test** directory, there is subdirectory named **spec** that contains the specifications for the different modules of your application. The **spec** directory exists because there can be another parallel directory called **e2e**, in which E2E tests are defined. This type of test is not easily generated because they vary wildly. Therefore, you have to create them yourself.

Modularizing Larger Projects

The directory structure which is generated by the generator is meant for smaller projects or modules. In larger projects, you should use the module system from AngularJS to structure your application and to divide it into technical components. Unfortunately, the AngularJS generator's generated directory structure is only useful for single-module applications. It is, however, possible to use the generator within individual modules. The management of multiple modules cannot be automated with Yo at this time. We will discuss how to structure our applications with the help of modules in Chapter 7, "Frequently Asked Questions."

You can provide a tool with the desired generator by passing a parameter. For example, to use AngularJS, use the parameter **angular**.

```
yo angular
```

If you do not include any further specification, Yo will generate the underlying project structure for an AngularJS application. You can select one of sub-generators on the list to generate application modules by separating it with a colon. If you want to add a new controller, you can execute Yo with the parameter **angular:controller**. You can define the name of the controller to-be generated using an extra parameter. The available sub-generators are listed in Listing 5.43.

Listing 5.43: Summary of valid AngularJS generator commands

```
yo angular [applicationName]
yo angular:controller controllerName
yo angular:decorator serviceName
yo angular:directive directiveName
yo angular:filter filterName
yo angular:route routeName
yo angular:service serviceName
yo angular:view viewName
```

Using CoffeeScript

Developers who prefer to write their applications in CoffeeScript can use the corresponding CoffeeScript templates by passing the parameter **--coffee**. It is also possible to use templates that will continue to work after the source code is minimized. This is done through the parameter **--minsafe**. It should be taken care of by the build process so that you do not have to worry about minimization during development.

You should pay special attention to the naming convention of components when using a generator. The name provided as a parameter is transformed from the Underscore.js JavaScript library into the CamelCase convention with the help of the **camelize()** function (https://github.com/epeli/underscore.string). This means that an AngularJS controller generated using the following command will be named **MyControllerCtrl**.

```
yo angular:controller my-controller
```

The generated file will have the name **my-controller.js** and can be found under **app/scripts/controllers/**. This can be confusing in some situations. Therefore, you should be familiar with this convention.

In addition to creating the components, the generator also makes sure that the generated file is automatically entered at the correct point in the **index.html** file. Since AngularJS has been developed with testability in mind, it is not surprising that the generator can also generate the required test files for your components.

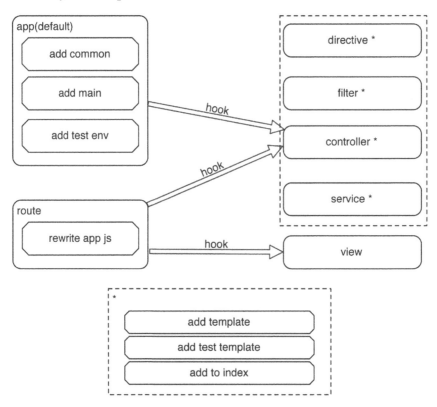

Figure 5.3: Overview of the modules of a Yeoman generator

Yo Angular

You can create a new AngularJS application with the **yo** command. Internally, it uses the sub-generator **angular:app**. **angular:app** is defined as the default sub-generator if no sub-generator is specified explicitly. You can determine the name of the application with an optional parameter. If you invoke the generator without a name, the name of the current directory is used as the application name. In both cases, the string "App" is added to the application name so that you will have an AngularJS application called **UserManagerApp** with the parameter **UserManager**. When this sub-generator is executed, the initial application it generates can already run. The following initialization tasks are thus completed.

- The underlying directory structure
- An **index.html** file with an already embedded AngularJS
- The first route including a template and a controller
- General files such as a 404 template or a .htaccess file
- Test environment for unit and integration tests
- Basic configuration for dependency management

In addition, you can optionally include the following modules:

- Twitter Bootstrap
- Angular Resource
- Angular Cookies
- Angular Sanitize

Additionally, Yo asks a relevant question when generating, which you can answer with an entry request. Finally, the script starts the script with the command **npm install**, which also installs the dependencies for the build process. These are defined in the **package.json** file. We discuss this aspect in more detail in the next section.

> ## Grunt In Yeoman
> In addition to the project structures for your project, Yo also generates a **Gruntfile.js** file, which defines a development and a build environments for your project. We will discuss using a Grunt server in Yeoman at the end of this chapter.

yo angular:controller

With the **controller** sub-generator, you can create a new controller. The name is provided as usual with the help of the first parameter. It is important to note that the name in the template is modified by the Underscore.js function **classify()** and is suffixed with the string "Ctrl". Thus, the file name **myController** and the internal component name **MyControllerCtrl** result from the parameter **my-controller**. Additionally, the generated file is entered in **index.html** and the corresponding test file is generated. You can understand the context by looking at the template's source code in Listing 5.44.

Listing 5.44: Template for yo angular:controller

```
angular.module('<%= _.camelize(appname) %>App')
.controller('<%= _.classify(name) %>Ctrl',
  ['$scope', function ($scope) {
    // Your logic here
  }]);
```

yo angular:directive

You can use the **directive** sub-generator to create a directive. The template in Listing 5.45 is used for generating a directive.

Listing 5.45: Template for yo angular:directive

```
angular.module('<%= _.camelize(appname) %>App')
  .directive('<%= _.camelize(name) %>', [function () {
    return {
      template: '<div></div>',
      restrict: 'E',
      link: function postLink(scope, element, attrs) {
        element.text('<%= _.camelize(name) %> directive');
      }
    };
  }]);
```

The generated file is stored in the **app/scripts/directives/** directory and is added automatically in the **index.html** file.

yo angular:filter

You create a filter with the command **yo angular:filter**. The generated filter will be stored in the **app/scripts/filters/** directory. The template for this can be found in Listing 5.46.

Listing 5.46: Template for yo angular:filter

```
angular.module('<%= _.camelize(appname) %>App')
  .filter('<%= _.camelize(name) %>', [function () {
    return function (input) {
      return '<%= _.camelize(name) %> filter: ' + input;
    };
  }]);
```

yo angular:route

You can use the **route** sub-generator to add a new route to your application. The script produces the files for the controller and the template automatically and adds the route automatically to the route provider's configuration. The controller is automatically added in index.html as usual.

Listing 5.47: Extending route configuration using yo angular:route

```
$routeProvider
.when('/', {
  templateUrl: 'views/main.html',
  controller: 'MainCtrl'
})

// this route has been generated by yo angular:route
.when('/myRoute', {
  templateUrl: 'views/myRoute.html',
  controller: 'MyRouteCtrl'
})}

.otherwise({
  redirectTo: '/'
});
```

yo angular:service

You can generate a new service using the **service** sub-generator. What makes this service unique is that it gives you the opportunity to choose a service type. You can select one of the following types:

- constant
- factory
- provider
- service
- value

If no type is provided, Yo generally selects **factory** as the default. You can see the corresponding template in Listing 5.48.

Listing 5.48: Template for yo angular:service

```
angular.module('<%= _.camelize(appname) %>App')
  .factory('<%= _.camelize(name) %>', [function() {

    var meaningOfLife = 42;

    // Public API here
    return {
      someMethod: function() {
        return meaningOfLife;
      }
    };
  }]);
```

yo angular:decorator

The Decorator pattern is a very useful way of expanding or modifying components. It allows you to belatedly modify an existing service. This could be an extension or a replacement of a particular function. With the **decorator** sub-generator, you can create a new decorator for the service that has been provided as a parameter. The decorator is generated in the **app/scripts/decorators** directory and its file name generally consists of the service name followed by the string "Decorator". Since multiple decorators can decorate the same service, it is possible that a file with the same name already exists. In this case, the sub-generator asks for an alternative name with an entry request. You can find the corresponding template in Listing 5.49.

Listing 5.49: Template for yo angular:decorator

```
angular.module('<%= _.camelize(appname) %>App')
.config(['$provide', function ($provide) {
  $provide.decorator('<%= _.camelize(name) %>',
    function ($delegate) {
      // decorate the $delegate
      return $delegate;
    });
  }]
);
```

Generated Grunt Configuration

Yo also generates a basic configuration for Grunt with the command **yo angular**. In this configuration, three primary tasks are defined. We will describe these tasks now. You can find a more detailed description of Grunt and especially the construction of the **Gruntfile.js** file in the section about Grunt in this chapter.

grunt server

When you start Grunt with the parameter **server**, a minimal web server is started to serve your web application. Additionally, Grunt opens your web application in the default browser. Grunt then connects to the default browser. The Grunt process monitors your project for changes continuously and causes a complete reloading of the application in the browser when a change occurs. Thus, arduous manual reloading is no longer necessary.

grunt test

With the command **grunt test**, you can execute a unit test in your application. Since the AngularJS generator embeds the test environment Karma in your project, you can also activate a continuous test execution in the **karma.conf.js** file with the parameter **singleRun**. When you use this function, your tests will be executed every time there is a change in the project directory. We have discussed Karma and its valid parameters in the configuration in detail in the section on Karma.

grunt

When you start Grunt without parameters, you can initiate your application's build process. In this case, the following tasks will be executed:

- minification of JavaScript code
- concatenation of JavaScript code
- minification of CSS code
- concatenation of CSS code
- embedding of AngularJS via CDN
- compression of JavaScript code (ugly)

The artifact created by this process can normally be found in the **dist** directory.

Summary

- Yeoman is a defined workflow for creating web applications.
- With the Yo tool, you can create new application components fairly easily with the help of generators.
- There are generators for all relevant JavaScript frameworks, especially for AngularJS components.
- Installation can be done through npm.
- These tools are automatically installed and configured for our projects by the dependencies to Bower, Grunt and Karma.
- The generator template for AngularJS gives you a complete configuration of Grunt tasks for the development, testing and delivery of your application.

Chapter 6
Debugging

Software developers make mistakes. You can avoid many of these mistakes by taking the test-driven development (TDD) approach. Nevertheless, you will still find yourself in situations where you have to manually debug an application. In this chapter, we introduce a few tools and methods to make our lives easier in this respect.

In order to debug an application, you need a tool that monitors the running of the application. With this tool, you can set breakpoints at which the application execution will stop. You can then analyze the current state of affairs. In addition, you can look into changes in the application states one step at a time.

Chrome Developer Tools

Without question, the Chrome Developer Tools are some of the most popular and frequently used web debugging tools. These tools come with the Google Chrome browser and offer a variety of useful utilities. We deal with some of these utilities in this section.

You can open the Chrome Developer Tools in one of these two methods. First, you can select the **Inspect Element** menu item on the context menu that appears when you right-click on a web page. Second, the keyboard combination **Ctrl+Shift+I** (or **Cmd+Alt+I** on the Macintosh) opens this view. As long as no other settings are currently open, you can open a new area at the bottom of the browser currently executing the program.

The Elements Tab

In the Elements tab you can analyze and manipulate the current document object model (DOM). As you can see in Figure 6.1, the DOM is rendered as a navigable XML structure. The syntax highlighting makes the HTML code very readable. If you move the mouse over one of these structures, you will see the corresponding container in your browser window with a partially transparent blue layer. If you select an element with a mouse click, you will see information about this element at the right portion of the window. This information is contained in various panes to structure a large amount of data about the HTML element. You can then examine the CSS styles applied to this element.

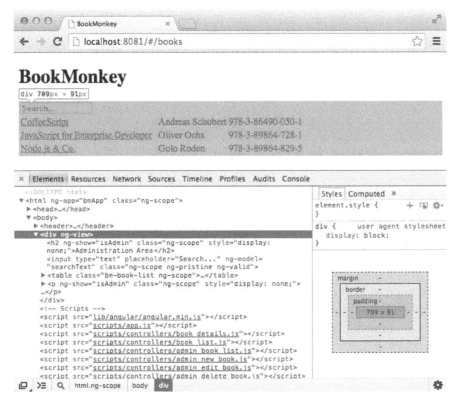

Figure 6.1: The Element Tab of the Chrome Developer Tools

Keyboard Control
The Chrome Developer Tools offer a few helpful keyboard shortcuts. You can find out about these shortcuts in their official documentation at https://developers.google.com/chrome-developer-tools/docs/shortcuts.

With a double click, you can manipulate an HTML element. If you double-click on an element or attribute, a small text box will open to allow you to change the current value. You can simply type a new value and press Enter. Numerical values can be incremented or decremented with the arrow keys.

The DOM Breakpoints submenu shows you the current registered breakpoints for DOM manipulation. This tool is very useful, because there may be situations where it is not fully clear which part of your JavaScript code modifies a certain HTML element. By right-clicking on the corresponding element, you can set a breakpoint under **Break on..** to modify an attribute directly, delete an element or modify a subtree. If a statement activates this breakpoint, processing is stopped and it jumps to the corresponding line of JavaScript code.

The Console

Under the Console tab, you can view the consoles of the currently opened tabs. Here, you can look at different log results and filter them by log level. In addition, you can enter a JavaScript statement in an entry field in the console. You can also evaluate these statements directly in the context of the current website. In this case, the console makes it easier for you by providing automatic completion. The return value of an executed statement is also provided directly after the execution. If the return value is an object, you can analyze it in the console. The console thus provides a tree-like view. The function **clear()** is also available in the console. This allows you to delete the current console results. With the console you can export and manipulate all variables that are defined in the current website. In addition, you can select HTML elements from the DOM easily using the function $(). The syntax should be familiar to most web developers. You can pass a string representation of a CSS selector to this function using the style made famous by jQuery. The return value is a reference to the first correct element or null if there is no match.

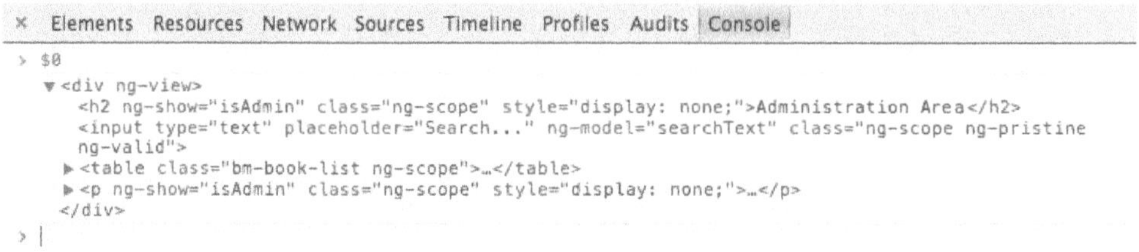

```
×   Elements  Resources  Network  Sources  Timeline  Profiles  Audits | Console |
>  $0
   ▼ <div ng-view>
       <h2 ng-show="isAdmin" class="ng-scope" style="display: none;">Administration Area</h2>
       <input type="text" placeholder="Search..." ng-model="searchText" class="ng-scope ng-pristine
       ng-valid">
     ▶ <table class="bm-book-list ng-scope">…</table>
     ▶ <p ng-show="isAdmin" class="ng-scope" style="display: none;">…</p>
     </div>
>  |
```

Figure 6.2: The Console tab of the Chrome Developer Tools

When analyzing an AngularJS application, you usually have access to the global variable **angular**. Through this variable, you can call the **angular.element()** function, which allows you to select DOM elements by passing a CSS selector. DOM elements returned by **angular.element()** include functions you can call to analyze specific AngularJS constructs. For example, you can call the **scope()** function to obtain the currently valid scope for the selected element.

You can learn more about **angular.element()** from this web page:

```
http://docs.angularjs.org/api/angular.element
```

The Sources Tab: Debugging JavaScript Code

The Sources tab provides an overview of all JavaScript files that have been loaded from the current website. In this tab you can define breakpoints in your source code at which the application would stop and you can analyze the current application states.

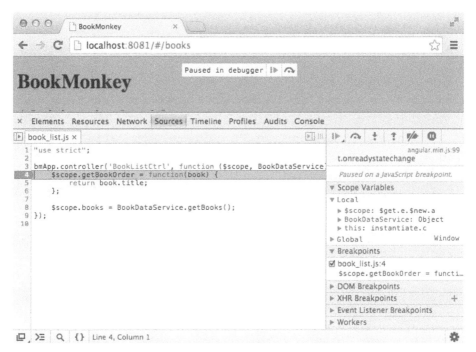

Figure 6.3: The Sources Tab of the Chrome Developer Tools

Like in any powerful integrated development environment (IDE), you can set a breakpoint in any line of code. Double-clicking on a line toggles the breakpoint on that line. If the runtime environment succeeded in executing your script on a line marked with a breakpoint, the application will stop at that point. You can then analyze the scope of the current function and possibly the inherited scopes too. When you are no longer interested in the current state, you can continue or run the program to the next breakpoint.

The following keyboard can be used to help you with debugging.

- F8 – Resume the program
- F10 – Step over the next function call
- F11 – Step to the next function call
- Shift+F11 – Step out of the current function call

> **Conditional Breakpoints**
>
> Sometimes, you may encounter an uncertain or erroneous behavior of a function that only occurs under certain circumstances. When the function is invoked countless times, but you are only interested in a particular case, you need conditional breakpoints. To add a conditional breakpoint, choose Edit Breakpoint. Alternatively, you can right-click on the gutter line and choose Add Conditional Breakpoint. In the input field, type a boolean expression. The breakpoint will pause code execution if the expression evaluates to true.

If you are debugging a website that serves minified JavaScript code, you can format the source code automatically using the pretty printing option. This also allows you to set breakpoints on any line in the minified source code. The option can be found in the editor and is represented by an empty JavaScript object in the object literal notation. To analyze general exceptions in a web application, you have these options on the pause function:

- Do not pause on exceptions
- Pause for all exceptions
- Pause for all uncaught exceptions

Thanks to this function, you can uncover errors that are swallowed by try-catch blocks and that have not been dealt with properly.

Summary

- The Chrome Developer Tools are a set of valuable tools for every web developer.
- In the Elements tab you can investigate and manipulate the current DOM. In addition, you can use breakpoints to pause DOM manipulations.
- The Console tab provides an interactive console that allows you to execute JavaScript code in the current context of the website. You can also select DOM elements with CSS selectors.

- You can examine the loaded JavaScript files and set breakpoints in the Sources tab.

Batarang: Inspecting A Running AngularJS Application

In addition to the established standard tools such as the Chrome Developer Tools, Firebug and various JavaScript debuggers, there is a special tool that you can use to inspect a running AngularJS application. With the Chrome extension Batarang, you can view information about the state and performance of an AngularJS application. You can investigate the server's individual dependencies, measure the execution times of controller functions and see relevant information about scopes. It is this last aspect that makes Batarang a must for so many developers. Project Batarang is an open source project created by Brian Ford. The source code is available from this GitHub site:

```
https://github.com/angular/angularjs-batarang
```

Scroll down to see the installation instructions. You can either install Batarang from the Chrome web store or from the source. The former is the easier method of installation, all you can do is click the link and confirm you want to install it. Once Batarang is successfully installed, a tab named AngularJS will be added to the tab collection of the Chrome Developer Tools. Within the AngularJS tab, there are five subtabs: Models, Performance, Dependencies, Options and Help. There is also a checkbox named **Enable** that you have to check to start using Batarang.

Looking into Scopes

As discussed in Chapter 2, "Basic Principles and Concepts," scopes form the connecting link between the model layer and the presentation layer. Many people soon wonder which data they can access on a view or which variables are defined within a scope. Since the states of a scope changes during program execution, it is sometimes useful to look into the scope when the program is running. Batarang offers exactly this feature in the

Models subtab. The subtab provides you with an overview of the current scope hierarchy of the running application.

By selecting a scope, you can look at the current variable allocation. The three digit number behind a scope represents the scope ID. It is worth mentioning that you can view your scopes and bindings in the Options tab. This occurs via simple CSS classes, which draws a red rim around the respective elements for which a new scope has been created. With this function, a developer who does not completely understand the concept of scope can see it visually. Also, after the installation of Batarang, you can find more features in the Elements tab of the Chrome Developer tools.

As soon as you select a DOM element in the overview, you will find the element's valid scope in the information column under the AngularJS tab. Unlike the model analysis in Batarang, the scope variables internal to AngularJS, which can be recognized by the prefixes $ and $$, are not hidden. In addition, Batarang stores a reference to the selected scope in the global variable **$scope**. You can then analyze or manipulate a selected scope by using the console.

Scope Manipulation via $scope
Using **$scope** to manipulate the scope in the console is very easy. However, note that the changes can only be seen after the next dirty checking cycle. It is thus necessary to activate it by calling **$scope. $apply()** or through an interaction with the application.

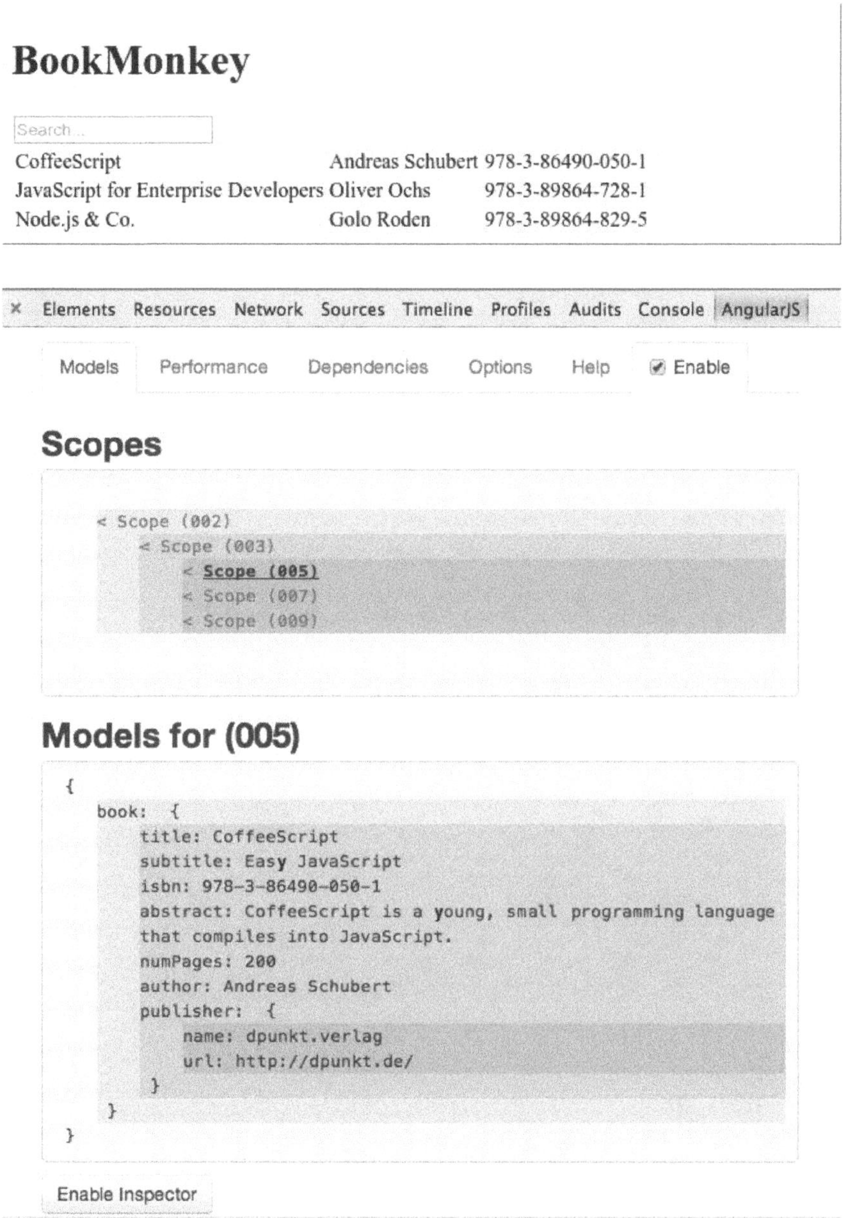

BookMonkey

Search ..		
CoffeeScript	Andreas Schubert	978-3-86490-050-1
JavaScript for Enterprise Developers	Oliver Ochs	978-3-89864-728-1
Node.js & Co.	Golo Roden	978-3-89864-829-5

× Elements Resources Network Sources Timeline Profiles Audits Console AngularJS

Models Performance Dependencies Options Help ☑ Enable

Scopes

```
< Scope (002)
    < Scope (003)
        < Scope (005)
        < Scope (007)
        < Scope (009)
```

Models for (005)

```
{
  book:  {
      title: CoffeeScript
      subtitle: Easy JavaScript
      isbn: 978-3-86490-050-1
      abstract: CoffeeScript is a young, small programming language
      that compiles into JavaScript.
      numPages: 200
      author: Andreas Schubert
      publisher:  {
          name: dpunkt.verlag
          url: http://dpunkt.de/
      }
  }
}
```

Enable Inspector

Figure 6.4: Scope Analysis with Batarang

Figure 6.5: Issuing scope in the console

Measuring Function Execution Time

Unlike most other similar frameworks, AngularJS uses dirty checking to create two-way data binding. This means that at any given time, all scopes that can be manipulated will be examined for changes in order to update the dependent components accordingly. This type of calibration makes developing with AngularJS very convenient and easy, because you can work with ordinary JavaScript objects in the data layer and not have to inherit from special framework constructs. In a complex application, however, dirty checking can lead to problems: as soon as examining the scope begins to take a long time, the application starts becoming slower.

Figure 6.6: The Run Duration Analysis of Functions

In the Performance subtab, Batarang allows you to analyze dirty checking in your application. When you activate this function, you will receive a detailed overview of the the functions that are retrieved from your application and how much time their execution takes. You can discover potential problems that can slow down your application relatively quickly.

Inspecting Service Dependencies

When an application has reached a certain size, it becomes more difficult to see through the tangle of service dependencies. This is nonetheless very important in the case that you want to split your application into different modules. In order to get an overview of the loaded services and their dependencies, Baratang provides you with a dependency graph, in which you can see how the services are dependent on each other.

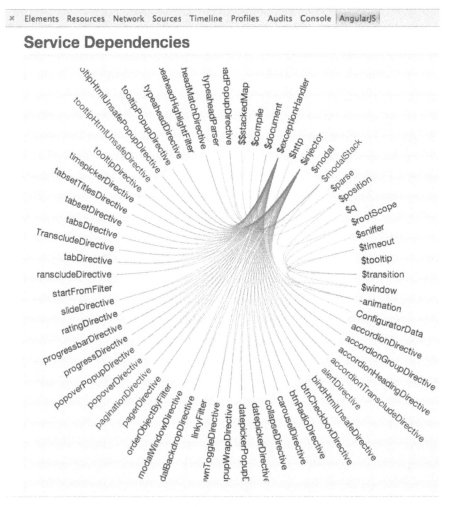

Figure 6.7: Analysis of the service dependencies

Summary

- Batarang is an extension to the Chrome Developer Tools that allows you to gain additional information about an AngularJS application.
- You can analyze and manipulate a scope in many ways.
- Since AngularJS uses dirty checking, it is important to look at performance. Batarang allows you to measure the performance of a function. You can easily uncover performance problems with Batarang.

The WebStorm IDEWebStorm is a professional IDE for development with JavaScript, HTML and CSS. It is one of the most popular development environments in this area and can be downloaded from this URL.

```
http://www.jetbrains.com/webstorm
```

> ### Zen Coding in WebStorm
> WebStorm allows you to use zen coding. This feature is provided by the Emmet plugin that you can download from
>
> ```
> http://www.jetbrains.com/webstorm/features/#zen_coding_&_emmet
> ```
>
> Emmet allows you to generate larger HTML structures by using a selector-like expression. This plugin can speed up development time, especially in web projects.

Although WebStorm offers many useful features, we will focus on its debugging feature in this chapter. WebStorm allows you to pause the running of an application at the desired spot and analyze the current program state.

First, you need to install WebStorm from Chrome web store by clicking this link.

```
https://chrome.google.com/webstore/detail/jetbrains-idesupport/
➥hmhgeddbohgjknpmjagkdomcpobmllji
```

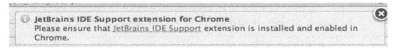

Figure 6.8: Jetbrains IDE Extension

When the extension is installed, the JB icon is displayed next to the Chrome address bar. Once you have installed the extension, you can create a new start configuration type JavaScript Remote Debug. You just have to provide a base URL and define a local map on your project structure.

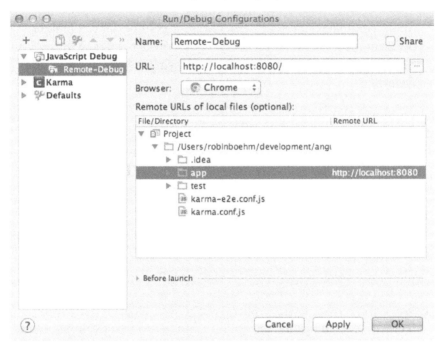

Figure 6.9: Configuring JavaScript Remote Debug

Now start Chrome in debug mode by using the debug icon or the keyboard combination shift+F9. You can easily set breakpoints inside the IDE by clicking on the left edge of the desired location. When the application reaches one of the defined breakpoints, execution will stop.

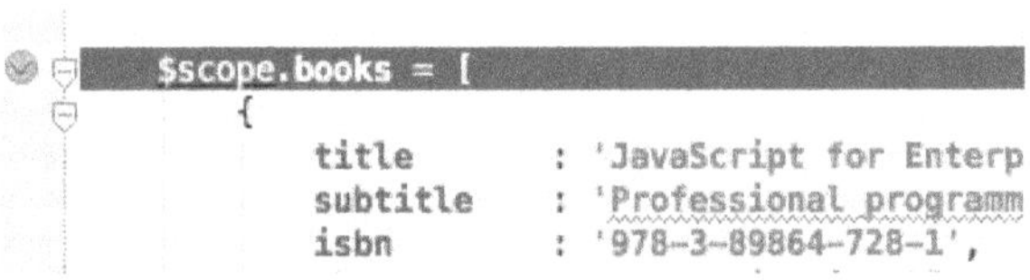

Figure 6.10: Setting breakpoints in WebStorm

You can then examine the current stack trace and variable allocation. In addition, you can control the program execution using the following keyboard shortcuts:

- F9 – Resume the program
- F8 – Step over the next function call
- F10 – Step to the next function call
- Shift+F8 – Step out of the current function call

Summary

- WebStorm is one of the most popular IDEs for JavaScript development. It provides tools for debugging web applications.
- To connect WebStorm with Chrome, you need a special Chrome extension called JetBrains IDE Support
- Setting up the debug configuration for an application is not a difficult task. During the debug process, you can control the course of execution using keyboard shortcuts.

Chapter 7
Frequently Asked Questions

AngularJS Modules: How Do You Structure Applications with Modules?

What are modules? In software engineering, modules are building blocks that form a closed functional unit and exhibit a high degree of cohesion. According to this definition, a module should be responsible for exactly one task and modules should form an entire system through loose coupling. Generally, you should always try to create modular software. This is especially true when encapsulated functionality is being reused or when a project needs to be more structural due to its complexity. In addition, a module has a clearly defined interface, which is used by its users to integrate with the module. The internal implementation of the module can then be changed without making changes to the module user.

Modules in AngularJS

In AngularJS, a module consists of a collection of framework-specific components such as services, filters or directives (See Figure 7.1). These components define the interface of a module.

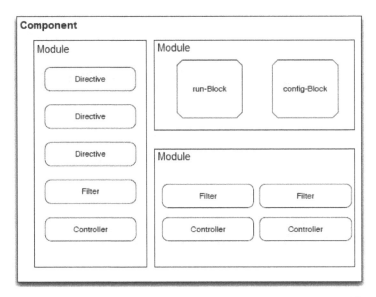

Figure 7.1: Possible module constellations in AngularJS

An AngularJS module always has a unique name that is specified by a string. In addition, a module can have one or more dependencies on other modules. The other modules must be loaded in such a way that they can be resolved. Listing 7.1 shows a small example.

Listing 7.1: The definition of a module with a dependency

```
// Init App Module
angular.module('yourAppName', ['yourAppDependency']);
// Define Dependency Module
angular.module('yourAppDependency', []);
angular.module('yourAppDependency').factory(...);
angular.module('yourAppDependency').filter(...);
angular.module('yourAppDependency').directive(...);
```

In the JavaScript code in Listing 7.1, a module named **yourAppName** is created. It requires the module **yourAppDependency**, which must also be loaded so that the dependency can be resolved. It does not matter which of the two modules is defined first, because AngularJS loads all defined and integrated modules asynchronously before running the application.

In the module **yourAppDependency**, the components that should be part of the module are registered using AngularJS functions such as

factory(), **filter()** and so on. After the registration, the components in **yourAppDependency** are accessible to **yourAppName**. Since **yourAppName** is now the module that AngularJS should execute after the DOM is fully loaded, you have two options. First, you can use the **ngApp** directive to declare that the **yourAppName** module is the start module. Second, you can use the function **angular.bootstrap()** to execute a module programmatically. Other options are explained in the official documentation of Bootstrap at http://docs.angularjs.org/guide/bootstrap.

> ## Module Loading in AngularJS
> AngularJS modules are loaded asynchronously. It does not mean modules can be asynchronously reloaded. Rather, it means AngularJS first loads all the modules defined or included in the document before it starts the application. In other words, all modules must be loaded by the time the application starts. There is no mechanism for lazy loading of modules in AngularJS.

When Is Modularization Useful?

Defining a set of modules is not an easy task, because they cannot be generalized and must be resolved differently depending on the application. You need a lot of experience in order to make the right decision. This is often associated with an iterative process. There are no formal rules.

However, we can derive a few guidelines from our experiences with large projects.

The official AngularJS documentation at http://docs.angularjs.org/guide/module suggests that modules should be structured according to technical points of view. This means you should create a module for all directives. Another module for managing the services and yet another module for the filters.

In our experience, however, we found that division based on technical aspects means that code reuse is almost impossible in most cases. This is because components that solve different technical problems are often managed in the same module. This means you have to implement the entire module even if you only need a small part of a component in the module.

Module Composition

At this point, it should be noted that the recommendation for module composition from the official AngularJS documentation is a relic from the early period of the framework. At that time, there were no concrete case studies on larger AngularJS projects. The team could thus only make a recommendation that was based on the knowledge they had so far. The AngularJS team has now acknowledged that a division based on technical criteria makes more sense.

In our experience, an elegant module composition can be achieved by dividing modules according to technical criteria. All components that solve a technical problem are thus part of a module. This means that it is fairly likely that most of the contained components will actually be needed when reusing the module composition.

Since version 1.0, AngularJS structures its modules according to this method. Many technical components that used to be part of the core have now been outsourced to their own modules. The following list shows a part of the current module structure in AngularJS.

- angular
- angular-animation
- angular-cookies
- angular-route
- angular-touch
- angular-...

You can also see in the module division of AngularJS that the development in a main module evolves towards non-essential parts being outsourced into their own modules bit by bit. You can use this method very successfully in your own projects. When you develop projects in a family of products, it makes sense to outsource common concepts that are useful for all projects into utility modules or common modules. You can thus significantly reduce development time and delay. However, this usually requires more synchronization effort.

For utility modules, you should remember that these concepts are not only helpful within the context of AngularJS. A good method should allow the development of some desired functionality independent from framework conventions and provide an adapter module for the corresponding framework (in this case, AngularJS). Thus, other teams that are working with different JavaScript frameworks can also benefit from the module.

If you are developing an open source module, you can use Bower to make it accessible to the public. At this point, you need a correct version control strategy. In the open source world, the semantic version control from Tom Preston-Werner has established itself as an unofficial standard. Its website is http://semver.org.

Due to the fact that a module in AngularJS is known by its name and there is no authority to determine who is allowed to use what prefix, name collisions cannot be avoided. If two modules have the same name, the most recently loaded module overwrites the previously registered module without warning. As such, you and your colleagues should agree on a naming convention for the whole organization. A good source for existing modules is the module repository at http://ngmodules.org. Listing 7.2 shows a possible pattern for naming your AngularJS modules.

Listing 7.2: Naming conventions for modules

```
// <namespace>.<name>-<optional-type>
angularjsde.bookmonkey
angularjsde.bookmonkey-i18n
angularjsde.bookmonkey-util
angularjsde.bookmonkey-auth
```

Directory Structure

In the world of JavaScript, there is no convention for directory structure. However, you can learn best practices from successful projects. The structure shown in Listing 7.3 is such an example.

Listing 7.3: Directory structure for a module

```
module-name/
    scripts/
    controllers/
    directives/
```

```
      filters/
      services/
      ...
      module.js
   styles/
   views/
   test /
      controllers/
      directives/
      filters/
      services/
      ...
```

This structure follows the recommendation of the official AngularJS documentation. However, there are advantages with regard to process automation, because you can use the wildcard patterns. In the file **module-name/scripts/module.js**, the module is initialized along with its dependencies.

Listing 7.4: A module.js file

```
angular.module('module-name', ['module-dependency']);
```

The following approach is highly recommended for the organization of various modules in an application.

Listing 7.5: Directory structure for various modules in an application

```
bower_components/
    bower-component-a/
    bower-component-b/
    ...
projectname_components/
    project-module-a/
   scripts/
    controllers/
    directives/
    ...
    module.js
    project-module-b/
common_components/
    common-module-a/
   scripts/
    controllers/
    directives/
```

```
    module.js
    ...
    common-module-b/
scripts/
  config/
    routeConfig.js
  module.js
```

In this structure, all components that are managed by Bower are located in the **bower_componenets** directory. Modules specific to your project can be managed in a directory named **projectname_components**, where **projectname** is to be replaced with the actual name of the project. Modules that are required by other applications and teams are located in the **common_components** directory.

> ### The Organization of Common Modules
> A very good method for organizing common modules (**common_components**) in a project or in a team environment is by managing the module in a separate repository. You can embed this repository as a subrepository in your project repository. When it exceeds a certain size and API stability, you can turn the common modules into components with Bower. To this end, you can either use the central Bower register or create a private register for your organization. Both options are discussed in the Bower section in Chapter 5, "Project Management and Automation."

Summary

- In this section we explained the general definition of a module and examined modules within the context of AngularJS.
- In addition, we introduced a directory structure for modules and projects.
- There are already numerous AngularJS modules listed in various ways. These modules usually can be downloaded from Bower.

Promises: How Do You Deal with Asynchronicity?

Asynchronicity and Non-Blocking Callbacks

A JavaScript application is executed in the browser in a single thread. This thread is often called the event loop. You have to make sure not to block an application's event loop for a long time. Otherwise, there would be a delay for the entire application.

There are, however, callbacks that require a certain amount of processing time before they can deliver valuable results for the application. These include HTTP requests. An HTTP request will block the entire application while the application is waiting for a response from the server. These blockages are not common, despite the fact that there is only one thread for the running application. How can an application respond quickly although there is only one thread for execution? The answer is asynchronicity and non-blocking command functions.

Asynchronicity and non-blocking command functions are ubiquitous in JavaScript. Listing 7.6 shows an example of an asynchronous function callback. The code sends a HTTP request to a server and prints the data from the HTTP response in the console. To achieve this, it calls the **makeHTTPRequest()** function with two parameters. The first parameter, **url**, specifies the target address for the HTTP request. The second parameter is a callback function that will be executed as soon as an HTTP response is received.

Listing 7.6: Calling an asynchronous function with a callback function

```
var url = 'http://mydomain.com/api/user/42';

var user;

makeHttpRequest(url, function(response) {
    user = response.data.user;
    console.log('User data', user); // user is defined!
}); // makeHttpRequest() is async / non-blocking!

console.log('User data', user); // user is undefined!
```

In the example, the variable **user** is used twice by the **console.log()** function. The first time is immediately after the calling of **makeHTTPRequest()** and the second time is in the anonymous callback function. The log output that immediately follows the **makeHTTPRequest()** call will be printed first. However, the variable **user** is still undefined at this point, because no HTTP response has been received.

Since **makeHTTPRequest()** is an asynchronous non-blocking function, calling it does not block the execution of your application, although the HTTP request is still being processed. As soon as an HTTP response is received, the callback function that was passed as the second argument to **makeHTTPRequest** will get executed. In this callback function, the variable **user** is assigned the value of **response.data.user** and its value is printed in the console. In this case, however, the variable **user** is defined, as long as there was no error in the processing the HTTP request and the corresponding **User** object is defined in **response.data**.

What Is A Promise?

Things become complicated if you want to execute multiple asynchronous callbacks that are dependent on each other. An asynchronous function callback is dependent on another asynchronous function callback if the former requires data for the callback that is first obtained from another callback. As you can see in Listing 7.7, the pyramid of doom arises in common source code indentation, which repeatedly pushes the script further to the right. Now imagine if you had to intercept and trace the errors in addition to the normal processing. It is obvious that a few asynchronous callbacks can lead to unreadable code.

Listing 7.7: A pyramid of doom

```
makeHttpRequest(url, function(response) {
  performOperation(response.data.user, function(result) {
    calc(result, function(calcResult) {
      doSomething(calcResult, function() {
        ...
      });
    });
  });
});
```

```
});
```

How do you deal with asynchronous callbacks elegantly? In the world of JavaScript, promises have been established as a way to tackle the problem. In other programming languages, promises are often called futures. There is an open specification of this concept called *promises/A+* (http://promises-aplus.github.io/promises-spec). This specification deals with the interoperability of various promise implementations. Listing 7.8 shows the same problem that was previously solved with the callback function. It now returns promises with the help of asynchronous operations. A promise represents an asynchronous operation where a result occurs and through it you can deal with asynchronous APIs elegantly.

As you can see in Listing 7.8, the return value or error is automatically passed to the next asynchronous callback (downstream value and error propagation). This means with promises you can write asynchronous callbacks in a much more readable way. Additionally, you can deal with errors more elegantly.

Listing 7.8: Asynchronous operations that return promises

```
makeHttpRequestPromise(url)
.then(function(response) {
  return response.data.user;
})
.then(performOperation)
.then(calc)
.then(doSomething, function(error) {
  console.log('An error occurred!', error);
});
```

In this example, **makeHTTPRequestPromise()** returns a promise object. The most important function of a promise is the **then()** function. You can use **then()** to define which function should be called back when the result of the asynchronous operation is available or when an error occurs. To achieve this, the **then()** function takes two parameters. The first parameter is a success function, which will be executed when the asynchronous callback is successfully executed and the result is available. The second parameter is an error function, which is executed when an error occurs during a callback. In the following listing, you can see a summary of an API that uses a promise.

```
// onSuccess and onError are functions!
```

```
promise.then(onSuccess, onError)
```

Because the return value is automatically passed to the next asynchronous operation and every operation returns a promise, you can chain **then()** callbacks as shown in Listing 7.8. However, you have to build in a transformation step between the callback of **makeHttpRequestPromise()** and **performOperation()** in order to provide the **performOperation()** function with the data from the **response.data.user** object (instead of the entire response object). You deal with any possible error in the last callback by giving the **then()** function an anonymous error function that merely prints a message in the console, in addition to the success function **doSomething**. Since potential errors are automatically provided, it is sufficient that you deal with the errors at just one location.

To show you how you can implement your own asynchronous operations that are based on promises, we will use Q. Q (http://documentup.com/kriskowal/q/) is a popular implementation of the promises/A+ specification. In addition, we decided to use Q because the AngularJS implementation of promises is also based on a subset of Q.

In Listing 7.9 we outline a possible implementation of the **makeHTTPRequestPromise()** function with Q. This function is a wrapper function that encloses the callback-based function **makeHTTPRequest()** in such a way that a callback contains a promise as response. To achieve this, we use the function **Q.defer()**, which returns a deferred object. This deferred object is the essential component needed to transform a callback-based call into a promise-based call. We store the reference of the object in the local variable **deferred**.

Listing 7.9: Transforming a callback-based call to a promise-based call

```
// Wrap makeHttpRequest
var makeHttpRequestPromise = function(url) {
  var deferred = Q.defer();
  makeHttpRequest(url, deferred.resolve, deferred.reject);
  return deferred.promise;
};
```

The **deferred** object offers access to the accompanying promise via the **promise** property. You pass this promise to the **makeHTTPRequestPromise()** function. Thus, you fulfill the requirement that **makeHTTPRequestPromise()** return a promise. Callers can now use

then() to register a success or error function, as shown in Listing 7.8. You now have to make sure that the promise is fulfilled or rejected, depending on the **makeHTTPRequest()** callback. You can achieve this with the functions **resolve()** and **reject()**. With **resolve()** you can treat a positive fulfillment, while the **reject()** function makes sure that the promise is rejected in the case of an error.

You have just seen that the **makeHTTPRequest()** function accepts a callback function as a second parameter that it will call back in the event of a success. Usually, callback-based asynchronous functions also offer an error handler. This is solved by using the respective callback function. It is thus assumed that the **makeHTTPRequest()** function expects an error function as a third parameter, as shown in Listing 7.9. This means that you can provide the **makeHTTPRequest()** with the respective function reference **deferred.resolve** and **deferred.reject** as the second and third parameters, respectively, in order to fulfill the promise or reject the error. This way, we have transformed our callback-based function **makeHTTPRequest()** to a promise-based function named **makeHTTPRequestPromise()**.Q also offers tools for formatting source code more elegantly with promises. These are, however, not relevant in the context of AngularJS.

Promises

To use Q to transform a callback-based function to a promise-based function, you use the deferred object created with **Q.defer()**. By using this deferred object, you can access the accompanying promise via **deferred.promise**. You then pass this promise to the callback. Now, you have to figure out why there is a division between a deferred object and a promise. Why can't you just work with promises? The answer is actually very obvious.

You usually do not want to give the callback control of when the promise is fulfilled or rejected. Therefore, you pass the promise and can then control when a fulfillment or rejection should happen in your function simplification with the help of deferred objects. If you just use a promise (without a deferred object), the callback could fulfill or reject the problem itself.

Promises in AngularJS

You can use promises in AngularJS. Practically all operations of the provided components return a promise. This includes the **$http** service, which simplifies the formulation of HTTP requests. The implementation of promises in AngularJS is based for the most part on a subset of Q. You can access this implementation by providing a **$q** service through dependency injection.

Compared to Q, there are a couple of differences in the internal implementation of AngularJS which is due to the fact that the framework must integrate the implementation in the context of dirty checking seamlessly. As was discussed in Chapter 4, "Extending the Application," scope manipulations that occur outside AngularJS require a manual callback of dirty checking via **$scope.$apply()**. To ensure that this does not force the browser to repaint the DOM elements after an asynchronous operation, these functions are executed with the help of a help function, which deals with this problem in **$rootScope**.

Listing 7.10 shows the **makeHTTPRequest()** example in an AngularJS service called **promisesService**. For this, we need our application's **$rootScope** in addition to the **$q** service, because we have to manually activate the dirty checking after the execution of the asynchronous function. If we did not do this, our AngularJS application would not be notified of changes triggered by this function.

Listing 7.10: Using $q in AngularJS

```
angular.module('app').factory('promisesService',
function ($rootScope, $q) {
  return {
    makeHttpRequestPromise: function (url) {
      var deferred = $q.defer();

      // manually trigger dirty checking
      $rootScope.$apply(function () {
        makeHttpRequest(
          url,
          deferred.resolve,
          deferred.reject
        );
      });
```

```
      return deferred.promise;
    }
  };
});

angular.module('app').controller('PromisesCtrl',
function ($scope, promisesService) {
  promisesService
  .makeHttpRequestPromise('http://server/user')
  .then(function(result) {
    $scope.user = result;
  });
});
```

By embedding **promisesService** at this point (See **PromisesCtrl**), we can use the **then()** function after the call to **promisesService.makeHTTPRequestPromise()** to handle successes or errors.

The **$q** implementation by AngularJS offers additional API functions to make working with promises easier. For example, the **$q.all()** function expects an array of promises and returns a promise. The returned promise is resolved after all promises in the array are resolved. **$q** thus allows you to execute a row of asynchronous operations synchronously, as long as they do not require one another. In addition, you can execute a resulting operation which then processes the individual results from the asynchronous operations. As usual you can specify the resulting operation in the form of a success function with **then()** (See Listing 7.11). This success function is thus executed when every individual asynchronous operation is completed and their result is available. In this case, AngularJS returns the individual results in an array. If at least one of the asynchronous operations causes an error and its promise is rejected, the resulting promise is also rejected.

Listing 7.11 presents the implementation of the **PromiseCtrl** controller. This time, we ask AngularJS to inject the **$q** service, which provides the function **$q.all**. We pass two promises to **$q.all()**, both returned by **promisesService.makeHTTPRequest()**. This is how we test two different user resources. We assign the returned array containing the individual results to the scope variable **users**.

Listing 7.11: The implementation of PromiseCtrl

```
angular.module('app').controller('PromisesCtrl',
```

```
function ($scope, $q, promisesService) {
  $q.all([
    promisesService
      .makeHttpRequest('http://server/user/1'),

    promisesService
      .makeHttpRequest('http://server/user/2')
  ]).then(function(resultsArray) {
    $scope.users = resultArray;
  });
});
```

$q.when() is another useful function in the **$q** service. This function allows you to simulate a promise-based API. You can pass a value to this function and it will return a promise that represents this value. In addition, with this function you can transform a promise belonging to a third party library into a **$q** promise. This only works when the foreign promise implements the promises/A+ specification.

To simulate an asynchronous API with **$q.when()**, let us use the **BookDataService** from the BookMonkey project one more time (See Chapter 3, "The BookMonkey Project.").

Before introducing the **$http** service in Chapter 4, "Extending the Application," we did not return a promise from a function. Instead, we returned the data directly. We did so because no asynchronous operations had been executed up to that point and we did not wish to make the example unnecessarily complicated. Our solution was problematic, however, because with the introduction of the **$http** service, we had to change every part of our application that had called our service. The API for **BookDataService** was finally based on promises after this change. Therefore, we had to deal with the corresponding **then()** callbacks. It would have taken less effort if we had simulated the soon-to-be asynchronous API with **$q.when()** before introducing the **$http** service.

Listing 7.12 shows the steps that would have been necessary to simulate a promise-based API. A rewrite of the **getBookByIsbn()** function is shown. We simply need to wrap the return value with the **$q.when()** function instead of returning it directly. The return value of **getBookByIsbn()** is now a promise representing the actual return value. We can now define our success and error functions with **then()**.

Listing 7.12: Simulating a promise with $q.when()

```
// BookDataService
bmApp.factory('BookDataService', function($q) {
  [...]
  // Public API
  return {
    getBookByIsbn: function(isbn) {
      var result = srv.getBookByIsbn(isbn);

      // use $q.when() to simulate Promise based API
      return $q.when(result);
    },
    [...]
  };
});

// BookDetailsCtrl
bmApp.controller('BookDetailsCtrl',
function ($scope, $location, $routeParams, BookDataService) {
  var isbn = $routeParams.isbn;

  BookDataService.getBookByIsbn(isbn).then(function(res) {
    $scope.book = res.data;
  }, function(error) {
    console.log('An error occurred!', error);
  });
});
```

> **Implementing Asynchronous APIs**
> It is best practice to implement every asynchronous operation with a promise. If you know that your API will work asynchronously sooner or later, it makes sense to simulate the future asynchronicity with **$q.when()**.

Testing Promises in AngularJS

Testing asynchronous functions is no easy task. Fortunately, you can use the Jasmine framework. Jasmine offers special functions such as **runs()** and **waitsFor()**. You use **runs()** to execute an asynchronous function. You use **waitsFor()** to wait for a certain condition to be met within a given timeout.

The details on the testing of asynchronous functions can be found in the official Jasmine documentation at http://pivotal.github.io/jasmine/#section-Asynchronous_Support.

AngularJS has another extension for asynchronous APIs that are based on promises. This significantly simplifies test formulation. By embedding the test module **ngMock**, you can perform the asynchronous execution of promises synchronously and thus decide when a promise should be resolved with a specific function callback.

Listing 7.13 shows the **BookDataService** that we artificially extended around the function **promiseFn()**. With the **$q.when()** function, this function returns a promise representing "BookMonkey".

Listing 7.13: Artificial extension of BookDataService for testing promises

```
bmApp.factory('BookDataService', function($q) {

  [...]

  // Public API
  return {

    [...]

    promiseFn: function () {
      return $q.when('BookMonkey');
    }
  };
});
```

To test this function, we create a new test as shown in Listing 7.14. In this test, we call the function **BookDataService.promiseFn()** and receive a promise as a return value. By calling **expect()**, we can test if the returned object is a promise. Subsequently, we define a variable **result** and pass it to the success function to the call to **then()** function. By passing **result** to the **expect()** function, we can inquire if **result** has the value **undefined** and thus has not yet received a value.

Next, we can invoke the promise synchronously by calling **$rootScope. $apply()**. Recall that using this function we can activate dirty checking manually.

After invoking the promise manually, we can test if we have a definite result and if this result corresponds to the string "BookMonkey". We do this by using two further **expect()** calls.

Listing 7.14: Testing a promise-based function with the synchronous invocation of the promise

```
it('should include a promiseFn() function',
  inject(function ($rootScope, BookDataService) {
    var promise = BookDataService.promiseFn();
    expect(promise).toBeDefined();
    expect(promise.then).toBeDefined();

    var result;
    promise.then(function (data) {
      result = data;
    });

    expect(result).toBeUndefined();

    // Resolve promise (execute success function)
    $rootScope.$apply();

    expect(result).toBeDefined();
    expect(result).toBe("BookMonkey");
  })
);
```

Summary

- In this section, we discussed how you can deal with asynchronous functions elegantly in JavaScript. Many asynchronous APIs are based on callback functions. Since the nesting of asynchronous callbacks can result in unreadable constructs (especially the pyramid of doom), we introduced promises to deal with the problem.
- There is an open specification for promises called promises/A+.
- This specification makes sure that different promise implementations are compatible with each other.
- We looked at the promise implementation Q.
- We can implement a subset of Q in AngularJS
- In AngularJS, we can access this subset via the **$q** service.

- At the end of this section, we looked at how to implement asynchronous operations based on promises with the **$q** service.
- We have also shown how we can simplify the testing of promise-based APIs in AngularJS. The framework allows us to synchronously invoke promises in a test.

AngularJS and RequireJS: Is This the Right Mix?

What Is RequireJS?RequireJS, which can be downloaded form http://requirejs.org/, is a JavaScript framework that enables the asynchronous loading of files and modules. It allows you to define modules and their dependencies. In doing so, RequireJS implements the asynchronous module definition (AMD) API, which is an unofficial standard for the definition of modules in the JavaScript world. The AMD API offers the following advantages:

- Dependencies no longer have to be manually sorted. Instead, they are resolved implicitly.
- Dependencies can be asynchronously loaded as soon as they are needed.
- AMD API deters the use of global variables.
- Module names can be saved over in order to be exchanged in a test by using a mock implementation.
- The framework automatically recognizes which dependencies are currently required and loads these in the correct order. RequireJS adds a **script** tag in the head tag of our application for every dependency. As soon as the tag is added to DOM, the browser attempts to load this file and execute it. This can speed up the initial loading.

A RequireJS Example

We demonstrate how to use RequireJS in a small project. The project's structure in shown in Listing 7.15.

Listing 7.15: The directory structure for the RequireJS example

```
index.html
```

```
scripts/
  app.js
  require.js
  helper/
    util.js
    i18n.js
```

The project contains an **index.html** file, in which we load our RequireJS script (see Listing 7.16). Note the extra attribute **data-main**, which defines the starting point of our application.

Listing 7.16: The index.html for our RequireJS example

```
<!DOCTYPE html>
<html>
<head>
  <title>My Sample Project</title>
  <!-- data-main attribute tells require.js to load
    scripts/app.js after require.js has loaded. -->
  <script data-main="scripts/app" src="scripts/require.js">
  </script>
</head>
<body>
  <h1>My Sample Project</h1>
</body>
</html>
```

After the browser loads the script, it starts executing RequireJS. The script defined with the **data-main** attributes (**script/app**) is now reloaded and executed. In **app.js**, we use the AMD API and introduce the execution of the provided function with **require()** (See Listing 7.17). The function, however, is first executed when all the dependencies have been completely loaded. The dependencies are provided as an array of strings via the first parameter. In our case, we require the module **helper/util** as a dependency. This module provides the function to be executed as a first parameter.

Listing 7.17: The starting point (app.js) of our RequireJS application

```
require(["helper/util"], function(util) {
  var output = util.translateFn("Hello World");
  console.log(output);
});
```

> ## Defining RequireJS Dependencies
> The path to a module's dependencies is defined relative to the entry point (defined by the **data-main** attribute). If you need it to behave differently, you can configure it using the parameter **baseUrl**. You can read the exact definition in the official documentation at http://requirejs.org/docs/api.html#config-baseUrl.

You define a module with the RequireJS **define()** function as shown in Listing 7.18. You can specify dependencies for a module in an array. In our **util** module, we specify the module **helper/il8n** as a dependency. In the **util** module we use the **translate()** function from the **il8n** module. In this example, the **util** module returns an API object that provides the public function **translateFn()**. As such, we can make the local function **translate()** available to other modules that want to use it.

Listing 7.18: The util module defined with RequireJS

```
define(["helper/i18n", function (i18n) {
  var translate = function(input){
    return "Translated: "+i18n.translate(input);
  };

  // Public API
  return {
    translateFn: translate
  };
});
```

You can therefore have a clean division of components in a simple JavaScript application by defining an AMD module for each component.

In addition, you do not have to deal with the correct loading order of various JavaScript files in your **index.html**, because RequireJS takes care of this.

> ## Loading External Dependencies
> Sometimes, you need to reload dependencies that cannot be found under the **baseUrl** path. To do this, there is a convention that overrides the standard behavior. You can then reload scripts whose paths can be specified to be relative to the current address. Reloading scripts from a CDN is also possible. In the following cases, the **baseUrl** convention is set aside:
>
> 1. The entered dependency ends with .js.
> 2. The entered dependency begins with a /.
> 3. The entered dependency contains protocol information such as http:// or https://.

Figure 7.2 shows the dependencies of our example project graphically.

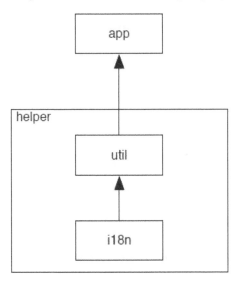

Figure 7.2: Dependencies Inside of our Example Project

AngularJS and RequireJS

In this section you will learn how to implement AngularJS and RequireJS together. To this end, you have to extend an AngularJS project to accept certain RequireJS-specific constructs. We have decided to implement these extensions based on our BookMonkey project.

The BookMonkey version from the last section of Chapter 3 acts as a basis for the introduction to RequireJS. Recall that in that section, we introduced navigation using routes. The idea now is to define the various AngularJS components in their own AMD modules. In addition, we will create a **requireConfig.js** file, which acts as the entry point to our application. We will also manage the dependencies with Bower. The directory structure is shown in Listing 7.19.

Listing 7.19: The directory structure for BookMonkey with dependency management with Bower

```
bower_components/
  angular/
    angular.min.js
  angular-route/
    angular-route.min.js
  requirejs/
    require.js
scripts/
  config/
    routes.js
  controllers/
    book_details.js
    book_list.js
  services/
    book_data.js
  app.js
  requireConfig.js
index.html
bower.json
```

As the first step, we include RequireJS in our **index.html**. We employ the **data-main** attribute to demarcate the entry point. As shown in Listing 7.20, this attribute references our AMD module **scripts/requireConfig**, which is defined in the file **scripts/requireConfig.js**. In addition, we remove or comment out the previous **script** tags, because RequireJS takes care of file loading.

Listing 7.20: The index.html of BookMonkey with RequireJS

```
<script src="bower_components/requirejs/require.js"
```

```
data-main="scripts/requireConfig"></script>

<!--
  These script tags are now obsolete!
  <script src="lib/angular/angular.min.js"></script>
  <script src="lib/angular-route/angular-route.min.js"></script>
  <script src="scripts/app.js"></script>
  <script src="scripts/controllers/book_details.js"></script>
  <script src="scripts/controllers/book_list.js"></script>
  <script src="scripts/services/book_data.js"></script>js
-->
```

Next, we configure the AMD module angular and **angularRoute**, which are required by our application (See Listing 7.21). To this end, we can use the **require.config()** function from RequireJS. This function receives a configuration object. In order to embed AngularJS, we require the attribute **paths**. This attribute allows us to enter dependencies that cannot be found directly under the **baseUrl** path. In addition, we give these dependencies a solid module name. Since AngularJS and the **ngRoute** module are external dependencies that we can only manage with Bower, we specify here the relative path to our **bower_components** directory.

To make sure that our AngularJS is correctly embedded, we have to tell RequireJS that it should assign AngularJS to the global variable **angular**. This is done by using the attribute **shim**. In order to achieve the correct initialization order, we define the AMD module angular as a dependency of the AMD module **angularRoute**.

Listing 7.21: AngularJS configuration in the context of RequireJS

```
require.config({
  paths: {
    angular: '../bower_components/angular/angular',
    angularRoute: '../bower_components/angular-route/angular-route'
  },
shim: {
  'angular' : {'exports' : 'angular'},
  'angularRoute': ['angular']
  }
});
```

You can load libraries through a content delivery network (CDN). The aforementioned RequireJS convention for modules are also important at this point. You can even specify a fallback (http://requirejs.org/docs/api.html#pathsfallbacks). This way, you can specify a CDN resource as the first parameter and a local resource as an alternative to be loaded in the case the CDN is not reachable. This is presented in Listing 7.22.

Listing 7.22: AngularJS configuration in the Context of RequireJS with a CDN and a fallback

```
require.config({
  [...]

  paths: {
  angular: [
    '//ajax.googleapis.com/ajax/libs/angularjs/1.2.0/angular',
    '../bower_components/angular/angular'
  ],

  [...]
});
```

There are other configuration options in RequireJS. Is is advisable to spend time to study its online documentation at http://requirejs.org/docs/api.html.

Listing 7.23: Definition of the AMD Module app

```
define([
  'angular',
  'angularRoute'
], function (angular) {
  return angular.module('bmApp', ['ngRoute']);
});
```

When we use our AngularJS application together with RequireJS, we must make sure that we define bootstrapping from AngularJS only when all scripts have been loaded. We can use the **require()** function from RequireJS to manage manual bootstrapping correctly (See Listing 7.24).

Listing 7.24: Manual bootstrapping of our AngularJS application in the context of RequireJS

```
// requireConfig.js
[...]
require([
  'angular',
  'app',
  'config/routes'
```

```
], function(angular, app) {
  angular.element().ready(function() {
    var elem = document.getElementsByTagName('html')[0];
    angular.bootstrap(elem, [app['name']]);
  });
});
```

In this function we can listen to the **DOMConteentLoaded** event by registering a callback function with **ready()**. As soon as this event is raised, we can begin the initialization of the AngularJS application in the callback function. To this end, we use the function **angular.bootstrap()**. As a first parameter, we specify the DOM element, which we annotate with the **ngAPP** directive in the event of automatic initialization. The second parameter defines the name of the application module that should be loaded. We can export the name of the application module from the AMD module **app**, which is available at this time.

In Listing 7.24, we specify the AMD module **config/routes** as a dependency. In this module, we define the routes of our AngularJS application. Listing 7.25 presents the module definition.

Listing 7.25: The route configuration of our AngularJS application as an AMD module

```
define([
  'app',
  'controllers/book_list',
  'controllers/book_details'
], function (app) {
  app.config(function($routeProvider) {
    $routeProvider.when('/books/:isbn', {
      templateUrl: 'templates/book_details.html',
      controller : 'BookDetailsCtrl'
    })
    .when('/books', {
      templateUrl: 'templates/book_list.html',
      controller : 'BookListCtrl'
    })
    .otherwise({
      redirectTo: '/books'
    });
  });
});
```

The AMD module **config/routes** requires three dependencies. First, it needs our AMD module **app** in order to provide the **$routeProvider** through the AngularJS **config()** function and configure the routes. Since we have to make sure that a specific controller has been loaded in the route configuration, we specify the AMD module in which we define the controller as a dependency. We can thus make sure that the two AMD modules **controllers/book_list** and **controllers/book_details** are both available.

Listing 7.26: An AngularJS controller as an AMD module in the context of RequireJS

```
define([
  'app',
  'services/book_data'
], function (app) {
  app.controller('BookListCtrl', function ($scope, BookDataService)
    {
    $scope.getBookOrder = function (book) {
      return book.title;
    };
    $scope.books = BookDataService.getBooks();
  });
});
```

As usual, we add a new AMD module to the **define()** function. In this case, we are dealing with an AMD module **controllers/book_list**. We also have a dependency on our **app** module so that we can add the controller as a definition. Since this controller also requires the **BookDataService**, we should also specify the corresponding AMD module **services/book_data** as a dependency. As usual, AngularJS internal mechanisms such as dependency injection are useable in the module definition. AngularJS can specify the scope (**$scope**) as well as the **BookDataService** without any problems.

For the sake of completeness, we show in Listing 7.27 another summary from the definition of the AMD module **services/book_data** for the **BookDataService**. It is worth mentioning that we are can also embed the AMD module **angular** and use the global API from AngularJS (e.g. **angular.element()**, **angular.copy()** etc.).

Listing 7.27: An AngularJS service factory as an AMD module in the context of RequireJS

```
define([
  'angular',
  'app'
], function (angular, app) {
  app.factory('BookDataService', function () {
    // angular.element()
    // angular.copy()
    // ...
  });
});
```

Therefore, we have shown how you can execute an AngularJS application in the context of RequireJS. As a summary, the dependencies of our application are shown in Figure 7.3. The diagram is not fully accurate technically, because we require our AMD module **app** in every other module. However, this would make the diagram very difficult to read. We have thus left these dependency relationship out of the diagram.

Testing with RequireJS

In this section, we look at the steps that are necessary in order for us to use an AngularJS application in the context of RequireJS. First, we have to install the RequireJS Karma adapter with npm. We also have to specify in our Karma configuration under **frameworks**. The installation of the Karma adapter is done with the following command in the command line:

```
npm install karma-requirejs
```

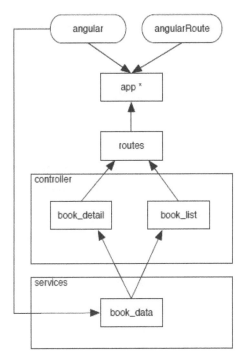

Figure 7.3: Module dependencies in BookMonkey in the context of RequireJS

When we have completed that, we have to adjust the **files** block in the Karma configuration.

Since RequireJS embeds the files and reloads them asynchronously itself, we have to provide the required files in the test suite without directly embedding them. We achieve this by setting the attribute **included** to **false** (see Listing 7.28). We can thus define that the web server that Karma started is allowed to send the files without embedding it using a **<script>** tag. Karma was explained in Chapter 5.

Listing 7.28: Karma configuration for testing an AngularJS application in the context of RequireJS

```
// frameworks to use
frameworks: ['jasmine','requirejs'],

// list of files / patterns to load in the browser
files: [
```

```
{
  pattern: 'app/bower_components/angular/angular*.js',
  included: false
},
{
  pattern: 'app/bower_components/angular-route/angular-route*.js',
  included: false
},
{
  pattern: 'app/bower_components/angular-mocks/angular-mocks*.js',
  included: false
},
{
  pattern: 'app/scripts/**/*.js',
  included: false
},
{
  pattern: 'test/unit/**/*.js',
  included: false
},

'test/testRequireConfig.js'

],

[...]
```

In addition, we have to specify a RequireJS configuration for our test that is adapted to execution in Karma (see Listing 7.29). In doing so, we note the following points:

- AngularJS must be included with all the required modules.
- The AngularJS module **ngMock** must be included.
- The path configuration must be adjusted for Karma.
- The **baseUrl** must be adjusted.
- Our tests must be specified as dependencies.
- We have to define a callback function that starts the test.

Since Karma delivers the loaded files under the path **base**, we have to watch out for this in the definition of our module. We should also adjust the path entries accordingly.

In addition, we group our tests in an array named **tests**. In the process, we iterate over all the files Karma has loaded to find a file that matches **spec.js**.

Listing 7.29: The testRequireConfig.js file for testing our AngularJS application in the context of RequireJS

```
// we get all the test files automatically
var tests = [];
for (var file in window.__karma__.files) {
  if (window.__karma__.files.hasOwnProperty(file)) {
    if (/spec\.js$/i.test(file)) {
      tests.push(file);
    }
  }
}

require.config({
  paths: {
    angular: '/base/app/bower_components/angular/angular',
    angularRoute:
      '/base/app/bower_components/angular-route/angular-route',
    angularMocks:
      '/base/app/bower_components/angular-mocks/angular-mocks'
  },

  baseUrl: '/base/app/scripts/',
  shim: {
    'angular' : {'exports' : 'angular'},
    'angularRoute': ['angular'],
    'angularMocks': {
      deps:['angular'],
      'exports':'angular.mock'
    }
  },
  deps: tests,
  callback: window.__karma__.start
});
```

When we are done with this, we can define our tests as AMD modules. As always, in this module we can work with a test framework of our choice (e.g. Jasmine).

The AMD module in Listing 7.30 shows some tests for our **DataBookService**.

Listing 7.30: An AMD Module with test cases for the BookDataService

```
define([
  'angular',
  'angularMocks',
  'services/book_data'
], function (angular, mock) {
    describe('Service: BookDataService', function () {
      var BookDataService;

      // load the application module
      beforeEach(module('bmApp'));

      // get a reference to the service
      beforeEach(inject(function (_BookDataService_) {
        BookDataService = _BookDataService_;
      }));

      describe('Public API', function () {
        it('should include a getBookByIsbn() function', function () {
          expect(BookDataService.getBookByIsbn).toBeDefined();
        });

        it('should include a getBooks() function', function () {
          expect(BookDataService.getBooks).toBeDefined();
        });
      });
    });
});
```

Testing an AngularJS application in conjunction with RequireJS initially requires a little more effort. However, after the early hurdles, you can define test cases as usual by providing them in the form of AMD modules.

The Answer

As you have just seen, it is possible to implement AngularJS with RequireJS. Unfortunately, RequireJS's biggest advantage–the asynchronous reloading of modules–is canceled out by the fact that every component (controllers, services, etc.) must be available at the start of the application for AngularJS. The problem also exists when embedding other AngularJS modules. Our application module's dependencies also have to be available and thus cannot be asynchronously reloaded.

Another problem for the combination of AngularJS and RequireJS is the fact that we cannot execute our E2E tests. The reason for this is that the **ngScenarioDSL** from AngularJS can only be implemented when we start the application with the **ngApp** directive. Since a manual Bootstrapping must be undertaken in combination with RequireJS, the condition for an implementation of **ngScenario** is no longer extant.

The mix of AngularJS and RequireJS can nevertheless be interesting. Because we attach every piece of information in RequireJS to its module definition via its dependencies and only have to work with one **<script>** tag, we do not have to manually make sure that the individual application components are embedded in the correct order. When using RequireJS, the order is provided to the dependencies implicitly by the meta information. With a clever build process, however, embedding order issue can be resolved without RequireJS.

Based on our experience, we do not recommend that you use RequireJS and AngularJS together. Instead, we recommend solving the loading order problem using an optimized building process. The reason for this is the fact that E2E tests can no longer be executed in connection with RequireJS. Because of this, an important mechanism for quality maintenance is no longer available. This is an inadequate ascertainment for large development teams, in which employees with the knowledge of the requirements create user story scenarios and developers program these in the form of E2E tests.

In addition, the source code is not so promising without the definition from AMD modules. It is therefore more difficult to understand. New developers that are not familiar with JavaScript or AngularJS must further understand another complex library in order to find a connection in a project when implementing RequireJS. The number of JavaScript developers who can work well in the entire ecosystem of language and thus know all of these frameworks is not very high.

> **Reloading AngularJS Components Asynchronously**
> You can find various blog entries on how to patch AngularJS in such a
> way that the application components can asynchronously reload when
> AngularJS and RequireJS are used together. Generally, we recommend
> against using such solutions. In the current version of AngularJS, these
> manipulations may work, however, no one can be sure that this will be
> the case for the versions to come. It is therefore advisable to wait and
> look if the framework comes with a mechanism to reload components
> asynchronously.

Summary

- RequireJS is a JavaScript framework that enables the asynchronous
  loading of files and modules. It implements the asynchronous module
  definition (AMD) API.
- By using a small example, we introduced the function and definition
  of AMD modules.
- We showed how AngularJS can be implemented in conjunction with
  RequireJS and what the implications are.
- We discussed the steps necessary to test applications that use
  AngularJS and RequireJS together.
- We generally advise against using AngularJS with RequireJS because
  this combination has many disadvantages.

Mobile Devices: Does AngularJS Support Mobile Devices?

Because of the increasing trend towards the use of mobile devices on the
web, many wonder whether AngularJS is specially compatible with such
devices.

In addition to the popular techniques for optimizing an application for
mobile devises (e.g. Responsive Web Design) which can be implemented
independently from AngularJS, AngularJS offers several extensions that

were specially developed for mobile applications. Thus, we can answer the above question in good conscience with a "yes".

Performance on Mobile Devices

Although AngularJS is suitable for creating web applications for phone and tablets, you should watch out for a few things. You should know what data you store within the scope of your application, because AngularJS dirty checking can otherwise take a very long time. You can optimize a few things with respect to rendering performance. As explained in Chapter 3, you should prefer the **ngBind** directive over equivalent expressions for template output. This is so that you can avoid the detour via the **$interpolate** service. Another advantage of the **ngBind** directive is that expressions that are not yet assessed are not shown when using it.

Supporting Touch Events

AngularJS comes with the **ngTouch** module, which contains extensions for interacting with touch devices. **ngTouch** is not a part of the core library. If you want to use it, you have to download and embed it with a **<script>** tag. If you are not using Bower, you can download the module at http://code.angularjs.org/ to manage the front end dependencies. In addition, you have to specify it as a dependency when defining your application module (see Listing 7.31).

Listing 7.31: Embedding the ngTouch Module.

```
angular.module('app', ['ngTouch']);
```

When you embed the **ngTouch** module, the **ngClick** directive is replaced with an alternative implementation, which is designed for touch interactions. The reason for this is that most browsers send a click event to the document first after 300 milliseconds after the tap and release event. Thus, click interaction appears to be slow when using the **ngClick** directive on mobile devices. On the other hand, the alternative implementation from the **ngTouch** module reacts immediately and the application thus appears to be much smoother. In addition, it suppresses the native browser event in order to avoid duplication.

You can test this behavior by using the **ngClick** directive in a simple template and call up the application with a touch enabled device (see Listing 7.32).

Listing 7.32: Using ngClick in the ngTouch module

```
<!DOCTYPE html>
<html ng-app="app">
<body>
  <div ng-click="click=click+1" ng-bind="click"></div>

  <!-- Scripts -->
  <script src="lib/angular/angular.min.js"></script>
  <script src="lib/angular-touch/angular-touch.min.js"></script>
  <script src="scripts/app.js"></script>
</body>
</html>
```

> **The CSS Extension for the ngClick Directive**
> When you embed the **ngTouch** module in your application, the alternative **ngClick** directive sets another CSS class named **ng-click-active** as soon as you press your finger on the appropriate element. This works with touch events as well as mouse click events. You can thus use this CSS class to set a special styling for the element in the pressed state.

The Swipe Directives

Another extension that comes with the **ngTouch** module is the support for swipe gestures. A swipe occurs when you stroke over a touch screen with one or more fingers. This gesture is often implemented to show a context menu for an element.

The implementation selected in AngularJS is based on jQuery Mobile. jQuery Mobile is not required as a dependency because **ngTouch** contains the relevant parts of the library.

The module comes with two directives for swipe gestures. The **ngSwipeLeft** directive deals with swipe gestures directed to the left, while the **ngSwipeRight** directive deals with swipes to the right.

Listing 7.33 shows the management of these directives.

Listing 7.33: Using ngSwipeLeft and ngSwipeRight

```html
<!DOCTYPE html>
<html ng-app="app">
<body>
  <div ng-swipe-right="right=right+1" ng-swipe-left="left=left+1">
    <div>Swipe-right: {{right}}</div>
    <div>Swipe-left: {{left}}</div>
  </div>

  <!-- Scripts -->
    <script src="lib/angular/angular.min.js"></script>
    <script src="lib/angular-touch/angular-touch.min.js"></script>
    <script src="scripts/app.js"></script>
</body>
</html>
```

The $swipe Service

If you want to implement more complex swipe interactions or have more control over what a swipe does, you cannot do that with **ngSwipeLeft** or **ngSwipeRight**. For this reason, the **ngTouch** module contains the **$swipe** service, which uses both directives internally. With it you can process the swipe events on a lower level.

The public API from this service includes a function called **bind** for listening to events. The different event types supported are listed in Table 7.1.

Type	Description	Activated by
start	Start of the interaction	mousedown, touchstart
move	The current position during interaction	mousemove, touchmove
end	End of interaction	mouseup, touchend
cancel	Occurs when the current interaction is canceled	touchcancel

Table 7.1: Events supported by the $swipe service

The function **bind()** takes as the first parameter a reference to a DOM element that should be monitored for swipe events.

As the second parameter, you specify a configuration object that defines callback functions for the events in Table 7.1. The callback functions for the **start**, **move** and **end** events return an object containing the swipe coordinates. As such, you can access the current x and y positions of the finger movement. In addition, during a callback, the service provides access to the native browser element that was activated by the swipe event. Listing 7.34 shows a sample **bind()** function.

Listing 7.34: A callback for the bind() function of the $swipe service

```
$swipe.bind(element, {
  'start' : function(coords, event) {
    console.log('start', coords.x, coords.y);
  },
  'move' : function(coords, event) {
    console.log('move', coords.x, coords.y);
  },
  'end' : function(coords, event) {
    console.log('end', coords.x, coords.y);
  },
  'cancel': function(event) {
    console.log('cancel', event);
  }
});
```

As an example, we use the **$swipe** service to create a directive that allows us to drag an element, i.e. to move it by using a finger gesture. Such an object would be said to be draggable, so we name our directive **draggable**.

Since we want to use this behavior on existing elements, we create a directive that we can implement as an HTML attribute (see Listing 7.35). In the link function, we can create the desired functionality by using a callback to **$swipe.bind()**. To this end, we use the **move** event and set the position of the element by using the attributes **top** and **left**. In doing so, we make sure that the CSS attribute position is set relative to its parent container. The element that is annotated by the directive must have this CSS attribute. However, for the element the value is **absolute**.

Listing 7.35: Our Draggable directive based on the $swipe service

```
angular.module('app').directive('draggable',
```

```
function ($swipe) {
  return {
    restrict: 'A',
    link: function (scope, element) {
      var width = element[0].offsetWidth,
        height = element[0].offsetHeight;

      var toggleActive = function () {
        element.toggleClass('swipe-active');
      };

      $swipe.bind(element, {
        'start': toggleActive,
        'move': function (coords) {
          element.css('left', coords.x-(width/2) + "px");
          element.css('top', coords.y-(height/2) + "px");
        },
        'end': toggleActive,
        'cancel': toggleActive
      });
    }
  };
});
```

In addition, we define a **toggleActive()** function to set the CSS class **swipe-active** on the element as soon as this gesture is active. This way, we can visualize this state better with a frame or transparent.

Now we can embed this directive in our example by creating an element that is annotated with the HTML attribute **draggable** (see Listing 7.36).

Listing 7.36: Using our draggable directive

```
<!DOCTYPE html>
<html ng-app="app">
<head>
  <meta charset="utf-8">
  <title>Usage of Draggable Directive</title>
  <link rel="stylesheet" href="css/draggable.css" media="screen">
</head>
<body>

  <div class="draggable" draggable></div>

  <div ng-click="click=click+1">
    <div>Click: {{click}}</div>
```

```
  </div>

  <div ng-swipe-right="right=right+1" ng-swipe-left="left=left+1">
    <div>Swipe-right: {{right}}</div>
    <div>Swipe-left: {{left}}</div>
  </div>

  <!-- Scripts -->
  <script src="lib/angular/angular.min.js"></script>
  <script src="lib/angular-touch/angular-touch.min.js"></script>
  <script src="scripts/app.js"></script>
  <script src="scripts/directives/draggable.js"></script>
</body>
</html>
```

Summary

- In this section, we discussed the extent to which AngularJS supports mobile devices.
- By using the **ngTouch** module, you can access extensions that AngularJS provides for mobile devices. It comes with a touch optimized implementation of the **ngClick** directive and also contains directives for dealing with swipe events.
- With the **$swipe** service, which is a part of **ngTouch**, you can implement touch functions such as drag and drop.

Index

AJAX...212
allowDuplicates property...189
Angular UI..32
angular-translate..32
AngularJS generator...269
AngularStrap...32
asynchronous module definition...313
automation...231
autoWatch property..262
Backbone.js..269
background-color property..8, 58
basePath property...259
Batarang...285
behavior-driven development..264
boilerplate code..25
Bower...268, 299, 301
bower install command..238
Bower register...239
bower.json file...235, 239
breakpoint...279, 281, 283
browsers property...260
browsing history..33
callback function..25
camel case notation..14, 52, 64, 67
CamelCase...271
Chrome..260
classic web application..23
click function..124
CoffeeScript..243, 258, 271
collection filter...20, 39, 109
column function..101
Common JS...234
compiler..137
configuration phase..87
constant function..48
continuous integration...257, 265
controller...10, 32, 83
data access object..32
data model...25
date filter..17

debugging...279
Decorator pattern...276
deep link...127
deep linking..33, 126
default task...244
dependencies property...237
dependency injection..........................27, 31p., 44, 87, 113, 121, 134p., 174, 192, 199, 215, 219
dependency resolution...135
describe function..93, 135
design pattern..21
devDependencies property...237
directive...6, 9, 51
directive definition object...14, 53, 56, 198, 206
directive function...13, 52
dirty checking...26, 201p., 204, 288p., 307
domain specific language...29, 91
double asterisks...259
duck typing...137
E2E testing...90
ECMAScript..76
element function..94, 124
Ember.js...269
Emmet..291
end-to-end test..29
endpoint configuration parameter...240
event..25
event handler...16
event listener...25
event loop...302
exclude property..259, 262
expect function...94
expression..6, 37p.
factory function..45, 52
fat client..23
files property...259
filter..38
filter filter...121
filter function...18p.
Firefox..260
formatting filter..20, 37
frameworks property...259, 265
future..304
gem...232
Git238, 241
Google...231
Grunt...242p., 268
Grunt API...243
Grunt server..273
Gulp...248
hashbang URL..132

History API...33
HTML5 mode..127, 132
HTTP..256
http-server module..76, 231
ignore property..236
initConfig function...245, 249p.
inject function..135
interface...295
Internet Explorer...260
inversion of control..27
isolated scope...15, 26, 60, 64, 71
it function...93
Jasmine.....................................93, 134, 137, 218, 259, 264, 269, 310, 325
JavaScript..256
Jenkins..265pp.
jQuerry...269
jQuery..25, 212, 234
jQuery Mobile..330
JUnit...266
Karma..94, 215, 231, 262, 264, 266
karma init command..260
karma start command..257
karma-junit-reporter plugin...266
link function...15, 53, 57, 67, 202
link property...15, 199
loadNpmTasks function..250
loadTasks command..248
long polling..257
loose coupling..295
main property..236
map function...99
matcher..94, 137
Maven...265, 267
max attribute...8
min attribute...8
min validator..172
minification..254p.
Mocha...149, 264, 269
mock object...90
Model-View-Controller..21
Model-View-ViewModel..23
module..31, 295
module composition...298
module function...87, 135
Module pattern..141
module repository...299
name collision...299
new operator...47
ng-app directive...7, 11
ng-bind attribute..84

ng-controller attribute..66
ng-controller directive...11
ng-init directive...8
ng-min plugin..256
ng-model attribute..6
ng-model directive..8
ng-repeat directive..40
ng-translate module..84
ngApp directive...79, 297
ngBind directive...84p., 88
ngBindTemplate directive..88
ngClick directive...130, 330
ngDisabled directive..168, 171
ngHide directive...163
ngHref directive...97, 126, 128, 132
ngInclude directive..177
ngMock module..134p.
ngModel controller...169
ngModel directive..81, 169
ngRepeat directive....................20, 98, 105, 112, 207
ngRoute module..35, 78p., 87
ngScenario..134, 137
ngScenario framework...77
ngShow directive.....................................163, 167, 170
ngSwipeLeft directive...330
ngSwipeRight directive...330
ngTouch module...329p.
ngView directive..87
Node.js...76, 231p.
Node.js installer..231
Node.js platform...257
novalidate attribute..168
npm..76, 232
observer..16, 26
Opera..260
orderBy filter..112
otherwise function..34
package.json file...241
path function...131
PhantomJS..260
pipe syntax..17
plugins property...262
polyfill..73
Polymer project..73
promise...212p., 304, 307
promises/A+..304p., 309
prototypal inheritance..26
Protractor project...93
Q 305, 307
Qunit...264

QUnit..149
Rails...269
readJSON function...252
register application...240
registerMultiTask function...246
registerTask function...244, 251
repeater..100, 116
required attribute..168
required directive..168, 171
required validator..168pp., 172
RequireJS...313p., 318, 327
REST API...23
restrict property...15, 57, 206
reusability..31
root scope..25, 59
round-trip principle..22
route..34, 88
routing..35, 79
row function...103
Ruby..232
Ruby on Rails..22
runtime environment...231, 235
Safari..260
scope...11, 25
scope property..15, 206
scope variable...8, 16, 18, 58, 80p.
searchpath configuration parameter...240
semantic version control...299
service...32, 44, 112
service factory...140
service provider..87, 140
shim..73
single asterisk...259
single page application...33, 35
singleRun property...262
Singleton pattern...44
snake case notation...14, 52, 64, 67
Spring MVC...22
SSH...240
step attribute..8
strict mode..141
Teamcity..265
template...35
template engine...16
template property...57
templateUrl property..15, 57, 206p.
test execution environment...95
test framework...77
test-driven development..29, 75, 89, 279
testability..29, 44, 214

thread...302
toBe matcher...94
toContain matcher...94
toEqual matcher...102
token input field..189
transparency..8
Travis...265
Trygve Reenskaug..21
Twitter Bootstrap...234
Twitter Flight..269
two-way data binding..................6p., 11, 18, 24p., 37, 59, 62, 80, 106, 175, 177, 189, 195, 288
type attribute...8
type mismatch...137
UI Router..35
Underscore.js...271, 274
unit test..29, 90, 134
uppercase filter..38
V8 engine..231
validator..168
version control...299
view...35p.
ViewModel..23
watcher..16, 70, 227
web server...256
WebKit...260
WebStorm..263
WebStorm IDE...262
when function..34, 104
wildcard...259
XML...267
XMLHttpRequest object..212
xUnit plugin..266
Yeoman..231
yo command..272
Zend Framework..22
.bowerrc file...239
.gitignore file..238
$compile service...192
$error property..173
$filter service...113, 121
$get function..49
$http service...212pp., 219, 307
$httpBackend object..214
$location service...131p., 184
$locationProvider component..127
$q implementation...308
$q service..307, 309
$rootScope...80
$route service..87
$routeParams service...146, 183

Johny Rachmanto
0811184981
johny_rachmanto@yahoo.com